Men against Time

Men against Time

Nicolas Berdyaev, T. S. Eliot, Aldous Huxley, & C. G. Jung

DOUGLAS KELLOGG WOOD

UNIVERSITY PRESS OF KANSAS

Published by the University Press of Kansas (Lawrence, Kansas 66045), which was organized by the Kansas Board of Regents and is operated and funded by Emporia State University, Fort Hays State University, Kansas State University, Pittsburg State University, the University of Kansas, and Wichita State University.

Library of Congress Cataloging in Publication Data
Wood, Douglas Kellogg, 1938—
Men against time.
Bibliography: p.
Includes index.
1. Time—History—20th century. I. Title.
BD638.W655   115   82-526
ISBN 0-7006-0222-4   AACR2

Grateful acknowledgment is made to the following for permission to quote excerpts from their material:

Chatto and Windus, Ltd.:
"The Burning Wheel," *The Collected Poems of Aldous Huxley.* Copyright 1970 by Laura Huxley.

E. P. Dutton:
Lawrence Durrell and Henry Miller: A Private Correspondence. Edited by George Wickes. Copyright © 1963 by Lawrence Durrell and Henry Miller.

Faber and Faber, Ltd.:
"John Marston," *Elizabethan Essays,* by T. S. Eliot. Copyright 1934 by T. S. Eliot.

Harcourt Brace Jovanovich, Inc.:
Excerpts from the poetry of T. S. Eliot are reprinted from his volume *Collected Poems, 1909–1962.* Copyright 1936 by Harcourt Brace Jovanovich, Inc.; copyright © 1943, 1963, 1964 by T. S. Eliot; copyright 1971 by Esme Valerie Eliot.

Harper & Row, Publishers, Inc.: from the following works by Aldous Huxley:
After Many a Summer Dies the Swan. Copyright 1939 by Aldous Leonard Huxley; renewed 1967 by Laura Huxley.
Antic Hay. Copyright 1923, 1951 by Aldous Huxley.
Brave New World. Copyright 1932, 1960 by Aldous Huxley.
Brave New World Revisited. Copyright © 1958 by Aldous Huxley.
Collected Essays. Copyright © 1959 by Aldous Huxley.
Crome Yellow. Copyright 1922, 1950 by Aldous Huxley.
The Doors of Perception and Heaven and Hell. Copyright 1954 © 1955, 1956 by Aldous Huxley.
Ends and Means. Copyright 1937 by Aldous Leonard Huxley; renewed 1965 by Laura Huxley.
Eyeless in Gaza. Copyright 1936 by Aldous Huxley; renewed 1965 by Laura Huxley.
The Genius and the Goddess. Copyright © 1955 by Aldous Huxley.
Island. Copyright © 1962 by Aldous Huxley.

for

Linn
Duncan
Meghan
Colm

CONTENTS

PREFACE

This book traces the early development of the twentieth-century revolt against time through the work and life-histories of four remarkable yet exemplary antitemporalists, Nicolas Berdyaev, T. S. Eliot, Aldous Huxley, and C. G. Jung. It analyzes their attempt to transcend the ontological dimension of time; their vigorous effort to move beyond history, time-philosophy, and any version of the idea of Progress; and their equally forceful struggle to overcome religious scepticism by "re-creating" the concept of eternity from the images and metaphors of symbolic language. It also stresses their engagement, their active involvement in the affairs of this world, and their attempt to solve what they think is the "spiritual crisis of the twentieth century," thereby demonstrating that their social concern should not be depreciated as the effort of escapists. And, finally, this study places the early phase of the antitemporalist movement—an important current of twentieth-century European thought—within its historical context.

In studying this movement, some intellectuals who might have been included have been left out. A case could be made, for instance, that the ideas of time held by Husserl and Heidegger, as well as those of the structuralists and such North and South American writers as Norman O. Brown, Marshall McLuhan, Kurt Vonnegut, and Jorge Luis Borges, should have been treated in depth. But there are several reasons why I have chosen not to include them here.

First, the work of Berdyaev, Eliot, Huxley, and Jung not only portrays all the hallmarks (similarities and diversities) of twentieth-century anti-temporalism in bold relief, but their life-histories, their "spiritual biographies," also frequently conform to the same paradigm, and hence they are instructively and conveniently studied together. In their reactions to time they represent the revolt in microcosm and are thus a preeminently suitable quartet to use in exploring the hostility toward time during the first half of this century. Second, this quartet is united in approaching the problem of time from a religious position. Even more importantly, each member of the quartet *spatializes* time in his attempt to destroy or transcend the temporal process (an epistemological procedure which Heidegger, as much as Bergson, for example, would condemn as an intellectual fallacy). Finally,

Preface

any comprehensive analysis of the time-concepts of the intellectuals I have excluded would require much more space than has been allotted here. And rightly so, since their place in the revolt against time—an intellectual movement that still shows signs of vitality—deserves examination in a separate volume.

While I do not claim to have presented the final treatment of anti-temporalism, *Men against Time* does provide a broad and detailed analysis of the movement from its beginnings at the turn of the nineteenth century through the 1950s, when the efforts of this quartet to transcend and abolish time reached a climax.

It is a pleasure to acknowledge my gratitude to Daniel Schneider, whose unceasing interest in this study was an invaluable inspiration, and to John Gillis, whose encouragement and generous assistance were present from its inception. I also wish to thank Franklin Baumer for the benefit of his insight and sympathetic criticism, and Warren Wagar for his unflagging support. Others I should like to thank are: Carl Schorske, who read and praised the first chapter of an earlier version of this book; Donald Harington, with whom it has been a delight to converse about time for many years; and Calvin Martin whose warm appreciation of *Men against Time* has been a source of encouragement.

Grafton, Vermont   D. K. W.
Princeton, New Jersey

CHAPTER 1

The Twentieth-Century
Revolt against Time

Time the leech, time the destroyer, time the bloody tyrant, the accomplice of death: mankind has persistently regarded this mysterious and inimical power, this exterminating force, as an enemy as formidable and relentless as pestilence, famine, and war. Time has been portrayed in a thousand forms (as a god devouring his young, a wizened graybeard turning the hourglass of centuries, a dancing skeleton threshing skulls on a field of corpses), hypostatized in a thousand metaphors, imprisoned or described in a thousand symbols (the shape-shifter, the eternal reaper of sorrow). From the *carpe diem* poetry of Mimnermus to the pessimistic stanzas of Spenser, Sidney, and Shakespeare—from the dawn of civilization to the present—the same lament, now strident and rebellious, now anguished and disillusioned, continues to be heard: Time is a devious slayer, a traitorous provider who gives only to take away, a patron of life who wears the black cowl of death beneath a disguise of light and laughter. For "Even such is Time," as an Elizabethan poet has said:

> which takes in trust
> Our youth, and joys, and all we have;
> And pays us but with age and dust,
> Which, in the dark and silent grave,
> When we have wandered all our ways,
> Shuts up the story of our days.[1]

In the twentieth century the lament against the eroding power of time not only endures, but frequently appears to have increased in intensity. On occasion it clearly resembles the melancholy protest of the Elizabethans. Dylan Thomas, for example, bitterly describes the "Grief Thief of Time" who sets "its maggot" on our track; in another poem, it

[1]

is the destructive "force that through the green fuse drives the flower"—a force which he equates with "The lips of time" which "leech to the fountainheads" of youth. The Scottish poet Edwin Muir, in "Variations on a Time Theme," registers his dismay with the apparently meaningless "sad stationary journey" of time which consumes each successive generation. Such expressions of hopelessness, of protest and impotent rage "against the dying of the light" inevitably wrought by time are not uncommon in any age: they are representative of the mutability tradition in literature. When Muir and Thomas recoil in horror or sadness at the spectacle of temporal decay, they are giving contemporary expression to a sentiment that can be found in the primitivist poetry of antiquity, in the verse of Lorenzo de' Medici, and in the stanzas of Lord Herbert of Cherbury. According to this tradition, time is synonymous with change, the process that exhausts life-forms and ensures the eventual decomposition of every sentient and inanimate object in the universe. It is the principal enemy whose very omnipotence often inspires a spirit of resistance. Thus, for instance, Muir and Thomas, like Shakespeare or other twentieth-century writers (e.g., Edward Thomas, Walter de la Mare, Robert Graves, Rupert Brooke, James Joyce, Nikos Kazantzakis, and C. Day Lewis), admit that they would like to "Make war upon this bloody tyrant, Time." But—and here is the rub—they also realize that, in the last resort, "nothing 'gainst Time's scythe can make defence." A private mythology, an exaltation of love and life, or a deliberate flaunting of death may enable the individual to reconcile himself to nothingness; but they are not enough, in Edwin Muir's phrase, to "put all Time's display to rout."

While the vitality of the mutability tradition continues in twentieth-century European literature, it does not represent the only protest against the destructive characteristics of the temporal process. In fact, this century has witnessed a far more dramatic and significant protest against mutability—an attack that demands and strives for transcendence and abolition of the temporal process. Thus, the major proponents of the twentieth-century revolt against time not only denounce the sad waste of the temporal process, but try to accomplish either a permanent or a temporary destruction of time itself. Their rallying cry is that of the hero of Kazantzakis's novel *The Rock Garden*: " 'I declare war on time! I declare war on time!' " Yet their protest—their desire, in the Greek author's words, to turn "the wheel back" and resuscitate the dead—is not simply a product of romantic sentimentalism, a spontaneous reaction of the heart. For while it may be exemplary of Everyman's objection to the inexorable cycle of life and death, this protest represents a confident and determined assault on the process of temporal corruption, a thoroughgoing and self-conscious attempt to eliminate the flux of events.

Four of the most outstanding protagonists of the twentieth-century revolt against time—namely, the Russian religious eschatologist Nicolas Berdyaev (1874–1948), the British poet T. S. Eliot (1888–1965), the British novelist Aldous Huxley (1894–1963), and the Swiss psychologist C. G. Jung (1875–1961)—aim their respective attacks primarily against the time of human experience—against what Georges Poulet has called *le temps humain,* i.e., psychological, qualitative, or subjective time. This is not to say that they are not also at war with what they regard to be scientific time; they are. Indeed they wish to eliminate or surmount any dimension, or variety, of time whether it be, for instance, what Heidegger refers to in *Being and Time* (1927) as *Innerzeitigkeit,* the banal round of "everyday time," or what astrophysicists describe as the periodic or aperiodic phases of the expanding universe.

It is important to note at the outset that each of these four men approaches the problem of time in a different way from the scientist. The latter is principally interested in constructing an "objectively" valid system of measurement; the quartet I have selected for study, however, is also concerned with the problems of measuring time, especially historical time, another form of temporality they yearn to transcend or destroy. Their methods of subdividing historical time are decidedly different from those of the scientist measuring cosmic time. Of course, scientific concepts of time do contain subjective elements, and some scientists have rebelled against "objective" conceptions of temporal process.[2] Nevertheless, most scientists try to remove their ideas of time from the subjective foundations of individual experience. Instead of being concrete, their conception of time is abstract; it is quantitative rather than qualitative, public rather than private, or personal. In other words, the scientist is generally preoccupied with the measurement of physical events, while the poet, novelist, or speculative philosopher of history (or the philosopher of physics) is chiefly concerned with the nature of time. The scientist is intent upon discovering an empirically verifiable concept of time that will enable him to calculate cosmic events—to construct a universal metric from which "calendars" and "clocks" can be derived—while the individual, who, like Berdyaev, Eliot, Huxley, and Jung, ultimately bases his notion of time upon personal, or subjective, experience, is concerned with the metaphysical dimensions of temporality, with the ultimate meaning as well as the ontological and axiological nature of time.[3]

Now although it is true that Berdyaev, Eliot, Huxley, and Jung derive their concepts of time from personal experience—and, concomitantly, that they direct their attacks on temporality primarily against subjective time (*le temps humain,* or what Einstein called *Ich-Zeit*) and secondarily against what they understand as scientific time—it is equally true that they believe in the objective validity of their own notions of time. When Berdyaev refers to the Beginning and End of historical time, when Eliot describes the cyclical revolutions of the temporal process, when Huxley discusses the dance of Shiva or Jung, the cycle of aions, each is referring to an objective structure of events which he considers to be a universal aspect of human existence. Such claims of objectivity are not uncommon. Individuals who shape their time-concepts on the foundations of personal experience usually extend their immediate perceptions of time (i.e., of succession, change, motion, supercession, simultaneity, and/or transitional intervals)[4] by interpreting time either as a linear progression or as a cyclical repetition. Linear time-concepts, no doubt, arise from the ability to anticipate or remember events; circular (or spiral) concepts of temporal process, from the observance of enduring and repetitive aspects of human experience. Yet, in both cases the ability to extend the "blooming, buzzing confusion" of time as an immediate datum of consciousness through the use of a symbolic form (circle, spiral, line) provides the individual with an "objective" model with which to interpret, order, and control events and a spatial diagram of time that may eventually enable him to destroy the temporal process itself.

The interrelation between the desire to abolish, or transcend, time and the transformation of experiential time into an objective (yet unscientific) dimension of human experience through the use of spatial symbols is a typical feature of Berdyaev's, Eliot's, Huxley's, and Jung's approach to the time-problem. Not only do they share a common and aggressively antipathetical attitude toward time (that is, not only do they regard time as an enemy who must be surmounted or destroyed), they also employ (spatial) concepts of time to annihilate the temporal process. They transform their subjective feelings about time into a personal concept of time (which purportedly has universal validity) and use their spatialized, or pictorial, representations of the temporal process to eliminate time. As Milič Čapek has observed, "The elimination of time and its spatialization are closely related." For in imposing a graphic symbol upon time, "in contemplating a spatial diagram of temporal process it is easy and psychologically natural to forget its underlying dynamic meaning."[5]

Spatialization of time transforms succession into juxtaposition and presents uncompleted moments of time as a completed, or simultaneous, whole. It represents time statically, depriving it of its inherent momentum. In Čapek's view, this Eleatic tendency can be discovered in early interpretations of Einstein's theory of relativity as well as in idealistic trends in contemporary metaphysics. Yet (as Čapek himself realizes) the use of spatial symbols to order, control, and destroy the temporal process is an ancient practice—one that can be found in archaic as well as modern societies, in the presuppositions of the *Enuma Elish* or in the writings of Berdyaev, Eliot, Huxley, and Jung.

When Berdyaev, Eliot, Huxley, and Jung use the verbal equivalents of spatial images to describe the time-process, they not only retrace the path of a venerable tradition—a tradition not seriously challenged until the end of the nineteenth century[6]—but they also achieve the same epistemological result as, for instance, "archaic man," the medieval eschatologist, the advocate of the idea of Progress, or the champion of dialectical materialism. In other words, by imposing a graphic symbol upon their immediate experience of time, they delimit the temporal process and establish its boundaries. This epistemological act (which orders and, in some cases, establishes direct control over the temporal process) in turn permits them to invest time with a teleological meaning or to formulate a sharp distinction between the time-process and eternity that may eventually precede and ultimately facilitate the transfiguration of time into timelessness.

Expressed concretely, when Berdyaev imposes a circle on cosmic time, a line on the historical process, and a point on existential time or when Eliot describes "The time of the seasons and the constellations / The time of milking and the time of harvest" as a series of cycles,[7] each is using a spatial image to clarify and focus the realities of the time-process. Yet their use of time-symbols does not end here. For once they have interpreted time in terms of spatial images, they are prepared to destroy or transfigure the temporal process. For example, Berdyaev gives the linear structure of historical time a "Beginning" and an "End" and, by making history finite and cosmic time subordinate to history (i.e., the unfolding of the divine-human drama), achieves the inevitable and irreversible abolition of every kind of time (cosmic, historical, and existential).[8] On the other hand, Eliot—who, unlike Berdyaev, rarely appears to examine the nature of time under the aspect of eschatology, especially apocalyptic eschatology—uses the circular structure which he imparts to astronomical, biological, and "moral" time to formulate a relationship between timelessness (the "still point") and time (the "turning world"). This relationship is then employed to reconcile the temporal process and eternity. By introducing a third term—namely, his notion of the "dance" (which is a poetic transcription of Bradley's concept of the Absolute)—Eliot not only reconciles time and eternity, but transforms the temporal process into a "pattern / Of timeless moments."[9]

Eliot's use of the circle demonstrates the way in which time-symbols are frequently transformed into eternity-images, or symbols of timelessness. It is not only, as Čapek observes, psychologically natural to eliminate time by portraying it as a spatial pattern; it is equally natural to suppose that the symbolic structure that makes time static and deprives it of its dynamic meaning must be related to, if not synonymous with, timelessness. The oldest symbol to portray both time and eternity has been the circle. This popularity is no doubt ascribable to the circle's basic and traditional function as an "ordering symbol." The perfect geometrical structure of the circle (all points equidistant from the center) has been used, of course, not only to clarify and order the temporal process. The circle can also be found demarcating the sacred precincts of a temple *(temenoi)*, delimiting the world-order (frequently in combination with a square representing the cardinal points of the compass), describing the movement of the planets (for instance, in Aristotle's "celestial world"), protecting man from inimical forces (for example, in the case of the magic circle), harmoniously rationalizing man's position in the universe (i.e., establishing the microcosm-macrocosm relationship), giving concrete expression to the emotions of a mental patient, or objectifying an individual's concept of eternity. Yet, while the evidence suggests the ubiquity and preeminence of the circle as an ordering symbol, it obviously is but one of many symbols (and, in fact, types of symbols) used by human beings to order their realities.

As a time-symbol the circle, like the straight line and its variants (Berdyaev's "undulating line" of history), is what Ernst Cassirer and Susanne Langer would call a nonlinguistic or nondiscursive symbolic form. Nondiscursive forms of symbolism (viz., ritual, myth, religion, and art) articulate feelings rather than rational thoughts; their meaning is essentially connotative because they lack the syntax, or grammatical structure, of linguistic symbolisms. But it is not just the circle or line—the graphic symbol or its verbal equivalents—that is nondiscursive, for often the prose used to elucidate a philosophy of history, or idea of time, is itself nondiscursive. In other words, although a description of the temporal process may be expressed in verbal symbols, in words which constitute a "language," their import may be nondiscursive because the meaning conveyed is metaphorical. It is undeniable that many linguistic treatises dealing with the problem of time often revert to a nondiscursive level, either to use the verbal equivalent of a pictorial symbol to express their philosophy or to employ metaphorical or poetic symbols (poetry is defined as a nondiscursive form of symbolism) to articulate feelings that cannot be expressed with the verbal precision and grammatical rigidity of analytical thought.

Berdyaev's numerous works on the philosophy of history provide a dramatic example of the use of nondiscursive prose to describe the time-process. Not only does he use spatial images to describe the time-process, but again and again, under the ecstasy of an overwhelming vision of man's destiny, he reverts to metaphorical expressions to convey the meaning of his apocalyptic interpretation of history. Underneath his discourses on Kantian epistemology, below his rational examination of objectification, lies the eschatological vision that permeates and unifies every strand of his thought. And his eschatology, like all eschatology, is created out of non-discursive symbols—images that belong to the world of myth, rather than to logic and science. The linear pattern of Western eschatology probably rests upon an extremely ancient structure of feeling. Like the emotions associated with the circular notion of time, this structure may ultimately be derived from the birth-death-rebirth pattern of primitive initiations—from what the French anthropologist van Gennep has called "the rites of passage." At any rate, Berdyaev's language is shot through with an emotional terminology (a vocabulary strikingly reminiscent of primitive initiation rites); and like Eliot, Berdyaev relies on graphic symbols to order, control, and eliminate time.

The same can be said of Huxley and Jung. They, too, appreciate the epistemological function of time-symbols and, like Berdyaev and Eliot, use nondiscursive images of the temporal process to express a group of interrelated ideas which they associate with the meaning of man's existence in time. According to Huxley and Jung, time is equivalent to physical change, to perpetual perishing and becoming; it is a process of growth and decay which conforms to the symbolic structure of a circular form. While, like Eliot, they recognize the existence of different historical ages, Huxley and Jung tend to play down or even ignore the linear pattern of historical time. Their reason for not stressing the past-present-future structure of historical time lies partially in the conception of a homogeneous human nature. Like Thucydides (and T. S. Eliot), Huxley and Jung infer the cyclical movement of time from the constancy of human nature. If man is the same in essence (as he is assumed to be), he will act essentially the same throughout time. Therefore, human time, like cosmic and biological time and like the changes experienced by societies or civilizations, necessarily repeats the same fundamental pattern.

Huxley, Jung, and Eliot recognize, of course, that although the formal pattern of the temporal process (what W. H. Auden calls the "general average way" of time) is constant, particular events—say an individual's life history—may not be identical in detail. An individual possesses the potential of imposing his own signature upon the repetitive rhythm of the cyclical process. Yet on occasion Eliot appears to deny even this limited definition of (individual) novelty. And it is not impossible to find him describing human activity as a result of divine predestination. This deterministic streak runs throughout his later poetry and all of his plays, and it helps elucidate his conception of "moral time." Because of Original Sin, Eliot assumes that man—natural man, man living in the fallen time of creation—remains essentially the same throughout history. The repudiation of the concept of a plastic human nature (coupled with the notion of primordial sin) implies that all historical periods are essentially identical. Yet identical only in the sense that they are equally corrupt or morally inadequate. Thus antiquity, the era of the metaphysical poets, and the twentieth century are all fundamentally the same because, in Eliot's view, Original Sin precludes moral progress under the aspect of time *(sub specie temporis)*. But, again, this does not mean that every temporal situation repeats itself in exactly the same manner ad infinitum. For there is a difference between, for instance, the Middle Ages and our own era. Indeed Eliot (like Berdyaev and Jung) believes that modern civilization has declined since the Middle Ages (particularly since the Age of Dante, or what Berdyaev and Jung refer to as the Age of Mystic Italy or the Age of Joachim of Flora), and that contemporary Western culture represents a tragic departure from the integrated society of medieval Europe. Even Aldous Huxley can be caught looking back nostalgically to an age of mystics which, he poignantly regrets, disappeared in the cannon smoke of seventeenth-century power politics. Yet despite their recognition of historical differences between cultures past and cultures present, despite their belief that we are (as a waggish Huxleyan mouthpiece says in *Eyeless in Gaza*) well on in the third volume of Gibbon, they tend to ignore particular differences and insist that since human nature is constant, time is cyclical (or spiral).

Initially puzzling as it may seem, Berdyaev—the linear eschatologist par excellence—also examines the rise and fall of civilizations under the aspect of circular time. Yet his concept of cyclical process (which, like Hegel, he employs to interpret cosmic time) cannot be used to describe the general pattern of history. For in Berdyaev's view, history is essentially a divine-human drama, a soteriological mystery play, that unfolds in a linear progression. But the pattern of cultural events, the history of individual civilizations, follows a spiral course.

Approaching the problem from the standpoint of analytical psychology, C. G. Jung arrives at a concept of cultural, or historical, transformation that bears a family resemblance to Berdyaev's. According to the Swiss psychologist, all time (biological, astronomical, and historical) is cyclical. The lives of individual men, the processes of nature, and the rise and fall of civilizations all follow a circular course. Yet, whereas astronomical and

The Twentieth-Century Revolt against Time

biological time perennially repeat the same pattern, historical time allows for minor variations. Its cycles never repeat themselves exactly, and therefore history develops as a series of spirals.

Although the implications of this theory are never fully developed, the end result of Jung's psychological interpretation of history is quite similar to Berdyaev's apocalyptic vision. Like Berdyaev, Jung gives the apparently meaningless process of growth and disintegration a meaning by assimilating the cyclical course of cultural history, the history of civilizations, into an inclusive pattern of universal history. Civilizations, like human beings, may inevitably be born only to die; but by imposing nondiscursive symbols upon the phenomenon of temporal flux, it is possible to see that they perish for a purpose. In Jung's schema the helix of historical time is transformed into the circle of timeless perfection—into a psychological condition, symbolized by the "mandala" (Sanskrit, *circle*) or the astrological symbol of Aquarius, a condition that is homologous with what Teilhard de Chardin would call "point Omega." In Berdyaev's system, on the other hand, the jagged line of history eventually smashes the cycle of cultural and cosmic time by reaching its appointed End. It resolves the antinomies of the historical process and accomplishes the return to timelessness—to eternity—which Berdyaev (like Jung, Eliot, and Huxley) describes as a timeless and spaceless circle.

If asked to interpret Aldous Huxley's concept of time, Jung would undoubtedly begin by observing the similarity between his own notion of the temporal process and that of the Englishman. For like Jung, Huxley imagines time and eternity as a circle. The Swiss psychologist might even have agreed (especially in later life) with Huxley's view, derived from Hindu and Buddhist sources, that the phenomenon of time is actually an illusion *(maya)* perceived by minds alienated from Reality. In any case, Jung would probably have concluded his remarks about Huxley's concept of time with a discourse on the nature of mandala symbolism because Huxley's cones and circles (like Yeats's gyres or Eliot's still point and turning world or Berdyaev's spaceless and timeless circle of eternity) perform all of the major functions that Jung ascribes to the mandala. That is, they impose order on the chaotic flux of experience, clarify the psychological relationship between the individual and the time-process, and (most significantly from Jung's point of view) represent the final achievement of man under the aspect of time—namely, the establishment of a permanent (or at least temporary) relationship between the individual and eternity. It is impossible to say whether Huxley, who was familiar with Jung's theories, ever recognized that his time-symbols and eternity-images could be interpreted as mandalas. Nevertheless his occasional (nondiscursive)

[9]

descriptions of the relationship between the temporal process and timeless Reality appear to correspond to Jung's definition of the mandala, or image of psychic wholeness. (Actually, Jung and his followers would regard most time-symbols and all eternity-images as mandalas, or what one disciple has called circles of the psyche—i.e., symbols that are analogous to, but one step removed from, genuine mandalas.) Whether or not Huxley's pictorial descriptions of time and eternity are really mandalas, however, it is important to point out that his use of graphic symbols to portray the temporal process offers a dramatic example of the intimate connection between the spatialization and destruction of time, on the one hand, and the transformation of time into eternity, on the other.

In his first full-blown mystical novel, *Eyeless in Gaza,* Huxley describes time and eternity as two cones which share a common apex. The temporal world (represented by the first cone) culminates in a point—a point which, like Berdyaev's point of existential time; Eliot's still point; or Jung's point, or center, of the mandala, marks the end of time and the commencement of eternity. As the world of time (or the first cone) converges on its apex, it is gradually transfigured into timelessness. The second cone in its turn expands toward a base whose circumference is equated with all being, eternal Reality, timelessness. This intricate image, which is reminiscent of Yeats's famous description of time and eternity in *A Vision,* is directly related to another symbol which Huxley uses to describe the temporal process: viz., the dance. For like Eliot (whose concept of the dance reconciles the still point with the turning world by transforming time into "a pattern / Of timeless moments"), Huxley uses the dance of Shiva-Nataraja[10] to explain the mysterious connection between perpetual perishing and eternal stillness. Shiva represents becoming and timelessness: he is at once the spinner of the cosmic illusion and the pattern of unmoving movement, or eternity. Unfortunately, however, the vast majority of human beings do not realize that the annihilating force of time is merely a product of their egocentric visions of reality. If only mankind could cast off the strait jacket of its collective ego, if only we could gain the experience of the mystic, we could see that time and eternity (*samsara* and *nirvana*) are one and the same, that Reality is an eternal dance, a process of timelessness.

Huxley's concept of "scientific religion"—his emphasis upon mysticism and empirical theology—is also found in the works of Berdyaev, Eliot, and Jung. In fact, mysticism is as important to the twentieth-century revolt against time as spatialization. Together they form the principal prongs of the offensive: they provide the essential method, or epistemological procedure, by which Berdyaev, Eliot, Huxley, and Jung (as well as other twentieth-century antitemporalists such as Charles Williams, W. B. Yeats, and Hermann Hesse) achieve their victory over the temporal process. But what is mysticism? Is it universally identical? And does it assume the same degree of importance in, say, Berdyaev's thought as in Huxley's, in Eliot's work as in Jung's?

According to William James (who realized that the words "mysticism" and "mystical" have a bewildering variety of connotations), there are "four marks" that characterize an experience as mystical: viz., ineffability, noetic quality, transiency, and passivity.[11] That is, a mystical experience defies expression, exemplifies a nondiscursive form of knowledge, lasts for a short while, and occurs only in passive states of mind—i.e., when the subject (or individual mystic) "feels as if his own will were in abeyance" or "as if he were grasped and held by a superior power."[12] Although these "four marks" characterize all forms of mystical phenomenology (including the mysticism of Berdyaev, Eliot, Huxley, and Jung), this definition of mysticism remains incomplete. For James leaves unmentioned the most typical, fundamental, and pervasive element of mystical experience: namely, the transcendence of time—the feeling of rising above, or being liberated from, the powers of temporality.

It is this archetypal characteristic of mysticism, more than any other single feature of preternatural experience, that receives the greatest emphasis by far in the writings of Berdyaev, Eliot, Huxley, and Jung. Eliot, for example, recognizes that the purest and most direct apprehension of Reality can be achieved only during a timeless state of mystical consciousness. For, "Time past and time future / Allow but a little consciousness. / To be conscious is not to be in time."[13] Aldous Huxley also believes that "deliverance is out of time into eternity," and that "men achieve their Final End in a timeless moment of conscious experience."[14] Berdyaev, while insisting upon an eschatological interpretation of human destiny, feels that in "creative" ecstasy man discovers "a way out from the time of this world, historical time and cosmic time."[15] And finally, Jung, who believes that man's end is self-awareness—a state of psychic wholeness attained only after the arduous integration of the "temporal" conscious and the "eternal" unconscious—confides that the richest moments of his life were nontemporal states of consciousness.[16]

Given this addition to James's definition, however, is it possible to say that mysticism is universally the same? Reports of mystical experiences appear to be unanimous in stressing James's "four marks," temporal transcendence, and the achievement of communion with a supernatural reality (to add still another element to James's definition). But is it accurate to say that mysticism is always identical in form and content? The answer is no; for while all mystics may, for example, wish to transcend time, their methods of attaining liberation—as well as their concepts of Reality—often differ. In a provocative book written in response to Aldous Huxley's *Doors of Perception,* R. C. Zaehner maintains that there are three fundamental types of mystical experience: viz., pan-en-henic, monistic, and theistic.[17] Ignoring for the moment both the Oxford don's ax-grinding and the probability that there may be other varieties of preternatural experience, it is possible to use two of Zaehner's categories to contrast the mysticism of Eliot, Berdyaev, and Jung with that of Huxley.

Eliot and Berdyaev are definitely theistic mystics. Their goal—the final cause of their spiritual quests—is to achieve personal communion with God in a timeless moment of consciousness, or "creative" ecstasy. While Berdyaev is a fairly consistent dualist and Eliot (especially in later life), a convinced monist, both agree that the personality is not destroyed during mystical experience. As they see it, the mystic (and it should be recalled that both of these men were convinced that they had actually transcended time during moments of mystical contemplation) establishes, in Martin Buber's phrase, an "I-Thou" relationship with God. God and man are joined together, united, but their communion precludes the elimination of their respective identities. They are one yet separate, united yet distinct. Aldous Huxley, on the other hand, denounces the "personalist" emphasis of Western theology, for he believes that it represents a disguised form of egotism. Behind the admonitions to worship the personality of Christ, behind the eloquent orations on the dignity of the human personality, lies the narcissistic self-image of Western man. In opposition to the theist's concept of communion Huxley proposes the Perennial Philosophy's notion of nonpersonal union with the divine Ground. According to Huxley, when the genuinely theocentric mystic establishes direct contact with eternity, his ego (as well as his "personality") is dissolved in the timeless and all-consuming depths of the Absolute (Brahman). He realizes that his individuality, his self, is an indissoluble and indistinguishable part of a larger and all-encompassing Self (Atman) and that, like time, the personality is an illusion which separates man from the divine Ground of all being. Huxley's mysticism is obviously monistic: he ultimately reduces every thing and every soul in the universe to one spiritual principle, Reality, the divine Ground, or eternity.

In contrast, C. G. Jung, while recognizing the similarities between his own analytical psychology and Eastern religious thought, repudiates the notion of annihilating the personality. The psyche must be transformed but not eliminated. A balance, a dynamic equilibrium, should be established between consciousness and unconsciousness—an equilibrium which Jung calls the self, i.e., that condition of psychic wholeness symbolized by the mandala. During his middle years, and especially in later life, Jung regarded individuation (the attainment of psychic integration) as an experience of timelessness. According to the Swiss psychologist, the collective unconscious and its contents (i.e., the archetypes) represent a spaceless and timeless mode of being. This statement is more than a hypothesis, for in Jung's view the intrinsic space-timelessness of the objective psyche has been proven by J. B. Rhine's ESP experiments.[18] The existence of telepathic phenomena, however, not only establishes the space-timelessness of the lower depths of the psyche, but indicates that there is another form of being behind the veil of the archetypes. Thus, when a person becomes individuated, he not only participates in the timeless dimension of the collective unconscious, but is provided with evidence of an "absolute object" upon which everything depends for its existence.

While Jung's mysticism is difficult to categorize because it is shaped by his unusual approach to the time-problem—i.e., by his concepts of archetypal configuration and synchronicity—his peculiar variety appears to be closer to theistic than to either pan-en-henic or monistic mysticism. Like the theist, for example, Jung not only defends the integrity of the personality, but stresses the notion of conscious communion, or participation in a timeless reality. Nevertheless, there remain two significant differences that preclude Jung's complete entrance into the theistic ranks: namely, his belief that Christ is a symbol of the self and his opinion that individuation is a psychological experience. And yet, Jung never denied the validity of Christianity. He not only believed that he had transcended time in a state of "completed individuation,"[19] but that the unconscious impinges upon a form of existence outside space and time.

Professor Zaehner tries to explain monistic and pan-en-henic mysticism (i.e., nature mysticism) in terms of Jungian psychology. (Thus, by implication, Zaehner equates monistic and nature mysticism with genuine or incompleted individuation and, by explication, emancipates theistic mysticism from psychology.) But it is obvious that Jung's kind of mysticism defies exact classification; and if it is to be categorized at all, it belongs on the fringes of the theistic variety of preternatural experience.

It is obvious that mysticism plays a cardinal role in Jung's relentless attack on the temporal process—a role more important than that of either synchronicity or myth. What priority, then, does mysticism assume in the thought of Eliot, Huxley, and Berdyaev? For Eliot and Huxley, mysticism —the direct experience of eternity here and now—represents the most significant method of overcoming time. As both authors state explicitly in their essays on aesthetics, while creativity may afford the individual a way of destroying time, mystical consciousness (even if it is only what Catholic theologians call "gratuitous graces" as opposed to full-blown mystical experiences) is by far the most exalted mode of temporal liberation. Time the destroyer can be eliminated by the artist or by the mythologist who, like Eliot in *The Waste Land,* transforms the chaos of temporal existence into an ordered pattern by using the timeless themes of myth and legend. But it remains for the mystic to achieve the highest and most comprehensive triumph over time. It is true that it is occasionally possible to detect an undercurrent of what appears to be eschatological expectation in the works of Huxley and Eliot; and yet neither author relies on eschatology to destroy time. Indeed, both Eliot and Huxley spurn eschatological visions of man's destiny; and if they seem to refer to the future in apocalyptic terms it is not in a spirit of exultation but of despair.

Berdyaev, on the other hand, does not interpret the apocalypse pessimistically. He regards it as the noblest creation of the divine-human partnership, the consummation of the story of man's estrangement from eternity. In Berdyaev's view, mystical communion with God may allow the individual to escape the power of time for an ephemeral moment in eternity (or to anticipate the eventual resolution of the conflicts of history in the Age of the Spirit), but mysticism cannot destroy the phenomenon of time itself. It enables the individual to transcend time, but it does not—it cannot—assure mankind of a final victory over the temporal process. The only way, Berdyaev insists, to abolish time irrevocably is to create a metaphysic of history—to accept the apocalyptic hope, the fervent belief, of an approaching End to the historical process which will destroy every kind of time and restore man to his former "theandric" status (or Godmanhood). The differences between Berdyaev's argument and that of Eliot, Huxley, and Jung should not, however, obscure the fundamental importance of their mutual agreement on the necessity of overcoming time. Not only do they each use spatial symbols to order, control, and destroy time; not only do they each base the belief that time can be eliminated on personal mystical experience; but all four insist that man can achieve redemption and save the world from suicide only by grounding his life in eternity.

"Spatialization" and "mysticism," "time-symbols" and "eternity-images," "apocalyptic eschatology," "creativity," and "the direct experience of eternity"—each of these terms is representative of ancient and yet enduring responses to the problem of transcending, or abolishing, time. And yet, if these patterns of reaction—if these epistemological procedures and methods—are merely symptomatic, or exemplary, of traditional responses, is there anything unusual about the twentieth-century revolt against time? In other words, what is the historical and sociological importance of twentieth-century hostility toward time?

The Twentieth-Century Revolt against Time

In the first place, this study is not simply concerned with four exceptional individuals who yearn to transcend, or abolish, time: such individuals can be found in almost any age. And while it is important to note the antiquity and pervasive continuity of the desire to transcend time, it is equally important to recognize the unusual configuration this desire has assumed in the twentieth century. For example, Berdyaev, Eliot, Huxley, and Jung were all at one time agnostics, atheists, or sceptics, who believed in the intrinsic value of temporal civilization and endorsed some form of "time-philosophy." Although the particular philosophies vary—Bergsonism for Eliot, the liberal idea of Progress for Huxley and Jung, Marxism for Berdyaev—for all, time is substituted for eternity and reality is equated with time, or becoming. Yet shortly before or after the First World War and the Russian Revolution, these (and many other) intellectuals began to reconsider their metaphysical presuppositions. As a consequence, the quartet eventually repudiated its secular world-views. This reappraisal ultimately took two forms: first, a strong revulsion against the time of human experience (expressing itself in both a revolt against time-philosophy in all its protean shapes and in a refusal to accept the identification of time with reality); and second, a denial of previous agnosticism, atheism, or scepticism, as well as a "conversion" to a traditional form of religious phenomenology, namely, mysticism. For Eliot and, to some extent, Berdyaev, the reappraisal also led to an acceptance of the dogma of an institutional religion.

This comprehensive reversal of attitudes (which in itself is an extraordinary phenomenon) exemplifies the experience not only of this quartet, but of religious antitemporalists in general. For the majority of the thinking men and women who revolted against time in the early decades of this century did so by attacking time-philosophies and by discovering (or returning to) religion. They rebelled against the secularization of modern consciousness by challenging the hegemony of the idea of (temporal) change in contemporary thought. Thus, their "conversions-in-reverse" were a direct reaction against the "Great Substitution" of the previous century; they rejected out of hand the ersatz religion that had substituted time for eternity, history for timelessness.

It is worth recalling here that "the word *secularization* came to mean what we now mean when we use it"—namely, "a growing tendency in mankind to do without religion, or to try to do without religion"[20]—in the forty or more years following the publication in 1859 of the *Origin of Species*. It was this period, rather than the late seventeenth century or the Enlightenment, that witnessed the secularization of the European mind[21]—a fact that underscores the revolutionary nature of the antitemporalists' dramatic change in outlook. They stood the secular movement on its head and pro-

[15]

ceeded to build a world-view *(Weltanschauung)* that had its roots in a prescientific age. And while it is not unusual to find in various historical periods intellectuals who criticize their societies for lacking spiritual values, it is striking to discover so many who, at the close of an era recognized for its optimistic appraisal of human affairs, abandon their secular world-views to adopt a hostile attitude toward time, history, and culture. Yet, it is here that the twentieth-century revolt against time most distinguishes itself from other efforts in the modern era to transcend temporality. In other words, not only do the religious antitemporalists attack the ontological limitations of time and condemn all varieties of time-philosophy, they also single out Time as a symptom of the "disease" afflicting Western civilization. Or, to put it another way, they couple their personal desire to transcend, or abolish, time with an attack on the secular, time-obsessed, values of Western culture.[22]

It would be a mistake, however, to regard the revolt against time and the rejection of the temporal values of Western civilization as the monopoly of religious antitemporalists, such as Berdyaev, Eliot, Huxley, and Jung. For in this century there have also been a significant number of intellectuals who have managed to rebel against becoming, as well as against the Western "time-ethic," within an entirely secular context.

Lawrence Durrell, for instance, talks of discovering a "Heraldic Universe" in which space annihilates time (both chronological time and "real duration"). Hermann Broch advances a comparable idea in his trilogy *The Sleepwalkers* (1931), when he insists that "whatever a man may do, he does it to annihilate Time . . . and that revocation [of Time] is called Space." H. G. Wells, on the other hand, explores the possibilities of surmounting historical time by traveling along the "fourth dimension" (1895); and D. H. Lawrence, proponent of a mystical view of human sexuality, describes states of erotic consciousness that transcend the flux of events (1927). Similarly, André Malraux sought to rise above the destructive pressures of duration. Like Théophile Gautier before him, Malraux found himself increasingly preoccupied with the enduring artistic achievements of mankind—achievements which themselves seemed to constitute or manifest an "Absolute" above time and history. Malraux's compatriot Marcel Proust also tried to counter time by transcending the chronological structure of duration. In his view, *Remembrance of Things Past* (1906–22) permits past moments to live again in the present and, thus, to transcend the apparently inexorable and omniverous *"ordre du temps."*

Proust's time-redeeming view of retrospection was inspired by Henri Bergson, who maintained that authentic time, real duration, did not consist of slab-like moments that could be separated and divided along a line into a past, present, or future. On the contrary, Bergson asserted that true time, nonchronological time, consists of an ever-moving, eternally flowing present which contains its own past. Bergson greatly influenced the work of other intellectuals either directly, through his description of *durée réelle*, or indirectly. Virginia Woolf, for instance, contrasts the time of the clock ("spatialized time" in Bergson's vocabulary) with "the unlimited time of the mind." At another point, she attacks as a "convenience" and a "lie" the "extreme precision," the "orderly and military progress" of measured time, and compares it to the rushing "stream" of impressions that fluctuate beneath the artificial ramparts of consciousness. Similar images of time are also found in the work of James Joyce. In the instance of the interior monologue, clock time is juxtaposed unfavorably against the stream of consciousness, which is itself synonymous with authentic (or living) time. Thomas Wolfe, author of an appositely entitled book, *Of Time and the River,* contrasts past and present time with "time immutable," "a kind of eternal and unchanging universe of time," which he can reconcile with the "transience of man's life" by achieving an "arrested or suspended moment" of intuition in which all kinds of time are fused together.

Finally, Martin Heidegger, who also manifests an antagonism for the deception and regimentation of quotidian time *(Innerzeitigkeit),* insists that one can achieve an authentic vision of time only by resolving to reevaluate the tripartite structure of our ordinary temporal experience. In *Being and Time* he argues that each phase of "our time," or life span (the "ontological" ground of human being, or *Dasein*), should be dynamically interrelated, for a person whose own time has been restricted to the mechanical time of an industrial civilization loses his humanity and becomes a mass man *(Massenmensch).* To achieve an authentic experience of time, Heidegger contends, we must realize that the past, present, and future are neither stagnant nor terminal categories of our being; they are vibrant and alive, and perish only with our death. To overcome *Innerzeitigkeit,* we will have to develop an "openness to the future" and realize that our past changes in relation to our anticipation of the future and that our present *(Gegenwart,* or "waiting-toward") as well as our future *(Zukunft)* are affected by our altering past. When this holistic and dynamic understanding of authentic time is achieved, we will be able to transcend the fragmented and static structure of everyday time.

No matter how compelling the arguments of the secular antitemporalists may be, no matter how determined their efforts to transcend chronological time may appear, it is undeniable that within a religious context the revolt against time is a far more persistent, serious, and radical development. This is immediately clear when one examines the reactions of religious anti-temporalists to Bergson's description of real time as unsegmented flux. The awareness of time as *durée réelle*—a concrete, immediate, but passing present—is viewed by most secular antitemporalists as the highest achievable form of time-transcendence. But for virtually all of their religious counterparts it is seen as only a step toward the ultimate goal of achieving victory over time. For them, the passing present is but a halfway house lying between the illusory flux of chronological time and the absolute timelessness of the eternal present. According to religious antitemporalists, even the passing moment is a subtle form of time; and as such, it must yield to an eternal, or timeless, present. As Wyndham Lewis points out in *Time and Western Man* (1927), real duration—however soothing to the longing agnostic or useful to the experimental novelist—remains a form of Time. Lewis (like Berdyaev, Eliot, Huxley, and Jung) looks upon such notions as *durée réelle,* "eternal or unlimited time," and "stream of consciousness" as dangerous symptoms of modern man's obsession with time, his adoption of "a mode of thinking that contemplates everything—nature, man, society, history, God himself—*sub specie temporis,* as not merely changing but as forever evolving into something new and different."[23] While awareness of real duration may represent a movement in the right direction, it falls short of the goal: the duration that secular antitemporalists view as promising to abolish time remains simply its most subtle form. It is, in fact, a symptom of a time-obsession and an example of a spiritually maiming passion for time-philosophy. As such, it encourages us (to borrow a phrase of C. E. M. Joad's) to "drop the object," to surrender the idea of an objective and absolute reality outside time which imparts validity to our lives. Time-philosophy abandons us, then, to epistemological and ethical relativism and prevents us from ever achieving knowledge (as opposed to opinion).

Most religious antitemporalists follow the same "methods," or epistemological procedures, as Berdyaev, Eliot, Huxley, and Jung in their attempts to transcend time and rediscover eternity: namely, "spatialization"—which, as we have seen, is also used by secular antitemporalists—and mysticism. Both methods of destroying time are interchangeable, and occasionally it is possible to find them being used simultaneously. Hermann Hesse, for example, describes a "Transformation from Time into Space"—a transformation which occurs by "means of music" and which, to the protagonist of *Steppenwolf* (1927), is equivalent to regaining eternity in a moment of mystical illumination. The French Jesuit paleontologist Teilhard de Chardin anticipates a comparable transformation toward the end of his book *The Phenomenon of Man* (1955) when, under the spell of an ecstatic eschatological vision, he describes the cosmic process as an irreversible linear regression and the path of evolutionary history as a rising line which eventually curves and turns into a circle around eternity, or "point Omega." Charles Williams advocates the "Way of Affirmations" as a means of overcoming time and perceiving the timeless dance of eternity; W. H. Auden describes sacred spaces, "gardens that time is for ever outside," and the "accidental happiness" that permits a perception of eternity; and W. B. Yeats writes of the "fiery moment" of mystical illumination in which the mind perceives "the trysting-place of mortal and immortal, time and eternity." Drawing both on what Wyndham Lewis calls "the 'spatializing' process of a mind not a Time-mind" and on the evidence of preternatural experience, Baron von Hügel, Evelyn Underhill, Dorothy Sayers, and Gerald Heard champion the merits of Christian mysticism, which allows the purified soul to transcend time and commune with eternal reality, or God. Christopher Isherwood, René Guénon, May Sinclair, and Ananda Coomaraswamy support the nonpersonal mysticism of the East as the authentic way to timelessness. And finally, Warner Allen, the "neo-Plotinian" mystic, who was strongly influenced in his pursuit of *The Timeless Moment* (1946) by E. Graham Howe, Dean Inge, and T. S. Eliot, insists that it is possible to transcend time (and space) through "the order of Consciousness and the world of Awareness." This conclusion was also reached by Maurice Nicoll, a proponent of the esoteric "Work" of Gurdjieff and P. D. Ouspensky. Nicoll urges us to "fight with time" and seek fulfillment *"Now"*—i.e., in "a state of the spirit . . . when it is above the stream of time-associations."[24]

Partially as a result of the First World War, twentieth-century theologians have likewise displayed a new (and quite often impassioned) interest in the problem of time. They have made a serious effort to establish the proper relationship between time and eternity—to discover whether it is possible to bridge the gap between the divine and the human—in a moment of timeless contemplation. The debate over time in twentieth-century theology is itself representative of a broader interest in the philosophy of history which developed in the apocalyptic atmosphere of post–World War I Europe. Indeed, as Emmanuel Mounier once observed, much of this century's thought betrays an "apocalyptic consciousness." And whether it reveals a desire to abolish time (as it does, for instance, in the writings of Berdyaev, Léon Bloy, Teilhard de Chardin, Evgeny Lamprecht, and E. M. Cioran) or whether it represents a premonition of doom, or the fear of imminent catastrophe, it is true that this apocalyptic current can be traced in the works of many twentieth-century intellectuals, including Albert Schweitzer, Arthur Koestler, Oswald Spengler, and C. Virgil Gheorghiu.[25]

The scope of the twentieth-century revolt against time and against religious scepticism grows further when seen as a revolt against Western history itself. Antitemporalism represents a partial or complete repudiation of the cultural and technological development of the West from the Renaissance and the Scientific Revolution to the present—a historical movement characterized (we are told) by cultural fragmentation, the depreciation of man's spiritual nature, the mechanization of human institutions, and the catastrophes of war. Far from revealing the triumphant march of human progress, as the apostles of meliorism contend, modern history reveals the disastrous hubris of Faustian man and the astounding frailty of human nature. In Joyce's *Ulysses,* Stephen Dedalus speaks for all religious antitemporalists when he declares, "History . . . is the nightmare from which I am trying to awake." Dedalus's cry of defiance complements that of the hero of Kazantzakis's novel *The Rock Garden:* " 'I declare war on time! I declare war on time!" Both statements are exemplary of the revolt's determination to challenge—if not abolish, or transcend—history itself (and the course of modern history in particular) and to give meaning to human life by penetrating historical time and restoring to modern consciousness the vision of existence under the aspect of eternity.

In this respect the antitemporalists' onslaught on history must also be seen as a rejection of historicism, a critique of the validity of history as a form of knowledge, and an example of the widespread "hostility towards the historical consciousness and the historian" which surfaced "in the decade before the First World War."[26] This antagonism, which constitutes an important part of the background to the twentieth-century revolt against time, had its origins in the last three decades of the nineteenth century. For example, in George Eliot's *Middlemarch* (1871–72), in Ibsen's *Hedda Gabler* (1890), and in Thomas Mann's *Buddenbrooks* (1901) history is characterized as a morbid discipline for escapists who dread living in the present. Even before the First World War Bergson described history as a defective, or invalid, epistemology, a charge repeated after the war by Paul Valéry. And the existentialists—André Gide in *The Immoralist* (1902) and Jean-Paul Sartre in *Nausea* (1938)—portray history as a debilitating subject which, because of its special relationship to the past and to chronological time, stimulates pathological symptoms.

Many of the intellectuals who attacked the discipline and process of history in the early years of this century went on to become thoroughgoing antitemporalists. (Thomas Mann is a case in point.) For them the struggle against history and "the historical consciousness" eventually also became a struggle against time—historical time and the diurnal dimension of time; and it is not unusual to find them using both terms interchangeably, Wyndham Lewis recognized this practice clearly when he blasted several members of the twentieth-century "Time-cult" for their "*chronological* philosophy": "There is Alexander, Gentile, Bergson, Croce, Wildon Carr. In its very heart and at its roots, for all of them, *reality* is 'History,' or reality is 'time,' which is the same thing."

In pursuit of their goal of re-creating a view of life under the aspect of eternity, religious antitemporalists also attack the preeminent value an advanced industrial civilization places on time—especially "clock time"—and its economic correlative, expressed in Benjamin Franklin's aphorism "time is money." Thus their cultural criticism is indicative of broadscale protests against the increasing complexity and materialization of modern life in the West.

Such protests are obviously not unique to the twentieth century. In fact, recent denunciations of the mechanization of human existence have their origin in different (yet related) currents of nineteenth-century thought. Although in most cases, nineteenth-century protests against the materialization and dehumanization of life do not involve a concomitant attack on the temporal process, they nevertheless exemplify a significant change in attitude toward Western culture. In the years following World War I this culminated in a repudiation of the overwhelming value placed on time by the optimists of *la belle époque*.

The period between 1871 and 1900, a time of great confidence in "materialism"—characterized by pride in material accomplishments, worldly pragmatism, and a "philosophy" dominated by material and mechanistic conceptions[27]—was simultaneously a period of growing dissatisfaction with the development of Western culture, in general, and the quality of nineteenth-century life, in particular. Yet the chorus of criticism, which gradually increased in volume from the depression years of the '70s onward, had already announced itself. Before 1870 Karl Marx and Charles Kingsley, for instance, excoriated the established classes for exploiting the poor laborer; Honoré de Balzac satirized the crass materialism of the bourgeoisie; John Henry Newman attacked the religious and political "liberalism" of his contemporaries; and Matthew Arnold noted the deracination and anarchy —the confusing whirligig of new and ever-swarming ideas—in nineteenth-century culture. Still, as Benedetto Croce once observed, there was an important "change in the public spirit of Europe" after 1870, an acceleration of the critique of nineteenth-century life already under way.

This change represents an intellectual and political response to the long-range effects of the "dual revolution"—the democratic revolution and the Industrial Revolution—as well as to the dramatic growth of Europe's population, the subsequent birth of the "masses," and the increasing rivalries among nations and classes. The growing standardization of life coupled with the rapid materialization of middle-class values, the depreciation of the "inner world" of the spirit and the glorification of the machine, the burgeoning discontinuity and dissociation of European culture, as well as the dangerously naïve equation of technological advancement with human progress—all combined to intensify the disaffection of intellectuals.

The growing antagonism toward nineteenth-century culture reached its apogee during the 1890s. This is not to say, however, that by this decade the majority of educated Europeans had renounced their materialism or their confidence in the future.[28] On the contrary, most Europeans seem to have remained steadfastly loyal to their faith in the inventiveness and productivity of Western civilization until 1916. Some, such as Walter Mehring's father, even thought that the turn of the century would bring the millennium. Nevertheless, the decade of the '90s inaugurated an intensive reevaluation of the direction and purpose of European civilization—a reappraisal marked not only by a "revolt against positivism," but by a new preoccupation with "spiritism" or the occult.[29]

In Germany, France, Italy, and England the renunciation of positivism took the form of "a growing awareness of the things of the spirit." The protest was registered in the works of philosophers, sociologists, historians, and poets—in the writings of such intellectuals as Wilhelm Windelband (who issued a "declaration of war against positivism"),[30] Henri Bergson (who attacked the quantitative and ratiocinative "fallacies" of modern thought), Max Weber (who stressed the priority of ideas in shaping the origin and development of "material" events such as modern capitalism), Benedetto Croce (who tried to emancipate history from science), or George Meredith (who championed the life of the senses and defended the achievements of the spirit at the expense of positivism).[31] Yet the desire to "escape from materialism"[32] was not limited to a repudiation of nineteenth-century scientism.

The "discovery" of spiritism also marks a change, although perhaps a minor change, in the spirit of *fin de siècle* Europe. As early as 1875, the world-traveling Russian occultist Madame Helena Blavatsky founded the Theosophical Society in New York City. She and her successor as head of the society, Annie Besant, were able to create a religious organization that continued into the twentieth century to influence European intellectuals like Berdyaev, Eliot, Huxley, Yeats, and Charles Williams. This new concern for mysticism and the occult (reflected more recently in the anthroposophical movement of Rudolf Steiner and the vogue of Eastern and Western mysticism) was given further impetus by the "spiritual" interests of Sir Oliver Lodge and Alfred Russel Wallace as well as by the founding of the Society for Psychical Research. (Established in 1882, this society's investigations and research activities anticipated some of the results of J. B. Rhine's ESP experiments done in the 1930s.)

Despite the attempts to "escape from materialism," despite the protests against the increasing "multitudinousness," "sick hurry," complexity, and mechanization of life, however, these sentiments were not indicative of any widespread dissatisfaction with the "bourgeois century."[33] On the contrary, the protests generally were made by a minority of exceptional, often hypersensitive, individuals. Yet significantly, the protesters failed to isolate Time in their diagnoses as an essential ingredient of the "modern malady." This point is important, for it is not until the First World War and the Russian Revolution that critiques of modern life single out Time as a symptom of the "disease" affecting Western civilization.

The correlation between the outbreak of the revolt against time, on the one hand, and the waning years of nineteenth century and the commencement of World War I, on the other, is not accidental. Europe had not known full-scale war for nearly a century when the guns of August shattered the Pax Victoriana in 1914. Of course, there had been the Franco-Prussian War in 1870 and the Crimean fiasco sixteen years earlier, but as of summer 1914, Great Britain and the Continent had experienced a hundred years of relative peace. The absence of a major war, however, could not disguise the existence of serious social, economic, and political problems—the wretched plight of most of the working classes, political revolution, many-faceted decadence, and the violent growth of nationalism.

It is striking that while evidently aware of the gravity and complexity of these conditions, three members of the antitemporalist quartet—Jung, Eliot, and Huxley—did not begin to translate their dissatisfaction with Western culture into an attack on time until the First World War. On the other hand, Berdyaev had become sufficiently unsettled by what he considered the decadence of nineteenth-century culture to advocate an idealistic version of Marxist revolution before the war. But even Berdyaev, who joined the Russian Orthodox Church in 1912, maintained a positive attitude toward historical time at least until the war and perhaps (although he is ambivalent on this issue) until as late as the Bolshevik assumption of power.

The delay in the commencement of their revolt against time can be partially explained by the fact that Berdyaev, Eliot, Huxley, and Jung (like antitemporalists in general) all came from the established classes of society. Although dissatisfied with the state of Western society, they tended to view the future with confidence or indifference because of their families' secure positions in the social hierarchy. Thus, the experience of an enormous catastrophe (the war or, in Berdyaev's case, the failure of the Russian

Revolution) was necessary before these men could renounce their allegiance to time-philosophy.

At first glance there would seem to be another reason for the delay: the factor of age. Whereas Berdyaev and Jung were nearing middle age at the beginning of the war, Huxley and Eliot were, respectively, only twenty and twenty-six years old. But, as an examination of their life-histories demonstrates, these discrepancies in age are not crucial. In fact, only a few years (and in some instances perhaps no more than a few months) separate the independent development of their antagonistic attitudes toward time and their identification of antitemporalism with an attack on Western culture.

The importance that Berdyaev, Eliot, Huxley, Jung, and other prominent religious antitemporalists ascribe to mysticism—perhaps even more than the importance they accord spatialization or the quest for timelessness in myth—has encouraged critics to regard the twentieth-century revolt against time as an example of sheer escapism—a manifestation of an invalid, if not cowardly, reluctance to confront the challenging complexities of modern life. Yet it would be a mistake to view the protagonists of the twentieth-century revolt against time as escapists trying to avoid the anxieties generated by a civilization in crisis.

Rather than experiencing a "failure of nerve" or withdrawing, like Koestler's yogi, from active participation in the affairs of the world, antitemporalists like Berdyaev, Eliot, Huxley, and Jung have responded energetically to the problems of our time. It might be true that they have, to borrow Charles Frankel's phrase, "re-discovered sin," or the constancy of human imperfection, and that they have abandoned the optimistic anthropology of the nineteenth century. But their abandonment of facile, anthropocentric optimism does not mean that they have abandoned humanity. For while they question the validity of Western culture, and while they are directly concerned with their own attempts to transcend, or abolish, time, they also suggest positive measures by which to improve the sad state of the West (and, by implication, the entire world). They refuse to accept the role of ivory-tower philosophers; they are vitally concerned with man's fate in the modern world. This engagement should not be depreciated, for although they believe that man's greatest achievement is the transcendence of time in mystical intuition, or the eschatological destruction of the temporal process, they would like every person to establish contact with Reality. Thus, they stress the necessity of a massive reorientation of human values, a universal endorsement of the belief in spiritual reality, and a thoroughgoing denial of the ultimate importance of things in time.

This quartet was not always confident that man would change the structure of his consciousness, effect a spiritual revolution, or transform the nightmare of history into sweetness and light. And yet, Berdyaev, Eliot, Huxley, and Jung persisted in diagnosing what they thought were the causes of twentieth-century ills; they continued to suggest remedies. They never gave up trying to convince human beings of their higher calling and spiritual dignity—they never stopped insisting that man's final End lay outside the ontological limitations of the ephemeral universe in an eternal reality that human beings could apprehend in time.

CHAPTER 2

Nicolas Berdyaev:
Twentieth-Century Apocalyptist

> The conquest of the deadly flux of time has
> always been the chief concern of my life.
> —*Dream and Reality*

"Dream and Reality"

Because his "way of thinking is fragmentary and aphoristic"—because it is not discursive "and moves by fits and starts"[1]—the religious philosophy of Nicolas Berdyaev often seems to be contradictory and paradoxical, a bewildering congeries of unrelated impressions and thoughts. And yet, underlying this aura of confusion, beneath this superficial semblance of distortion, there is a clear and unified vision, a coherent metaphysic, which is held together and sustained by the dynamic thread of a basic theme: the abolition of time and the realization of eternity. All of the problems with which Berdyaev deals, all of his particular philosophical conceptions—objectification, "meonic freedom," personalism, creativity, Godforsakenness, and theandrism—revolve around and are derived from this fundamental eschatological concern, this passionate and tenacious desire to deliver mankind from "the tragedy and torment of time"[2] into the unfettered freedom of eternity.

Berdyaev himself recognized the centrality of the eschatological issue for his thought. In his spiritual autobiography, *Dream and Reality,* he confesses, "The conquest of the deadly flux of time has always been the chief concern of my life." Thus, he could never "acquiesce in the ephemeral," he could never accept the fact that "Man is nailed to the cross of time with its tormenting contradictions." Consequently he knew "moments of almost desperate impatience with time," moments in which he "would fain have quickened and forestalled the end—not the end in death, but the end beyond time in transcendence and eternity."[3] Again and again, Berdyaev found himself trying to cure "the disease of time," trying to destroy the temporal process which "is the nightmare and torment of our life in the world."[4] He persistently fought against time—against the destructiveness of contingency—because he believed that "unending history would be meaningless" and that "history has meaning" only "because it comes to an end."[5] He constantly insisted that time (which he considered indissolubly linked with history)[6] must have a final and irreversible stop if humanity is to succeed in conquering the absurdity of the fallen world. "History must come to an end"—"time must come to an end"—if eternal life is to be won and death conquered.[7]

Berdyaev's eschatological concern did not spring solely from a personal fear of time or a terror of history. Nor did it derive entirely from an egotistical desire to achieve immortality. For he strove genuinely to liberate not only himself but all humanity from the "tormenting contradictions" of time. As a consequence he consistently related his eschatological metaphysics to the spiritual and social problems he found confronting the modern world. His eschatological view of human affairs may have been rooted in his subjective awareness of the transitoriness of human life and his hypersensitive recognition of the catastrophic nature of world history, but he never allowed his apocalyptic viewpoint to become "an invitation to escape into a private heaven." Rather, it led him to translate his personal yearnings for timelessness into a peremptory and sustained demand for universal salvation. It deepened his compassion for other human beings who suffered from the "unspeakable pain" caused by the "perpetual flux" of time and intensified his efforts "to transfigure this evil and stricken world."[8]

The compassionate impulse which frequently dominates Berdyaev's thought is firmly grounded in his acute psychological analyses of the spiritual and social conditions of modern life, as well as in his experience as an active participant in many of the great social and political unheavals of this century. Born in 1874 of parents who belonged to the upper class of the Russian nobility, Nicolas Alexandrovich Berdyaev was raised as an aristocrat, a fact to which he consistently attributed great importance because it "left its mark on" his "mental make-up"[9] and influenced the development of his religious philosophy. His mother, *née* Princess Kudashev, was half French; and though born a member of the Russian Orthodox Church, she always considered herself to be a Roman Catholic. Berdyaev's father, on the other hand, was a free-thinker, or Voltairian deist, who strongly disapproved of Church dogma and ritual. And since his scepticism prevailed at home, the customary Orthodox atmosphere of the Russian household was absent from Nicolas's childhood. Yet even though an enlightened rationalism held sway over the household, the parents often clashed over religious issues. These arguments, however, seem only to have increased the father's influence over the son. And though Berdyaev

[28]

later refused to admit that he had "ever been a Voltairian," he recognized that he "nevertheless shared" the French philosopher's "concern for the emancipation of man and even his revolt against religion."[10]

When Nicolas was "on the threshold of adolescence," he experienced his first "conversion," not a "violent confessional conversion"—indeed in a strict sense it was not even "religious"—but simply a "spiritual re-orientation" that led him to embrace philosophy, the search for truth and meaning, as his life's work.[11] He still shared his father's (or Voltaire's) sceptical attitude, and he had not come to believe in God per se. But he had undergone an experience that shifted the focus of his life. He had been "shaken to the depths by the thought that, even though there may be no such thing as a meaning in life, the very search for meaning would render life significant and meaningful." Henceforth he dedicated his life to this quest for truth; and, as he later saw it, "This insight marked a true inner revolution which changed my whole outlook." It changed "my whole life . . . and I felt as if carried on the wings of some spiritual rapture."[12]

At the time Berdyaev turned to philosophy, he was attending the military Academy of Kiev. His forebears on his father's side had been prominent in the tsarist army since the days of the Napoleonic Wars. Thus, it was quite natural that Nicolas should have been destined for a military career. But he was not prepared to follow in the Berdyaev tradition. And shortly after he joined the Cadet Corps, he revolted against the stringent discipline of his surroundings.

This early confrontation with military regimentation may help to explain the development of Berdyaev's later "spiritual anarchism," his hatred of any institutional or ontological restriction of personal freedom or liberty. At any rate, he felt alienated from his fellow cadets (ostensibly because they did not share his intellectual interests) and attempted to withdraw as much as possible from the society of the academy. Nevertheless, the years Berdyaev spent as a cadet were extremely important. It was during this period that he "discovered" his father's library, read Kant's *Critique of Pure Reason* and Hegel's *Phenomenology of the Spirit* (works which were to play a significant role in shaping his religious metaphysic), and eventually experienced his "conversion" to philosophy.

Because his intellectual and philosophical pursuits set him apart from the other cadets, and because he professed an interest in studying natural science, Berdyaev decided to leave the academy and enter the University of Kiev. There he pursued his philosophical studies—studies which soon led him to enter "the Marxist fold." He had already developed revolutionary and Socialist sympathies before entering the university, but the experience of being a student and meeting active Marxists (the most famous of whom was Anatoli Lunacharsky) accelerated his acceptance of Marxist theory. "The encounter with Marxism," which "took place in 1894," proved of enormous significance for Berdyaev.[13] For although he later repudiated the doctrine of economic determinism, he never lost his admiration for Marx's "genuine moral passion and . . . his repudiation of class-morality." Berdyaev never forgot the "sheer genius of Marx" and the spell-binding image of a classless society, a new Golden Age, at the end of the historical process.[14]

Berdyaev particularly appreciated what Sir Isaiah Berlin calls Marx's "monism"—i.e., his reduction of all phenomena in the universe to one theoretical hypothesis capable of explaining every occurrence, every vicissitude or event that transpires in the manifold world. And it is this monism, this historical universalism, that probably provided Nicolas Berdyaev with his first taste of messianic eschatology.[15] For even though Marx purports to be a "scientist," his theory of history—especially as it is occasionally described in the footnotes to *Das Kapital*—is highly emotive and nondiscursive. It is essentially a secularized transcription of Judaic eschatology. Yet while Berdyaev "accepted the materialist interpretation of history over against the bourgeois illusion," he "repudiated the metaphysical implications of materialism" (especially Marx's conception of "super-structure") because he could not believe that truth can "be imprisoned in any social net," that all ideas are determined by economic and political conditions.[16] Still, he liked Marx's identification of the "chosen-people motif" of Judaism with the industrial proletariat. And at a later date, when he described *The Origins of Russian Communism* (1937) and *The Russian Idea* (1946), he recognized the important contribution Marx and the Russian Communists had made to historical theory, even though he criticized the latter for their "distortion of the Russian messianic idea."[17]

During his student years, Berdyaev did not develop what might be termed a "traditional religious outlook." For although he believed in "the supreme reality of spirit and of absolute values independent of the material world"[18]—a position which he had gradually attained after his adolescent "conversion" to philosophy and which he was able to maintain simultaneously with his Marxist view of history—he did not believe in God. But even while he denied the existence of God, Berdyaev's disaffection from the mundane "two dimensional world" led him to adopt the "ethical idealism" of Fichte; "during and after my university years," "the God in whom I believed was the God of German Idealism, a God who is involved in the process of becoming," and who (in Berdyaev's opinion) is more of an evolving moral principle than a transcendent deity. Thus, at the same time Berdyaev accepted the Marxist theory of history, he also accepted the ethical God of German Idealism. He attempted to overcome this apparent contradiction in his first book, *Subjectivism and Individualism in Social Philosophy* (1901), by endeavoring "to show the possibility of a synthesis of critical Marxism and the Idealist philosophy of Kant and partly of Fichte."[19]

Berdyaev wrote this book while he was an exile in the province of Vologda. He had joined a Social Democratic cell (which was in contact with Plekhanov, Axelrod, and Vera Zasulich) when he entered the university and had also participated in student demonstrations. In fact, his first arrest was the outcome of his participation in a student demonstration—a demonstration which he had gone to evidently believing that he would be shot and perhaps killed. Fortunately for Berdyaev, he and his fellow students were treated gently by the patriarchal prison governor. In 1898, however, he did not fare as well when he was arrested in connection with the Social Democrats' first big demonstration: he was expelled from the university and subsequently exiled to Vologda in northern Russia for two years.

"The period immediately preceding the exile to Vologda was probably one of the most exhilarating, enthusiastic and creative in my life," Berdyaev recalled. "It was a time . . . of an experience of living in a world smouldering and almost bursting into flame—a time" when "I became increasingly aware of the transcendent dimensions of life." And this sense of elation, "this mood, which prefigured my later spiritual re-orientation, persisted into the early period of my exile."[20]

At Vologda Berdyaev spent most of his time reading (he especially enjoyed Ibsen because, like himself, the Norwegian playwright seemed to be striving to transcend "the closed circle of one-dimensional, flat, mundane existence")[21] and writing. His first articles were written at this time, and an essay on "F. A. Lange and Critical Philosophy in Its Relation to Socialism" was published in the German Marxist journal *Neue Zeit* (edited by Karl Kautsky). Yet Berdyaev had already taken a step further away from Marxism toward Idealism, a transition signaled not only by his first book, but by an article published during his early Vologda period entitled "The Struggle for Idealism." These and subsequent articles incurred the disfavor of orthodox Marxists and further alienated Berdyaev from their ranks. But he still accepted aspects of Marxist theory, and although (for the moment) he approved of Eduard Bernstein's revisionism, Berdyaev still "shared Marx's prophecy concerning a new world" at the end of the historical process.[22]

After Berdyaev's term of exile was over, he went through a period of deep depression and weariness—a period in which "all creative energy seemed to desert me."[23] It was a time in which "I became . . . the prey of spiritual and cultural decadence . . . a tendency which was characteristic in some measure of the whole movement that began in the nineties and entailed a substitution of beauty for truth and of individualism for social responsibility."[24] This fallow and inactive phase terminated when he moved to St. Petersburg to assume the editorship of a new periodical. The Russian capital that greeted him in the autumn of 1904 was in a dynamic state of flux, full of intellectual ferment and political agitation:

> Following an amnesty under Svatopolk Mirsky, the majority of political exiles, their ideas sharpened by long years in Siberia, flooded into the capital. Scores of new "thought-systems" arose. More quasi-religious cults appeared. The hitherto clandestine political parties began to emerge from hiding and were later joined by half a dozen new ones.[25]

At first Berdyaev entered the environment of the Russian cultural renaissance enthusiastically. He participated in the discussions of several of the twenty or more intellectual circles and coteries that had sprung up in St. Petersburg. And he soon made the acquaintance of the symbolist poet Andrey Bely, of Dmitri Merezhkovsky (author of the famous *Romance of Leonardo da Vinci*) and his wife, the poet Zinaida Gippius. Initially the Merezhkovskys, who were identified with a contemporary religious movement (the New Religious Consciousness) exerted a strong influence over Berdyaev, encouraging his continued progress from Marxism to Idealism. And it was from the Merezhkovskys that he and the philosopher Sergy Bulgakov ("another religio-idealist fellow traveler of Marxism," who later became a priest and a controversial Orthodox theologian)[26] took over the editorship of the radical political and religious journal the *New Way (Novy'put)*. The enterprise folded, however, after a number of issues were printed, and Berdyaev and Bulgakov subsequently associated themselves with another periodical, *Problems of Life,* which continued to publish into the early days of the Russian Revolution.

While the atmosphere of ferment in St. Petersburg definitely excited Berdyaev, he recognized that "there were unmistakable signs of incipient decadence in the whole movement."[27] The proliferation of pseudo-mystical cults, the artificial pursuit of "culture," and particularly the failure of the intelligentsia to relate its ideas to current social and political realities cast the oppressive atmosphere of a greenhouse over the entire movement. The St. Petersburg intelligentsia, of course, was preoccupied with "socialism" and "sought to build an ethical foundation within socialism." But it directed its "search for an absolute toward religion instead of revolution. From Plekhanov (whom Berdyaev had met and argued with in Geneva in 1904) and other materialists" these "intellectuals turned to Tolstoi and Dostoievsky."[28] And it appears that the avowed intentions of the intelligentsia's new social ethic—this rare concoction of idealism, occultism, and socialism—were rhetorical rather than practical. This impression is substantiated by a letter Berdyaev wrote from the country, in which he expresses his dissatisfaction with the hypocrisy of the St. Petersburg intelligentsia:

> In all St. Petersburg literary society I have scarcely met any purity or nobility. I am so painfully surprised at the impurity and shallowness of this milieu, that I am resting my spirit in the country, and dream of living at least one winter away from St. Petersburg. . . . In this musty mess of "circles," there is no interest in God's world and in world-problems . . . and they esteem themselves to be the salt of the earth![29]

Berdyaev may have been unhappy with this state of affairs, but he continued to live in St. Petersburg. He was there in 1905 when the Russo-Japanese War concluded, after the Battle of the Tshushima Straits, with the "disgraceful" treaty of Portsmouth and when, on Bloody Sunday, the Cossack guard fired on the unarmed workmen (led by Father Gapon) in front of the Winter Palace. He was in the capital in June 1905 when the crew of the *Potemkin* mutinied and when the tsar issued his eleventh-hour October Manifesto, guaranteeing civil liberties and announcing formation of a Duma. And Berdyaev was still in St. Petersburg when the abortive uprising occurred in Moscow in December of the same year.

As to the revolution of 1905 itself, Berdyaev's attitude seems to have been divided, if not somewhat confused. For while he tells us many years after the event that it was inevitable, he actually appears to have been caught off guard and deeply perplexed not only by the appalling bloodshed but by the abject failure of the Russian intelligentsia to provide the revolution with any sort of effective leadership. Berdyaev's own immediate (and totally unself-critical) contribution toward remedial action was a scathing denunciation of the cultural elite for their remoteness "from the wider social movements of the time."[30] But while he may have urged his fellow intellectuals to overcome their political naiveté by rejecting liberalism and pacifism (and evidently the gradualism of Bernstein and the Mensheviks) in favor of a commitment to violent social change in the immediate future, Berdyaev himself was equally guilty of political myopia. In fact, for a short period he was almost completely oblivious to the march of events that was bringing revolution to Russia. Yet this apathetic condition was only temporary and is partially explained by Berdyaev's involvement with his own spiritual struggle. This preoccupation may have been inspired by his deeply religious wife, Lydia Yudifovna, who had resolved her own spiritual crisis by converting to Catholicism shortly after their marriage in 1904. In any event, the anguish and confusion of this period in his life was partially dispelled after the summer of 1907 when Berdyaev experienced a near-conversion to Russian Orthodoxy.

Berdyaev insists that his "second conversion" was not really a conversion in the traditional Western sense. Nevertheless he remembered a moment in which he became conscious of himself as a Christian, a moment

> when some strange knowledge and light were communicated to me: it happened one summer in the country; at a moment of great anxiety and depression, I went into the garden at twilight. Heavy clouds hung overhead, and the shadows were falling, when suddenly a burning light flared up in my soul. But I do not call this experience a sudden conversion, although it happened at a time of intense spiritual conflict, because before it I was neither a sceptic, nor a materialist, nor an agnostic; and because thereafter the conflicts within me did not vanish.[31]

This sudden illumination, which precipitated Berdyaev's spiritual reorientation eventually steered him into the fold of Russian Orthodoxy. And though he denied that he was ever a sceptic, materialist, or agnostic, he occasionally admitted that his acceptance of Christianity "delivered me from atheism."[32] It must be remembered, however, that to Berdyaev the term "atheist" was as appropriately applicable to Idealists as to Marxists. Moreover, it is important to remember that Berdyaev had not been raised in a religious tradition. He "could never, as the expression goes, return to the faith of my fathers"[33] for his father had no faith, and his home life was almost entirely devoid of religious sentiment. Hence it is far more accurate to say that Berdyaev discovered (rather than returned to) faith.

Berdyaev's encounter with Christianity coincided with his final departure from St. Petersburg. Initially he visited the country (the site of his "conversion"); and then, after a winter in Paris, he moved to Moscow, where he spent his last days in Russia. In Moscow Berdyaev reestablished his friendship with Sergy Bulgakov, who had recently converted to Orthodoxy. It was Bulgakov who helped to confirm Berdyaev in his newly gained faith by reassuring him that the doctrines of Orthodox Christianity would not conflict with his social concern. But when Berdyaev eventually became a member of the Church, he was scandalized by its rampant corruption and bureaucratic politics. And thus, in 1913 he published a scathing polemic aimed at the hierarchy of the Holy Synod. For this vituperative exercise, Berdyaev was charged with blasphemy—a charge usually punished by permanent exile to Siberia. Fortunately World War I helped prolong the proceedings, and his case was ultimately abrogated by the February Revolution.

Berdyaev welcomed the Russian Revolution (for more than the obvious reasons), but he did not participate in the early February phase, even though he had been friendly with members of the Kadet party. Though the Kadets were too "bourgeois" for his liking, Kerensky's government, which subsequently replaced the "democratic" regime, was sufficiently Socialist in its orientation to attract Berdyaev's attention. "As a result of a number of circumstances," he found himself "for a short time a member of the Council (*Soviet*) of the newly proclaimed Republic (pre-Parliament)." The council sessions were dominated by Kerensky, who "indulged mainly in hysterical ravings," and were especially distasteful to Berdyaev.[34] When the Kerensky government was ousted in October, it was Berdyaev's opinion that the Bolsheviks "showed greater awareness of the situation and a greater courage in facing the revolutionary storm."[35] Thus, even though he sharply disagreed with their interpretation of religion, his commitment to radical social change and his profound faith in the messianic vocation of the Russian people persuaded Berdyaev that the economic and political policies of the Bolsheviks were (at least for that particular period) essentially correct.

In 1918 Berdyaev established the Free Academy of Spiritual Culture in Moscow; two years later he was appointed to the chair of philosophy in the university of that city. But shortly thereafter, with a proverbial shift of Soviet policy, Berdyaev was arrested by Dzerzhinsky's Cheka and, after a brief delay, was exiled in 1922. With his wife, Lydia Yudifovna, and his sister-in-law, Eugenie Rapp, Berdyaev went to Berlin (they left on the same boat as N. O. Lossky and Pitirim Sorokin). There he worked for the Y.M.C.A.; made the acquaintance of Max Scheler, Count Keyserling, and Oswald Spengler; and founded an academy devoted to the study of religious philosophy. Four years later he moved to Paris where he established his academy and, with financial assistance from friends, started a review entitled *The Way (Putji)*.

The French capital made a great impression on Berdyaev, and as he later recognized, "I came to share the life of the West fully only in Paris."[36] In Paris he met the neo-Thomist philosopher Jacques Maritain, through the widow of Léon Bloy. And not long after their first meeting he and Maritain helped establish a religious discussion group which met periodically for about three years and included such prominent members of the Catholic intelligentsia as Charles du Bos, Gabriel Marcel, and Etienne Gilson.[37]

During the interwar years, Berdyaev also had the opportunity to meet other members of the French intellectual aristocracy at the gatherings sponsored by the de Jardins. These intellectual conclaves took place on the de Jardins' estate in Pontigny. Here, in the Gothic surroundings, Berdyaev "came to know André Gide, George Philippe, Fernandèz, Groethuysen, Martin Buber, Buonalotti, and many others."[38]

In addition to the de Jardins' discussions, Berdyaev participated in the Union pour la vérité, an organization with a left-wing bias, which was actively supported by Nizan and Malraux. These meetings were extremely fruitful for Berdyaev, giving him a solid grounding in both the atheistic and religious forms of existentialism, and they undoubtedly played a role in shaping the existentialist emphasis of his eschatology. Actually, Berdyaev did not believe that the philosophy of atheistic existentialists really represented existential philosophy: he thought that philosophers like Sartre misrepresented the ultimate spiritual destiny of man. In Berdyaev's view, the atheistic existentialists, the apostles of the "Godlessness of the night," who strait-jacket mankind to time and history are even more misguided than the optimistic atheists of the eighteenth and nineteenth centuries, the apostles of the "Godlessness of the day." For while both deprive man of God, at least the "daylight godlessness of enlightenment"[39] provided man with a non-tragic ersatz religion.

Yet Berdyaev regarded optimistic liberalism and especially the idea of Progress with the same fundamental distaste that he exhibited for atheistic existentialism. His appreciation for religious existentialism, however, enabled him to make still another significant contact with a group of French intellectuals, the religiously oriented thinkers associated with the "personalist" periodical *Esprit,* under the editorship of Emmanuel Mounier (himself the author of a famous book on the personalist movement). The activities of this movement (which were inspired by the ideas of Maritain and Berdyaev, as well as the Spanish historian Alfredo Mendizabel and Gouverneur Paulding, a member of the staff of *Commonweal*) were especially dear to Berdyaev's heart, for its essential aim "was to work out a social programme on spiritual foundations"—a concept he later described in his own terms in *Slavery and Freedom.* Unfortunately, however, the *personalisme communautaire* of the *Esprit* movement "was confined to a comparatively small group, unable to do anything which could effectively influence its environment."[40]

Its failure and the failure of all reformist movements in the thirties were dramatically attested to by the outbreak of World War II. Berdyaev viewed the war as another indication of the bankruptcy of humanism, a tragic episode in the conclusion of "modern history," and a confirmation of his 1924 prophecy that the world had entered the trying time of "The New Middle Ages." With the exception of a brief interruption, Berdyaev remained in Paris throughout the war. And even though he had frequently attacked national socialism, the Gestapo allowed him to continue his speculations at his home in Clamart. After the war he resumed his educational work, and in 1947 he found himself "in the company of Mr. Bevin and the ex-Viceroy of India," in an academic procession at Cambridge University where he was awarded the degree of Doctor of Divinity.[41]

In one respect, the honorary degree symbolized a chief irony of Berdyaev's life, for in the West he had been persistently and erroneously regarded as the principal spokesman for Russian Orthodoxy, while the officialdom of the Russian Church in Europe and the Soviet Union had continually regarded him with suspicious animosity. On the other hand, the honorary doctorate was a moving tribute to the esteem in which many members of the English intellectual community had always held Nicolas Berdyaev. Had he lived longer, perhaps France (which had been his home for over twenty years) would also have recognized his contribution to the intellectual life of Europe. But England was the last country to honor him. On March 24 of the following year this "spiritual anarchist," this rebellious religious philosopher—whose "chief concern" in life had been the "conquest of the deadly flux of time"[42] and the "evocation of the image" of a regenerate world at the end of history—died at the age of seventy-five.

"The Meaning of the Creative Act"

Objectification

From this biographical sketch one can see that with few exceptions Berdyaev continually took a personal interest in the affairs of this world, that he was, in every sense of the current phrase, an engagé intellectual. Not content to contemplate his essence like an Aristotelian Prime Mover, Berdyaev abandoned the ivory tower for the marketplace. He let himself get caught up in the problems of a world ravaged by bestial cruelty, a world vitiated and dehumanized by collectivism, mass culture, and the inevitable "machine."[43] He concerned himself with a society which gloried in "uncurdled" experience, which deified (to use another of John Dewey's terms) the "humdrum": the monotonous enemy of the creative, of the aesthetic. This pronounced social concern, this spirit of commitment and involvement (which is illustrated by his political and educational activities as well as by his eloquent diagnoses and criticisms of modern society), derives from Berdyaev's passionate desire to deliver mankind not only from the terror of contemporary history, but from history itself. It results from his unceasing wish to solve not only the seemingly insurmountable problems of our time, but the problem of time itself. In short, this commitment springs both from his role as a social reformer and from his vocation as a prophet.

Berdyaev believed that the disastrous consequences of modern history (viz., war, revolution, mechanization, Godforsakenness, mass psychosis, and dehumanization) were primarily the results of the Fall, of man's original severance from the divine dimension—his loss of spiritual wholeness and subsequent enslavement in the space-time categories of an "objectified" world. This fall had shattered man's "God-manhood" (i.e., his primordial state of "theandric" perfection) and had, thus, forced him to externalize and forsake the spiritual freedom he had enjoyed before the creation of the cosmos. Yet, he, and only he, had been responsible for the original rupture, for his fall into time, and for the beginning of history. The Fall itself had not occurred in the traditional Garden of Eden; it had not taken place in the phenomenal world at all. On the contrary the reverse is the case: "This phenomenal world and its time are a product of the Fall."[44]

Thus, the Fall was a pretemporal affair, ultimately responsible for the Creation, which itself is a symbol of man's estrangement from God. This tragic event disrupted the harmonious conditions under which man had previously lived, and it turned him away from the very source and ground of his spiritual being. Man's personality had originally been complete, but now it was divided and deranged. Berdyaev believed, as did the Pythagoreans, the Platonists, the Hermetics, and the Alchemists, that man had formerly been an androgynous anthropos, a cosmic man, who, at the disruption of the primal unity, had lost his original ontic status as a self-contained being.

Indeed for Berdyaev, sex, as opposed to love (either eros, philia, or agape) represented "a cleavage within the complete androgynous form of man." "Sex," he wrote, "is a fall, it is a disruption which seeks to re-establish wholeness but does not succeed in doing so." And it is only at the end of time—"outside objectification, outside the determinate world of phenomena"—that man will be able to overcome the duality of sex and thus reestablish his intimate connection with God. History, then, becomes a drama in which fallen and "divided" man, ever "nailed to the cross of time,"[45] attempts to recapture his former condition of spiritual wholeness.

Although man may have fallen from God, Berdyaev emphatically believes that every man is a "potential God-man,"[46] that in spirit man is "the image and the likeness of God," a "microcosmos and a microtheos," who can once again attain "divineness."[47] For him redemption necessarily entails divinization. The primary obstacle and evil in the way of man's return to God is what Berdyaev alternatively refers to as "externalization," "objectification," or "thingification" of the spirit. When the spirit of man fell it was objectified, and thus "Life . . . is, as it were, the dying of the infinite into the finite, of the eternal into the temporal."[48] Berdyaev believes that in its pure form, spirit is not concretely manifested, that it is "non-being" rather than "being." Yet to avoid misinterpreting Berdyaev, it is necessary to distinguish between the traditional meanings of "non-being." Going back to Greek conventions, non-being may be defined in two ways: as *ouk on* or as *me on*, "the non-being that flatly negates being and can have no commerce with it, and the non-being that, as potentiality, enters into a dialectical relation with being as the other pole of a genuine antithesis."[49] Berdyaev uses "non-being" in the second sense: "'Objective' things are devoid of ultimate reality."[50] As Will Herberg succinctly puts it,

> He thinks of being as definition (finitude), limitation, restriction, and brands objectivity as unreal. True reality he sees in non-being *(me on)*, the creative principle of freedom, which he designates as "meonic freedom."[51]

Thus Berdyaev denies the existence of the Parmenidean world of Being and the Platonic world of Forms or Ideas. In fact he equates the realm of Being (traditionally distinguished, of course, from our world of Appearance, which is but a faint reflection, or copy, of the perfect world of Forms) with the external, commonsense world. Thus, Being is identified with the objectified world of the Fall, which to him exists only as a painful illusion in the minds of men estranged from God.

Berdyaev's iconoclastic equation of "Being" with "phenomena" rests on his repudiation of essentialist philosophy and his aversion to ephemerality. For while he could think of "nothing more sad and barren than that which the Greeks expressed by the phrase *ouk on*," he could never "believe in or be the servant of time."[52] His "equation" served him well, enabling him to dispose of ontological metaphysics and empirical epistemology in one blow. In his attempt to refute the empiricists, Berdyaev enlisted the support of his favorite philosopher, Immanuel Kant. Accepting Kant's conception of an active mind that formulates the content of its own thought, Berdyaev rejected the correspondence theory of truth. It rests on both a passive conception of mind and a belief that the external world of objects represents the ultimate source of reality and the sole criterion of validation. And though Kant remained agnostic about the noumenal world *(Ding an sich)*,

Berdyaev used the concept of noumena to undermine the empiricist's belief in the reality of the perceptual universe.

Berdyaev maintained that the distinction between a phenomenal universe, on the one hand, and an unknowable (but nevertheless real) noumenal dimension, on the other, deprived phenomena of ultimate reality. Thus it is only possible to speak of the "reality" of the object-world in a pejorative sense. This contention closely parallels the argument of the post-Kantian idealists, who maintained that since only noumena are ultimately real, it is misleading and useless to regard phenomena as constituents of "knowledge." Yet while the idealists thought that they could penetrate the inscrutable veil of the "thing in itself" by reason, Berdyaev believed that a priori logic prevented man from reaching spiritual reality. He thought that reason distorted noumena and that only ecstasy, concrete mystical experience, could transcend the spatial and temporal limitations of the world of objects.

Berdyaev's distaste for ontology and logic, his belief that discursive thought represents an aspect of man's fallen nature, places him within the existentialist camp. For like the existentialists Berdyaev not only repudiates the a priori as the way to truth, but emphasizes the importance of the individual, the subject, and the particular over the general, the object, and the universal. Similarly he maintains that existence is prior to essence, that a person's life is not predetermined by an abstract definition of man. This position dovetails with his belief that reality (the spiritual "reality" of man included) can only be described in terms of potentiality, meonic freedom, or "creativity." Yet although he stresses that man and the universe cannot be explained in terms of Being, like other religious existentialists (Marcel, Maritain, Buber, and Tillich, for example), Berdyaev nevertheless believes in a "human nature." Man possesses a divine image and is "a microcosm and a microtheos."[53] He is involved in a divine-human drama, and plays a decisive role in realizing the return to eternity. Still, Berdyaev's general position—especially his "Kierkegaardian" revolt against idealist metaphysics[54] and his emphasis upon subjective experience in the attainment of spiritual truth—establishes him in the vanguard of contemporary religious existentialism.

Both the "Being" of the idealist, then, and the ephemeral, "blooming, buzzing confusion" of the empiricist were anathemas to Berdyaev. For whereas the abstract "reality" of the ontologists implied the elimination of existence and the "congealing" of spirit, the fluctuating universe of the "anti-Eleatics" entailed the equally inimical notion of death—the inevitable exhaustion of all life-forms in the devouring time-process. Hence, he identified the Eleatic realm of Being with the world of objects; he made both of them conditions of man's existence in the fallen world. And since he believed in the eventual abolition of the "objectified" universe—since he had faith in an eschatological resolution of the historical process—he skillfully provided for the inevitable destruction of both the logical Reality of the idealist and the empirical universe of the scientist.

The Creative Act

Yet man need not wait until the end of time to transcend the ontological limitations of the "objectified" world, for Berdyaev believed a person can soar above the dimensions of the universe at any given moment, at any "now," in the time-dissolving fire of creative ecstasy. "The Kingdom of God or eternity is not separated from me by the length of time which is to pass before the end of the world," because it is possible to transcend time by mystical intuition—to grasp the eternal now and "escape from life" by achieving "communion with another, free world in which there are no cares and burdens."[55] Thus, there are really "two ways to eternity—through the depth of the moment and through the end of time and of the world."[56]

Berdyaev's conception of mysticism, his belief in the possibility of transcending time in "the depth of the moment," derives from his special notion of "creativity." He dealt with the idea of creativity in an early book, *The Meaning of the Creative Act,* which he completed in Moscow in 1914 upon returning from a trip to Italy. Berdyaev always regarded this book with reverence and profound appreciation, not because it represented a final resolution of the problem of creative activity, but because of the conditions under which he wrote it. For, as he tells us in his autobiography, "*The Meaning of the Creative Act . . .* was written at a time of well-nigh intoxicating ecstasy." It is "a book in which my thoughts and the normal course of philosophical argument seemed to dissolve into vision." And although "it is an impulsive, unpremeditated and unfinished work . . . it contains in that raw form all my dominant and formative ideas and insights."[57] Philosophically, Berdyaev considered this book to be so important because his interpretation of creativity enabled him to transcend and abolish time; it provided him with a theory by which he could destroy necessity, fate, and the other disrupted conditions of the objectified world. "In essence," he maintained, "creativity is a way out, an exodus; it is victory"—i.e., "spiritual liberation from 'the world,' the liberation of man's spirit from its bondage to necessity."[58] When an individual "creates" he is capable of surmounting the inimical forces of the fallen world. For

> Creativity . . . is not an "insertion" in the finite, not a mastery over
> the medium, or the creative product itself: rather it is a flight into

the infinite; not an activity which objectifies in the finite but one which transcends the finite towards the infinite. The creative act signifies an *ek-stasis,* a breaking through to eternity.[59]

Berdyaev rested his belief in the individual soul's ability to transcend time through "creativity" on the foundations of a faculty psychology. He believed that human beings possess a subconscious, a conscious, and, most significantly, a supraconscious. The subconscious, which, viewed historically, is a remnant of man's primitive mental biography, expresses itself in nondiscursive symbols and is responsible for the creation of fantasies, dreams, and myths. Berdyaev had read Freud and Jung,[60] and was equally well acquainted with the theories of the French sociologists, notably Émile Durkheim, and with the work of the German anthropologist and historian of religion J. J. Bachoffen. Berdyaev drew on all of these sources, as well as Frobenius, in formulating his concept of the subconscious.

Berdyaev believed in the value (and, in some cases, in the reality) of myth. For, in his words, "The myth-creating process which belongs to the fountain head of human nature and from which human nature has not emancipated itself even today" possesses "a greater element of truth . . . than . . . the individual power of concept and thing."[61] This statement displays Berdyaev's basic antipathy to discursive reason, or rational discourse—that mental activity carried on by the second faculty of the human soul, the conscious. He disliked conscious reasoning, which objectifies its concepts in words and is based on the logical distinction of subject from object, because it is indicative of man's fallen nature.

He felt that the verbal expression of concepts was analogous to the Fall of man itself, for just as the Fall externalized human spirituality, the concrete articulation of thought in discursive symbols objectifies and debases the spirit of mankind. Words are divisive; they destroy the harmony and unity of religious insights by dividing them up into syntactical categories—into subjects, objects, and predicates. And as such they are demonstrative of man's loss of wholeness, of his disrupted and dissociated nature. But words also take place in time, in the temporal process, which itself is likewise a reflection of the severed and shattered character of the objectified universe. And hence, conscious reasoning is far inferior to subconscious perception; for unlike the symbols of dream and myth, rational thought is incapable of grasping reality in its entirety.

Mythology, however, is not superior to the form of perception carried on by the third faculty of the soul, the supraconscious. For the supraconscious, which expresses itself in images, is not only capable of rendering a unitary vision of reality, it can attain communion with eternity itself.

[42]

And it is the supraconscious that carries on the creative activity that allows a person to transcend the limitations of the finite world.

Berdyaev himself believed that he had succeeded in communing with eternity through the medium of supraconscious creativity. As he tells us in *The Beginning and the End:*

> There are such things as moments of communion with eternity. These moments pass, and again I lapse into time. Yet it is not that moment which passes, but I in my fallen temporality: the moment indeed remains in eternity.[62]

He attributed these experiences of timelessness, these transcendent moments, or eternal nows, to the power of the creative act conceived in the supraconscious, an act which is, "as it were, a link between the noumenal and phenomenal worlds, a way out beyond the confines of the phenomenal world" and an ecstatic "experience of transcendence."[63]

It is noteworthy that Berdyaev represents his moments of "creative" insight, his mystical illuminations, as acts of communion with eternity. For the relation of "communion" is a characteristic of the theistic variety of mysticism. Berdyaev himself always opposed the "false mysticism" of the monists because he believed in the value of personality. Consequently, he rejected the Hindu and Buddhist concepts of "liberation" via annihilation of the soul, for it obviously precluded personal communion with God. To this devaluation of the human personality he opposed his notion of an intimate or "creative" contact with God—a confrontation which he sometimes described, borrowing the words of Martin Buber, as an "I-Thou" relationship. At the same time he insisted that "the task that faces me" and every other human being "is that personality as a whole should enter into eternity."[64]

Similarly, Berdyaev discounted the pan-en-henic concept of submersion in, or union with, nature, for he believed that God transcended the physical stuff of the universe. Nevertheless he always felt sympathetic toward mystics of other persuasions (including Bergson and Proust), for he not only recognized "the predominance in himself of *homo mysticus* over *homo religiosus*," but believed "in the existence of a universal mystical experience and a universal spirituality which cannot be described in terms of confessional differences."[65] In this respect, he always held the German mystics—Meister Eckhart, Angelus Silesius, and Jakob Boehme—in high esteem. And although he could not accept their respective doctrines totally, he did adopt Boehme's notion of *Ungrund*—i.e., "the dark nature of God" or the "primal dark abyss" in whose "inmost depths occurs a theogonic process or that of divine genesis"—to validate his own contention that there was movement within "the inmost depths of the divine life."[66] This notion was useful to Berdyaev for it not only reinforced his definition of God in terms of meonic non-being, but helped him explain the historical process as the partial outcome of a process of movement within the divine life itself.

Yet although mystical creative ecstasy enables a person to transcend time and space, to achieve personal communion with God, it is ultimately an unsatisfactory form of experience: mystical intuition allows an individual to escape from time only temporarily. A "vertical" apprehension of eternity, or (to use another of Berdyaev's favorite phrases) a vision of "four-dimensional" reality, only permits a brief respite from the disruptive forces of contingency. Berdyaev resolved this problem by distinguishing between two fundamental types of creative activity. While insisting that "every creative act of man is eschatological in character and brings this world to an end,"[67] he differentiated between the temporary abolition of time, attained through mystical experience, and the permanent destruction of the temporal process, achieved through the joint creative cooperation of God and man. Indeed, "the creative act of man is an answer to the call of God" and helps "prepare the way for the end of this world and the beginning of another."[68] "Creation is," he writes, "a divine-human work. And the crowning point of world creation is the end of this world." For, "The world must be turned into an image of beauty, it must be dissolved in creative ecstasy."[69]

The realization of the end of time—the creation of the supreme work of art—will mark the pinnacle of the divine-human partnership. All creative activity points in this direction: "Every creative act, whether moral or social, whether in the sphere of art or in the realm of knowledge, is an act which has its share in the coming of the end of the world," in helping to prepare the advent of the third epoch in the religious history of the world, the Age of the Spirit.[70] In fact, our creative acts in the present already participate in the "existential time" of the "religious epoch of creativeness,"[71] or the aeon of the Holy Spirit. For, "Creative ecstasy," which "is a way out from the time of this world . . . takes place in existential time." But here Berdyaev seems to contradict himself, for he also insists that "the results of every true creative act of man enter into the Kingdom of God."[72] Apparently, however, he believed that man's creative acts occur both in existential time—i.e., that timeless time of the last historical epoch which, though it is not identical with eternity, is nevertheless "a participant in several moments of eternity"[73]—and in the Kingdom of God, or eternity, itself. The creative act is allowed to take place in existential time as well as eternity because it is assigned a special role in the historical drama. Indeed, it not only permits man to destroy time in "the depth of the moment," but prepares the way for "a great revolution in human self-consciousness"—a revolution or spiritual transformation that will be marked by "the awakening of super-consciousness or of the higher consciousness."[74]

Thus, creativity is a stimulus, or transforming agent, that effects the awakening of supraconsciousness—a spiritual awakening that enables man to create (with God's help) the third and final epoch of world history, the Age of the Spirit, or aeon of existential time—as well as an "eschatological energy" that allows man to transcend time in the immediate present. And in this sense the creative act already participates in existential time as well as the Kingdom of God: it is already united with the final epoch through creative anticipation and preparation of the irrevocable End of time and joined to God, or eternity, through the personal act of mystical communion.

Personalism, Society, and Culture

When Berdyaev was writing *The Meaning of the Creative Act,* he actually believed that the third, or creative, epoch of world history was close at hand. Subsequently, however, he was forced to revise his optimistic opinion:

> The hope in the advent of an age of creativity . . . was shattered by the course of historical events: by the catastrophe of the first world-war, by the Russian Revolution, by the cataclysm in Germany, by the general and ominous decline in creativity in the inter-war years, by a second world-war and the threat of a third one to come.[75]

Yet, although he may have lost hope for the immediate realization of a creative religious epoch, Berdyaev insisted that after his "intense experience of ecstasy" in writing *The Meaning of the Creative Act,* he "never went back on my faith in the creative vocation of man."[76] He continued to believe that although man was "a mixture," "a combination of creature and creator . . . compact of matter, absurdity, and chaos," he was also the possessor of sufficient "creative power" to rejuvenate the defunct spiritual carcass of society.[77] Even though he believed that spirit had been degraded into objectivity on every level of existence—psychological, ontological, and social—even though he felt that man's "being" and objectified social institutions testified to the disruption of the divine dimension, Berdyaev fervently believed that by sharing in the creative non-being of God, by turning from the objective world of actualized being to exercise one's potential meonic freedom, man could prepare the way for a new outpouring of the spirit that would bring spiritual "alienation and objectification to an end." But to achieve the realization of this new era, man must prepare to change the present structure of his own consciousness.[78] At the moment his personality is still enslaved in the external world. "The world of slavery," as Berdyaev points out, "is the world of spirit which is alienated from itself"; and the "source of slavery is always objectification." To free himself man must once again become a "person" as opposed to an "individual." The person is he who "does not allow the ejection into the external of his conscience and his judgment."[79] The individual, on the other hand, is he who has lost his religious moorings, who has compromised with materiality, with collective society, and who has, hence, lost his spiritual dignity.

Like his friend Jacques Maritain—as well as many other contemporary "personalists" (for example, the Jewish religious philosopher Martin Buber, the Protestant theologian Paul Tillich, and the Catholic existentialist Gabriel Marcel)—Berdyaev regarded "individuality" as a state of incompleteness, a condition of slavery in which the temporal obsessions, cravings, and revulsions of the ego eclipse the cardinal significance of spiritual values. On the other hand, Berdyaev considered "personality" to be the state of spiritual wholeness (analogous to the androgynous form of man before the Fall) that accompanies religious enlightenment, or the awakening of supraconsciousness. This spiritual condition characterizes the existence of a man who has renounced his exclusive attachment to material objects by grounding his life in God. A person, in contrast to an individual, is ultimately free—undetermined by the coercive forces of objectified existence. And, within the context of the temporal world, the person (like the *Jivan Mukta* or Nietzsche's *Übermensch*) is a law unto himself.

Here Berdyaev's social radicalism comes to the fore. As we have noted, he detested the complexity of modern society and believed that it destroyed and externalized human spirituality, that it created "individuals" and not "persons." But because he realized that man needed some sort of society to carry on the practical necessities of life, Berdyaev developed (for example, in *Slavery and Freedom* and *Solitude and Society*) a theory of society by which he sought to preserve the integrity of his personalism. He distinguished between two different types of socialism: "collective socialism, which is based on the supremacy of society and the state over the personality . . . and personalist socialism, which is founded on the absolute supremacy of the personality, of each personality, over society and the state." In the latter, the personality can preserve its freedom and can have "communion" with others without losing its dignity because personalist socialism maintains that "only economics can be socialized," that "the spiritual life cannot, nor can the consciousness or conscience of man."[80]

Although Berdyaev believed that man could create a society anarchic enough to preserve spiritual integrity, he did not believe in the ultimate value of society itself. The "perfect" society (i.e., personalist socialism) is not really perfect because nothing in time or the objectified universe can ever attain that state of perfection: "The nature of history and all that it contains is such that nothing perfect can be realized in time."[81] And hence, perfection is realizable only outside the confines of the phenomenal universe, that is, in eternity.

Berdyaev regarded his personalist society as a "staging-ground" for the return to eternity—for the realization of the Age of the Spirit and the achievement of the End of the historical process. This is not to say that he did not possess an intense social concern. He did. Yet all of Berdyaev's social efforts—his occupation as a revolutionary in Russia and his educational and critical activities in the Soviet Union, Germany, and France—were the outcome, and not the cause, of the essential goal and purpose of his philosophy: the abolition of time and the fallen universe and the realization of a return to eternal life. Consequently, he attacked the concept of a terrestrial Utopia as vigorously as he did the idea of Progress for, "The Utopia of a terrestrial paradise contains the same fundamental contradictions as those involved in the doctrines of progress, insofar as it also postulates perfection within time and the limits of the historical process"[82]

In Berdyaev's view, "perfection in time" is an absurdity because it is connected with the notion of endless history or eternal time. And history has meaning only "because it comes to an end. Unending history, be it as progress or as regress, is the epitome of meaninglessness."[83] Thus, the concept of Utopia is an illusion; the notion of achieving harmony and perfection in time through the creation of "perfect" social institutions is untenable and erroneous. Similarly, the belief in the preeminent value of "culture" is misleading and fallacious. For all cultural activity *sub specie temporis* is doomed to failure. And, in Berdyaev's words, if we are ever "to create beauty in this world we must situate the real center of mankind in another world."[84]

Berdyaev always felt the poignancy of what he believed to be the "unavoidable" failure of culture. While traveling in Italy, however, shortly before the First World War, he was "completely carried away" by the beauty of the Renaissance: "Though I knew that the Renaissance was a failure, I realized that this was the most sublime, significant and tragic failure experienced by European man."[85] It was a failure because, like all cultural achievements, it transpired in time and expressed itself in the corruptible medium of the objectified universe.

Still, there is a sense in which the Renaissance was not a complete failure, for though Berdyaev thought (and this justifies his belief in the eschatological value of creativity) that "creative *works* are within time, with its objectifications, discords and divisions," he also insisted that "the creative *act* is beyond time: it is wholly within, subjective, prior to all objectification."[86] Thus, while the "works" of the Renaissance were failures. because they were externalized in time, the "inspiration" that led to their material embodiment was, to a certain extent, successful because it transcended the limitations of the temporal universe. Hence, "culture" is synonymous with the material form assumed by a creative act and as such represents the externalization, or objectification, of the spirit.

In this respect, Berdyaev's definition of creativity is analogous to Benedetto Croce's. In fact, Berdyaev acknowledged that the Italian philosopher was correct in seeing "the essence of art in self-expression."[87] True art is transcendental, whereas its object, the material embodiment itself, is a graphic example of the tragic failure of creation under the aspect of time.

The act of creation is indeed nontemporal; and in its ultimate sense, the only successful "work" it can ever achieve is "the creation of eternity." But "the creation of eternity means bringing all culture to an end";[88] it means a destruction of terrestrial society, and the abolition of the temporal process. Thus, although Berdyaev insisted that man "ought not to . . . disregard the world and humanity outside and disembarrass himself of responsibility for others,"[89] he did not believe in the ultimate value of either culture or society. Even though he wished to ameliorate man's fate in the world, he subordinated his social concern to his ultimate goal: the realization of eternity. And it is this desire to redeem all mankind from the disastrous consequences of the historical process that explains his unshakable belief in "the creative vocation of man." By saying that he believes in man's creative vocation, Berdyaev means that he has faith in man's ability to create eternity. And thus, in this sense, his image of man is "optimistic," for it invests man with the capacity to make a creative response to God's calling, to join with Him to abolish time and "create" eternity.

Berdyaev translated his early Marxist concern for achieving the freedom and equality of all men in time into a desire to realize the collective emancipation of all men outside time. But this did not stifle his persistent preoccupation with social problems: indeed it only served to intensify it. For though he did not believe in the ultimate value of any form of objectified existence (whether social or cultural), he nevertheless wished to lead mankind away from the meaninglessness of destructive behavior. He wished to rechannel human efforts in the direction of creative activity—activity which he hoped would eventually transform human consciousness, prepare the way for the coming of the Age of the Spirit, and enable mankind to return to the freedom of eternity. And thus, he envisaged the establishment of a "personalist socialism" and a spiritual culture, an anarchic society with religious moorings, wherein man would be free to pursue his eschatological destiny, to create the fire of his final redemption.

"The Beginning and the End"

Myth and History

Berdyaev's repudiation of social utopianism, his rejection and condemnation of the objectified conditions of the fallen world, derive, as he willingly admitted, from his " 'anarchistic' instincts and convictions"—convictions and instincts which themselves "are born of a realization of the conflict and tension between history and the end of history, of a belief in eternity, and of an inability to believe in or be the servant of time." He remained a confirmed "mystical anarchist" after his first confrontation with Orthodox Christianity, for he could never "regard the social categories of power and domination as applicable to God or to God's relation to man and the world."[90] And it was because he believed in an eternal "kingdom of freedom and anarchy"[91] beyond the dimensions of the phenomenal universe—because he wished to do his share to free man from the slavery of time—that Nicolas Berdyaev sought to create a philosophy of history that would permit humanity to regain eternity. He emphatically believed that "man ought to rebel against the slavery of history," that "the resultant and consistent demand of personalism, when thought out to the end, is a demand for the end of the world and of history, not a passive waiting for this end in fear and anguish, but an active, creative preparation for it."[92]

Yet a philosophy of history, a theory of temporal process, that will eventually enable man to destroy the shackles that bind him to the externalized universe cannot be constructed scientifically: "It is indeed beyond dispute that it is impossible to construct a purely scientific philosophy of history." Still, if we are to emancipate ourselves from "the tragedy and torment of history," which "are above all else the tragedy and torment of time," we must recognize that "the philosophy of history can be nothing but a religious metaphysic of history," that it must deal with eschatology —that is, with the end of time and the resurrection of the dead. For, "One can become reconciled to the horrors of history," to "death, only if one cherishes the great hope of a resurrection of all who have lived and are living, of every creature who has suffered and rejoiced."[93]

Thus, to ensure the eventuality of this resurrection, we must want to destroy time itself—to accomplish the permanent elimination of the temporal process. For, "It inflicts grievous wounds upon human personality and is the cause of measureless suffering among men. In fact, history has become something like a crime."[94] It is a source of evil, of destruction, that must be abolished before redemption is possible. Hence we must let our will, and not our reason, guide us. We must will to believe (regardless of empirical and logical evidence to the contrary) that suffering in time not only deserves but will receive a reward outside time. We must accept this belief, this philosophy of history for a time of crisis, upon faith, upon our thirst for justice, and ignore the laughter of the hollow men.

According to Berdyaev, a philosophy of history is based not only upon a "religious metaphysic of history," but upon a mythological description of the historical process: "History is not an objective empirical datum; it is a myth."[95] This is not to say that myth is a fictional form of knowledge, a naïve and false contrivance of the primitive mind. For Berdyaev, "the greatest realities, the original phenomena of spiritual life," are "concealed in the myths of mankind—realities that are more real and more concrete than the concepts and ideas of discursive reason." Thus, "the current identification of myth with invention and make-believe" is erroneous.[96] It is simply a further example of the misleading nature of rational consciousness. For it is an undeniable fact that "the deepest mystery of spiritual life . . . cannot" be approached "through the superficial criteria of formal logic," that "the real way to approach spiritual reality and the knowledge of the divine life . . . is not through abstract philosophy but through concrete mythology." And, analogously, it is only possible to discuss the fate and destiny of man in time in terms of an eschatological myth—a concrete "myth which situates world destiny as a stage of the divine destiny in man, and thus predetermines its main spiritual forces."[97]

The ultimate source of this myth, and the original source of all varieties of eschatological myths, is found in man's dream of paradise—his perennial "dream of joy and freedom, of beauty, of soaring creative power"—in his "dream of love." Sometimes it takes the form of evoking the memory of

> a golden age in the past. At other times it finds its expression in messianic expectation which is directed towards the future. But it is one and the same dream, the dream of a being who has been wounded by time and who longs eagerly to make his way out of time.[98]

This dream, which epitomizes man's perennial desire to transcend the temporal process, "lies at the basis of all Utopias of heaven on earth."[99] Archaic societies, of course, placed the Golden Age in the past and, fortified by their cyclical conception of the temporal process, hoped for an eventual return to those special times of the beginning, just after the world's creation, when man lived in a timeless paradise and enjoyed an intimate association with his gods.[100]

Recently, however, utopian philosophies have usually been based on forward-looking views of history. In fact, in many cases, they have assumed the essential characteristics of messianic eschatologies. And, as Berdyaev points out, "It is not only the philosophy of history contained in the books of the Bible and in St. Augustine which is prophetic and messianic, so also is the philosophy of history of Hegel, Saint-Simon, Auguste Comte, and Karl Marx." This is also true of "the nineteenth-century doctrine of progress, which was so non-Christian externally," for it too "springs . . . from the same source of messianic expectation."[101] These philosophies of history all derive from the same messianic hope—a hope "born in suffering and unhappiness" that "awaits the day of righteous judgment, and, in the end, of messianic triumph and the messianic reign of a thousand years." And Berdyaev recognized that "from the psychological point of view," these conceptions of historical time represent a "compensation" for terrestrial adversity:

> The sufferings of the Hebrew people, the sufferings of the Polish people, of the Russian people, the sufferings of the German people (and I say of the people, not of the State), and of the labouring classes of society operate favourably to the rise of a messianic frame of mind.[102]

Understanding the psychology of the messianic mind, however, does not invalidate the reality of messianic aspiration, or eschatological mythology. Nevertheless, there are false types of messianic eschatology. For example, Marxism, Saint-Simonism, Comtism, the idea of Progress—indeed, any secular eschatology which posits the goal of history within the confines of the temporal process, or the objectified universe—are erroneous philosophies of history, concepts of time that are guilty of what Berdyaev terms "bad or evil infinity," i.e., an indefinite prolongation of the temporal process or a false identification of "infinite time" with "eternity." Even Judaic eschatology, which was the fountainhead of all messianic speculation, is not above reproach, since it does not accept the singular role of Christ in the historical drama. Nor, in Berdyaev's view, are all varieties of Christian eschatology secure from criticism. Calvinism, for example, and St. Augustine's *De Civitate Dei*—while they properly understand the goal of history to be beyond time—do not stress the important role man plays with God in realizing the "creation" of eternity. Similarly, other Christian theologians misinterpret the nature of the historical process by overlooking the apocalyptic nature of history or by stressing the constant immanence of God in time.

The Time-Controversy in Twentieth-Century Theology

This criticism of other forms of religious eschatology reflects Berdyaev's disagreement with other twentieth-century eschatologists, a disagreement that derives from his radical interpretation of the Christian philosophy of history. Berdyaev is an apocalyptist; he constantly stresses the culmination of the historical process. And although he does not proclaim "the end of the world in the near future,"[103] he not only devotes his most ecstatic prose to a description of the inevitable destruction of cosmic and historical time, he admonishes his fellow men to join God in creating eternity. The concept of Apocalypse, however, means more to Berdyaev than the irrevocable cessation of the historical and cosmic processes. For it "is not merely the revelation of the end of the world and of history. It is also the revelation of the end within the world and the historical process, within human life and every moment of life."[104] The term "apocalypse," to Berdyaev, is applicable to an "end" of any thing, event, or series of events: "There is an individual eschatology and apocalypse, and there is an historical eschatology and apocalypse."[105]

Occasionally Berdyaev also speaks of an internal versus an external apocalypse. And, in his description of *The Fate of Man in the Modern World,* he expresses his belief that today

> we are witnessing a judgement upon not one epoch in history, but upon history itself. And in this sense only, and not in the sense of the swift arrival of the end of the world. There is such a thing as the internal apocalypse of history. The apocalypse is not merely a revelation of the end of the world: it is also a revelation of the inner events of history, of the internal judgement upon history itself. And this is what is happening now.[106]

The result of this "internal apocalypse" will be determined by man's creative efforts and by his ability to emancipate himself from the oppressive forces of modern civilization. In other words, the preparation of the historical Apocalypse rests squarely on man's shoulders. For until he chooses to terminate the nightmare of history, the Apocalypse will simply remain a perpetual possibility.

Thus, while Berdyaev established his entire religious philosophy on an apocalyptic center, he made mankind responsible for abolishing time. And though he fervently wished the final End were immediately at hand

("I would fain have quickened and forestalled the end—not the end in death, but the end beyond time in transcendence and eternity"),[107] he realized that man will have to endure the torment and tragedy of contemporary history until he voluntarily decides to transform his consciousness. The suffering will continue until he changes his values, sheds his old skin, and creates (with God's help) "the new 'heaven and the new earth.' "[108] Berdyaev would no doubt have granted that this reorientation of human energies might seem remote, not to say practically unrealizable. But, he would have intransigently insisted, it will occur—not in the present age but at some point in the future. There has been a beginning, and, therefore, there must be an end.

Berdyaev began to develop his apocalyptic philosophy of history shortly before the outbreak of the First World War; as he stated in his foreword to *The Meaning of History,* "The World War and the Russian Revolution only served to stimulate my interest and to concentrate my researches preeminently in this field."[109] But Berdyaev was not alone in possessing a fresh and vital interest in the philosophy of history. Other European theologians, who had also been profoundly affected by the catastrophes of the 1914 to 1918 years, had become increasingly preoccupied with the problem of time and the interpretation of history. Yet while (like Berdyaev) their initial reaction had been to deny the idea of Progress, to repudiate Hegelian idealism, and to condemn theological liberalism (that optimistic form of theology popular in Britain and Europe before the war which stressed God's immanence in history and man's perfection in time), they invariably accepted a nonapocalyptic view of the historical process. The neo-orthodox theologian Karl Barth, for example, who began to expound his "theology of crisis" after the war, developed an "upward-looking" philosophy of history which minimized the significance of the final judgment. In contrast to apocalypticism, upward-looking, or axiological, eschatology stresses the possibility of establishing contact with eternity here and now. It maintains that although there will someday be a definite End to history, it is possible for individuals to anticipate that End in an encounter with God in the present. And axiological eschatology opposes its conception of the immediacy of eternity to the "illusory" notion of infinite progress. Men do not have to wait indefinitely for the dawning of a new era in which the perfect society will be born—they can achieve a timeless apprehension of the divine in the present, here and now.

This idea of the relationship between the temporal and the eternal (which bears the marks of Platonic mysticism and resembles Berdyaev's notion of anticipating the end of time through the creative act) became popular after 1918—it was advanced, for example, by Dean Inge in England

and Paul Althaus in Germany—and remained the dominant eschatological position on the Continent until 1926. In that year Paul Althaus published the third edition of his *Last Things,* in which he admitted that he had overemphasized the axiological nature of the Christian message. His admission inaugurated a decade of vigorous debate over the relationship between time and eternity in Christianity.

Karl Heim entered the fray in 1930 when he examined the problem of time and eternity in his famous book *The New Divine Order.* The German theologian favored a teleological position in regard to eschatology—i.e., he believed that the End of time will come in the future—but he attempted to take a position between the Platonism of the axiologists and the advocates of progressive immanentism by stating that although "an *end* of history will come *in* history, whereby the time-form of our fallen creation will be abolished," "the whole meaning of time will be gathered and fulfilled in the eternal life which then will begin for all the world."[110]

Although Heim's eschatology is teleological, however, it is not really immanentistic. For there are actually two types of teleological, or forward-looking, eschatology. And, indeed, there is a significant difference between an immanentist teleological eschatology of history—advocated, for example, by R. J. Campbell in his *New Theology* (1907)—and the eschatology of Karl Heim. The immanentist believes that God works out His divine plan *in* time. And although as a Christian, he might not deny the possibility of an eventual end of time, the immanentist usually disregards such a concept and tends to believe that the goal of history is achieved within the temporal process. This notion—which was influenced by, and partially derived from, Hegel's identification of the historical process with the self-realization of the Absolute—was particularly popular in a time of substantial peace and relative prosperity, the late nineteenth century.

Karl Heim's teleological eschatology, on the other hand, is nonimmanentistic. For though he believes that God manifests Himself in time (for example, at the *Incarnation*), Heim does not think that the Deity is immersed within the temporal process—that is, constantly (or almost constantly) in time supervising the perfection of the world (and, by implication, His own greater glory). Indeed, like Barth, Heim believes that God represents an entirely other, or incommensurably different, form of being than the "being" of our fallen world—from the material universe with its limiting space and time-forms. And Heim maintains (also like Barth and the Swedish theologian Gustaf Aulen) that the radical ontological cleavage between man and God can only be transcended with the assistance of divine intervention.

After Heim's discussion of "Time and Eternity" in *The New Divine*

Order, the popularity of axiological eschatology declined steadily. Even former axiologists such as Karl Barth disavowed upward-looking eschatology in favor of a forward-looking view of history. Perhaps the idea of a nonimmanentist teleological eschatology had not presented itself to Barth in the early years after the Great War because such a perspective could only have appeared to be dangerously close to the Christian immanentist's view of history and the secular idea of progress.

In any event, quasi-Platonic eschatology carried the day until 1926 and the publication of Althaus's controversial essay *The Last Things* (third edition) and Karl Heim's *The New Divine Order.* Althaus returned to the debate in 1936 (a year after Barth had published his reinterpretation of Christian philosophy of history in *Credo*); and in the second edition of *Dogmatics,* Althaus assumed a synthetic position incorporating both axiological and teleological views. And while he still stressed the immediacy and nearness of God to every generation (in a manner reminiscent of Ranke), Althaus recognized the eventual termination of the historical process: the death of this world and the commencement of eternal life.

A view quite similar to Althaus's was expressed as late as 1955 by Rudolf Bultmann in his Gifford Lectures on *History and Eschatology.* For while the German "demythologizer" accepts a teleo-eschatological view of the time-process, he also stresses the immediacy of eternity in the present. In support of this view, Bultmann cites a passage from Erich Frank's *The Role of History in Christian Thought* which, he believes, excellently describes "the paradox of Christ as the historical Jesus and the ever-present Lord, and the paradox of the Christian as an eschatological and historical being."[111]

To the Christians the advent of Christ was not an event in that temporal process which we mean by history today. It was an event in the history of salvation, in the realm of eternity, an eschatological moment in which rather this profane history of the world came to its end. And in an analogous way, history comes to its end in the religious experience of any Christian "who is in Christ." In his faith he is already above time and history. For although the advent of Christ is an historical event which happened "once" in the past, it is, at the same time, an eternal event which occurs again and again in the soul of any Christian in whose soul Christ is born, suffers, dies and is raised up to eternal life.[112]

While insisting that history is eschatological, that in a sense the true believer is "already above time and history," Bultmann does not dwell on the inevitable end of the historical process. Bultmann's reticence to speak at length and in detail about the End of time is also shared by other Protestant theologians such as Paul Tillich and Reinhold Niebuhr. While accepting a teleological eschatology and (as they say in, respectively, *The Interpretation of History* and *Faith and History*) believing in an ultimate culmination of the historical process, Tillich and Niebuhr do not pretend to know when the end will come. The neo-Thomist Jacques Maritain is likewise agnostic about the occurrence of the eventual end of time. But he is confident that it is far off. As Maritain points out in his essay *Humanisme intégral,* the history of mankind and the unfolding message of Christianity are still in an extremely primitive stage of development. Similar disavowals of accuracy in determining the approximate cessation of the historical process can be found in the speculative works of academic historians: for example, in Basil Willey's *Christianity Past and Present* (1952), in Herbert Butterfield's *Christianity and History* (1950), and in Arnold Toynbee's *Civilization on Trial* (1948).

While accepting a nonimmanentist and forward-looking view of history, the apocalyptist—in contrast to the teleologist—is obviously not unwilling to discuss the end of time in great detail. And while a teleologist and an apocalyptist—say, Niebuhr and Berdyaev—would agree that the opposites of history are reconciled at the end of time, the apocalyptist (Berdyaev) would be much more interested in forecasting, anticipating, and actually planning the final abolition of the historical process than would the teleologist. However, an apocalyptist like Berdyaev is also closer in outlook to axiologists (Dean Inge) than he is to teleologists (Niebuhr or Barth). For like Althaus and Bultmann, Berdyaev acknowledges the possibility of anticipating the End of time in the present. But, it is important to note, he differs from the axiologists in stressing the overwhelming importance of the final cessation of cosmic and historical processes.

Berdyaev, and apocalyptists in general, then, differ first from axiological eschatologists (for example, Dean Inge, the early Althaus, and Barth) by insisting that man's ultimate end is realized only at the end of time. Second, Berdyaev and the apocalyptists differ from the teleological immanentists (such as the early R. J. Campbell) by emphasizing God's transcendence, His qualitative difference from the objectified world of becoming. Finally, Berdyaev and the apocalyptists differ from the nonimmanentist teleological eschatologists (namely, the Protestants Bultmann, Frank, Tillich, Heim, the later Barth, Brunner, and Niebuhr, as well as the Catholic Jacques Maritain) by elaborately discussing and passionately yearning for the abolition of the temporal process, calling on men to join God in the creation of the greatest work of art: the destruction of time.[113]

Nicolas Berdyaev

The Twentieth-Century Apocalypse

Though Berdyaev may be the most dramatic and outspoken apocalyptist of our time, he is far from being the only one. In fact, as Franklin Baumer has demonstrated, the twentieth century has its own version of the apocalypse.[114] Like Berdyaev, many other contemporary European intellectuals have discerned an apocalyptic message in the catastrophic events of our century and have been stimulated to speculate about the future of Western civilization.

The impetus of Berdyaev's eschatological speculations, of course, "came from a vivid experience of the transitoriness of human life and of the complete lack of solid ground under man's feet." For, "Both in my personal life and in the life and history of the world around me I tended to await and anticipate catastrophes." Berdyaev believed that the Apocalypse—the End of world history—was "closest to" us "in the catastrophic moments of our personal life and of the life of peoples, in wars and revolution; in creative ecstasy; in nearness to death." And he felt that these apocalyptic occurrences, these "catastrophic moments," were "particularly propitious for the elaboration of a philosophy of history."[115] Thus, it was his own proximity to many of the century's major upheavals that led him to his apocalyptic theory of history. As he acknowledged in 1923, "The World War and the Russian Revolution only served to stimulate by interest and to concentrate my researches pre-eminently in this field."[116] Even when he was still an idealist, he felt himself drifting "closer and closer to the eschatological nature of Christianity" in his "attempt to understand" the "predicament" of current history.[117] And analogously, many other intellectuals living in this century have been brought closer and closer to an eschatological (though not necessarily a Christian or even a religious) view of the historical process in their attempts to comprehend the bewildering instability and cataclysmic nature of contemporary events.

The development of what Emmanuel Mounier calls the "apocalyptic consciousness" of our time (an attitude already anticipated toward the end of the nineteenth century in the works of Burckhardt, Nietzsche, and Dostoievski) can be traced in a variety of works—literary, theological, philosophical—which began to appear shortly after the First World War. Vying with Berdyaev for recognition as the most energetic of contemporary apocalyptists was Léon Bloy, who spurred Jacques Maritain on to Catholicism and whose wife corresponded with Berdyaev's wife, Lydia Yudifovna. Bloy announced as early as 1915 that the world was on the verge of the Apocalypse. Similar (though not identical) conclusions stressing the collapse of civilization, the decline of Western culture, or the commencement of a new dark age can be found in the works of such diverse intellectuals as Albert Schweitzer, Arthur Koestler, Germain Bazin, H. G. Wells, Johan Huizinga, and George Orwell. The list could easily be extended, but it is sufficient to indicate the wide spectrum of the apocalyptic state of mind in contemporary European literature. The apocalyptic mood, of course, was engendered, or given impetus, by the cataclysmic events of our century: the eruption of two world wars, the rise and spread of totalitarian governments, and, of course, the staggering evidence of man's inhumanity to man. This pessimistic spectacle—reinforced by a broadcast antipathy for mass-culture, the "Machine," and "time"—has convinced many intellectuals "that the West has entered a 'time of troubles' and that it may even conceivably 'go under,' as Spengler predicted, unless the crisis is properly diagnosed and a cure provided."[118]

Berdyaev himself accepted Spengler's analysis of the decline of the West and used his cyclical conception of time to account for the deterioration of modern culture. He interpreted the cultural history of Europe from the Middle Ages to the present dialectically, maintaining that contemporary "culture" had already shifted into its senescent phase—into what Spengler termed "civilization." In Berdyaev's view,

> culture does not develop eternally. It contains the seeds of its own destruction. It is based upon principles which inevitably transform it into civilization. And the latter is the death of the spirit of culture.[119]

Berdyaev believed that the evidence provided by the First "World War already illustrates the downfall of European civilization,"[120] a downfall that began during the Italian Renaissance. Yet the term "Renaissance" can be applied with more accuracy, in Berdyaev's view, if it is used to describe the entire period of modern history—that is, if it defines the course of European history from the fifteenth century to the early twentieth century. Modern history, as he tells us in *The End of Our Time* (1924), is swiftly rushing to its conclusion: the "Renaissance" is over; "our epoch is the end of modern times"; and it brings in its wake "the beginning of a new middle age."[121] In Spenglerian terms, modern "culture" has turned into "civilization," its life-cycle has been virtually exhausted. And in Berdyaev's view, it is only because we refuse to face the truth, because we cannot detach ourselves from our commitments and our vested interests, that we persistently believe that our dying age continues to flourish.

While modern history has terminated, however, history itself is not at an end—only a culture of a world civilization. The Middle Ages, which were based on an integral religious ethos, gave way to their dialectical opposite: the Renaissance, the era of modern secularism. It, in turn, developed centrifugally, destroying the harmony of medieval culture. Today, however, the Renaissance is a shambles; and we are entering a new middle age, "a period of transition" that will be marked initially by terrible suffering and agony.[122] A new dialectic has emerged, generated by the explosive forces which created the First World War and the Russian Revolution. Communism now confronts Christianity in the decisive struggle of the historical process.

It is important to remember that in a sense Berdyaev was an enthusiastic supporter of the Russian Revolution because Bolshevism opposed all the modern or "Renaissance" ideals and instructions he considered anathemas: capitalism, liberalism, democracy, and humanism. On the other hand, while he loathed "the spirit of modernism" and appreciated Russian efforts to remake the world on principles of justice, he looked upon communism (especially as represented in the "distorted" doctrines of Lenin and Stalin) as a satanic force which could only lose its "falsehood" if it were synthesized with Christianity. This, then, is the project and goal of the dialectic of the New Middle Ages. When the goal has been achieved, a new and regenerate epoch of world history will unfold: the New Middle Ages will be followed by the Age of the Spirit.

Berdyaev thought that the final sapping of modern culture had been achieved by the subversive ideas of heroic individuals and not, as the "materialists" would have it, by the impact of economic and social forces. Modern culture was undermined in particular by creative antihumanists such as Dostoievski and Nietzsche, himself *"the forerunner of a new religious anthropology."*[123] Berdyaev always appreciated Nietzsche's role as a destroyer of "humanism," for he believed that the false values of our secular society had to be annihilated before the "creative epoch" could dawn. And though he thought that "Nietzsche's ideas are false and must be rejected," Berdyaev felt that "the true prophetic spirit was in him," that his work (especially *Thus Spake Zarathustra*) indicated the arrival of a new religious aeon in the history of humanity.[124]

The End of Time

But Berdyaev also appreciated Nietzsche for other reasons. As he confessed in his autobiography, he realized that

> something which has been said of Nietzsche is equally applicable to me: he is said to have been in need of ecstasy to enable him to live; he was driven by a sense of dissatisfaction and disappointment in the actuality of existence. I too felt the need of, and

longed for ecstasy, and I have, indeed, known it. I have known the rapture of creative ecstasy.[125]

Berdyaev felt this need for creative ecstasy, for an experience of transcendence and deliverance, because he "could never be reconciled to the fact that time is a perpetual flux and that each moment is devoured by, and vanishes into, the succeeding one." This ephemeral "aspect of time," he admitted, "has caused me intense and unspeakable pain." He continued, "To part with people, with things, with places, has been a source of agony to me as dreadful as death."[126]

Like Shakespeare, Sidney, and Spenser, like Nietzsche and many of his contemporaries, Berdyaev felt the horror of mutability. And thus, he demanded that time must have a stop, that history must come to an end, for "unending history . . . is the epitome of meaninglessness"; indeed history only "has meaning because it comes to an end." For, "the meaning of history is beyond the confines of history," beyond the temporal process and the sickness of "time which is torn apart into past, present and future."[127] History is a source of illusion, evil, suffering, and despair. In fact, hell itself "is that which remains in time" or "that which, obsessed by its evil nightmares, does not pass into eternity." Hence, history must be irrevocably destroyed—not simply the history of a particular epoch, not only the "Renaissance" or "modern times," but the very structure of history itself. For only then can mankind escape the merciless "pressure of historical processes," only then can mankind "stem the torrent of time's disintegrating flux."[128]

Thus, because he was intensely aware "of suffering in the world and in human existence," because he had always been "struck by the unspeakable pain and destructiveness of time," and because all his life he had "re-echoed Zarathustra's immortal words: 'Eternity, I love thee,'" Nicolas Berdyaev "desired that time should cease to be, that eternity should contain and conquer time."[129] He believed that time was the cause of terrific "religious anguish," of a desperate "longing for immortality and eternal life, for redemption of the finitude of existence."[130] And thus he imposed a formal order upon the temporal process. He subordinated the content of time to a symbolic order that he thought described the realities of human, cosmic, and terrestrial destiny. He accomplished this by using the verbal equivalent of the nondiscursive, undulating line ("human development . . . does not take place along a straight ascending line")[131] to fix the boundaries of time. Just as the medieval alchemist or the necromancer in Benvenuto Cellini's *Autobiography* described magic circles about themselves to ward off demonic influences, or just as Nietzsche metaphorically "drew" a circle around the temporal process to make himself invulnerable to time, Nicolas Berdyaev forced symbolic boundaries or precincts *(temenoi)* upon the divergent flow of ephemeral events. He limited the temporal process so that it would come to an end; for only then would "the tragedy and torment of history"—"the tragedy and torment of time" itself—come to a close.[132]

Man may still exist in time; he may still be forced to suffer the horrors of other historical tragedies in the future. But if he can restore his personality, if he can create a society anarchic enough to preserve his spiritual integrity, and if he can accept the burden of freedom, the freedom that demands the end of time (which, according to Berdyaev, is the true meaning of Dostoievski's story of "The Grand Inquisitor" in the *Brothers Karamazov*), then man will be able to participate in the meonic freedom of God and will be ready to receive the Aeon of the Spirit. As Berdyaev tells us, there is a third and final historical age, the Age of the Spirit, which is close at hand. "We are not yet entering into the era of the Spirit," however. "We are entering into the dark era,"[133] the era that serves as the cataclysmic preface to the epoch of the Paraclete. In Berdyaev's view, we are now in an age of darkness, a period of hellish suffering, which Berdyaev rationalizes by believing that "one must die in order to come to life again," that one must endure agony in order to be reborn. But even though "there will be darkness and suffering in the future such as there have not been . . . there will also be unprecedented light, there will be the appearance of a new man, of a new society, a new cosmos."[134] Just as the novitiate in primitive initiation ceremonies or the neophyte in the Isidic or Mithraic mysteries (or, for that matter, the novitiate in any baptismal ritual) undergoes a symbolic death in order to be reborn, so Nicolas Berdyaev believed that man must endure temporal suffering before he could be reborn into the New Kingdom of the Spirit, which itself would prepare the way for his return to God-manhood.

Berdyaev appears to have acquired his conception of a New Aeon, of an apocalyptic era to presage man's return to God, from several sources. He often acknowledged, for example, that the Russian eschatologist N. F. Fedorov had greatly influenced his thinking by "realizing the conditional nature of apocalyptic prophecy." Yet while recognizing that "there will be a transformation of the world and the resurrection of every creature that has lived," Fedorov "did not arrive at a philosophical expression of this problem."[135] Berdyaev received further inspiration in developing his conception of a third epoch from reading the Calabrian monk Joachim of Floris. In fact, if we discount Berdyaev's adoption of the Orthodox view that every particle, every manifestation, of existence in the cosmos is slowly but inevitably progressing toward ultimate perfection, it is possible (although conjectural) to suppose that he derived his general chronology from the Calabrian. Indeed, Karl Löwith's description of "Joachim's discriminating interpretation" of history "based on the trinitarian doctrine" could easily be mistaken for Berdyaev's classification of historical epochs.

> Three different dispensations come to pass in three different epochs in which the three persons of the Trinity are successively manifested. The first is the dispensation of the Father, the second that of the Son, the third that of the Holy Spirit. The latter is beginning just now . . . and is progressing toward the complete "freedom" of the "spirit."[136]

This temporal genealogy is obviously similar to Berdyaev's. In Berdyaev's scheme, the first epoch, the Age of the Father, is identified with the Old Testament. It also corresponds to the first stage of revelation (i.e., "revelation in nature") which precedes the second epoch, the Age of the Son. It, in turn, is identified with the New Testament and the second stage of revelation ("revelation in history"). A third dispensation, or epoch, also "that of the Holy Spirit," which corresponds to the last stage of revelation ("eschatological revelation") and is characterized by apocalyptic expectation, prepares the world for a return to eternity by achieving the complete meonic freedom of humanity and ushering in the Kingdom of Heaven.[137] And there are other indications that Berdyaev may have borrowed from Joachim—or at least recognized the similarity between the Calabrian's basic time-schema and his own. For as early as 1914, Berdyaev stressed the importance of "Mystic Italy," or the "Christian Renaissance," of "the thirteenth and fourteenth centuries." This movement, which took place "within the framework of the Middle Ages," was, in Berdyaev's words, "one of the most extraordinary movements in the spiritual culture of Western Europe." It is associated with the works of Dante, St. Francis of Assisi, Giotto, and—most significantly from our standpoint—with Joachim of Floris, the chiliast, in whom "the prophetic hope of a new world-epoch of Christianity was born, an epoch of love, an epoch of the spirit."[138] This notion, of course, is synonymous with Berdyaev's "epoch of creativeness" or "Age of the Spirit." Even if he did not draw directly from Joachim, it is nevertheless significant that Berdyaev identifies his conception of the last era with Joachim's "prophetic hope"—his great hope of a new aeon, which unfortunately, like "the hopes of Mystic Italy" in general, "were ahead of their times" and consequently doomed to failure.[139]

Apart from these basic and important similarities, however, Berdyaev's philosophy of history is far more sophisticated than Joachim's. And it ultimately rests upon a critical analysis and complex interpretation of time.

There are, in Berdyaev's view, three principal forms of time: cosmic, historical, and existential.

> Cosmic time is calculated by mathematics on the basis of movement around the sun, calendars and clocks are dependent on it, and it is symbolized by the circle. Historical time is, so to speak, placed within cosmic time and it also can be reckoned mathematically in decades, centuries and millenia, but every event in it is unrepeatable. Historical time is symbolized by a line which stretches out forward into the future, towards what is new. Existential time is not susceptible of mathematical calculation, its flow depends upon intensity of experience, upon suffering and joy. It is within this time that the uplifting creative impulse takes place and in it ecstasy is known. It is symbolized above all by the point, which tells of movement in depth.[140]

Berdyaev correlated his interpretation of time with his "Joachimite" conception of three historical Ages. And he believed that the future Aeon, the new Spiritual epoch of the Holy Ghost (i.e., that third and final episode of the "trinitarian drama"), would occur in existential time, not in the cosmic or historical time that characterized, respectively, the Ages of the Father and the Son.[141] Yet this imminent Age of the Spirit—in which time itself (i.e., "eternity which has collapsed in ruin") will eventually be destroyed—still lies in the future.[142] It is to be preceded by our stage of "Godforsakenness, by yearning anguish, by the mechanization and secularization of history, and by transition through a period of godlessness."[143]

It is Berdyaev's view that we are on the verge of the last stage of revelation, on the threshold of that glorious epoch when "God finally and fully reveals Himself." But at the present, we continue to live "in the cosmic time of the natural kaleidoscope of life and in the disrupted historical time." Yet, Berdyaev emphatically believes that we are swiftly approaching the epoch of "the beginning and the end," and thus we must not despair. For when the end finally does come, it will mark "the conquest of both cosmic time and historical time. There will be no more time." From that conclusive epoch of the Spirit—that age and time which have their "roots in eternity"—"the end of things" will "take place."[144] Man will overcome his personal dichotomy; he will regain his androgynous spirituality, his pneumocentricity; and all manifestations of the objectification of the spirit (Being, temporality, social institutions) will cease to exist. Hence, the "end is the triumph of meaning," for only by envisaging an end to finite existence and temporality can man regain his theandric status; only thus can he achieve eternity. The end of time "is the union of the divine and human, and the eschatological consummation of the existential dialectic of the divine and the human."[145]

Thus Nicolas Berdyaev, while believing that man is a fallen spirit, a degraded soul enmeshed in the net of objectivity, still believed that man could regain his paradise; he believed that all of history was inevitably rushing toward that end; and he believed that man, by spiritually regenerating himself, by changing the structure of his own consciousness, could help prepare for and achieve that end. Hence, while there is pessimism in his image of man, there is also optimism. Berdyaev looked for a better world, a world in which man would not have to compromise the integrity of his own spirit, and he molded his thought accordingly.

He believed in the apocalypse because he felt that if the "world" and "history" did not come to an end, life would be "devoid of meaning."[146] The apocalypse would end the sickness and suffering of this world; it would destroy "the flux of time"—that nightmarish "symptom of the disrupted, fallen state of our world." He thought that the new "'heaven and the new earth' betokens victory over this disrupting temporal flux, which splits human existence into extraneous moments and experiences." He sought to eradicate "history's hostile and alien character" by effecting "the end of history," the end of time. That act itself "signifies a victory over all objectification and alienation—a victory by which man ceases to be determined from without."[147] Berdyaev ordered and limited the temporal process by imposing on it what Franklin Baumer has called "the jagged line," so that he and the rest of humanity could satisfy their "Love of Eternity," could "become reconciled to the horrors of history," by cherishing the "great hope of a resurrection of all who have lived and are living" at the end of time. He wanted "to put an end to the old world and to begin the new." For, "In that is the breath of the Spirit."[148]

CHAPTER 3

T. S. Eliot and the Transfiguration of Time

To be conscious is not to be in time.
—"Burnt Norton," *Four Quartets*

The Need for Roots

When Thomas Stearns Eliot was born on 26 September 1888 in St. Louis, Missouri, Nicolas Berdyaev was just beginning to explore the intricacies of Kantian epistemology and Hegelian metaphysics. When Berdyaev was encountering Marx at the University of Kiev and dreaming of transforming the world into an earthly paradise, Eliot, aged six, was writing his first play. When T. S. Eliot was studying as an undergraduate at Harvard, discovering the Symbolists, and laying the foundations for his subsequent career as a poet and critic, Berdyaev was gradually resolving his spiritual crisis, slowly but inevitably realizing that he would be a religious eschatologist. And during and shortly after the First World War, when Eliot was formulating an aesthetic which stopped "at the frontier of metaphysics or mysticism,"[1] criticizing the monotonous sterility of modern life, and trying desperately to discover some pattern in the nightmare of contemporary events, Berdyaev was examining the meaning of the creative act, attacking the chaos of twentieth-century culture, and describing the meaning of history in crowded Moscow lecture halls. In the next few years (especially after 1926 when Berdyaev had arrived in Paris to inaugurate the most productive phase of his career and after 1927 when Eliot had declared himself a British citizen and an Anglo-Catholic), these two began to speak with increasing unanimity on what they considered to be the essential problems facing the twentieth century. And while the son of the Marshal of the Nobility for southwest Russia and the son of the president of the Hydraulic Press Brick Company of St. Louis were not always in precise agreement on every issue, their proffered solutions to the problems of secularism, God-forsakenness, dehumanization, and mechanism began to assume a basic identity. This family resemblance was also observable in the writings of many other intellectuals of the time.

Both Eliot and Berdyaev believed that the "modern malady" had been caused by the erosion of spiritual values (a process both thought "began soon after Dante's time"), the diffusion of ersatz religions (such as Godless humanism), and the failure of our industrialized society to "judge temporal values in the light of eternal values."[2] But they also insisted that if the tendency to substitute time for eternity represents a typical feature of the modern era, it cannot be denied that human beings usually exhibit a predilection for the ephemeral over the eternal. And although it is true that thirteenth-century Europe (and especially Italy) possessed a remarkable religious ethos—a degree of order, spiritual coherence, and integrity which Europe and the West have not witnessed since—it cannot be forgotten that this medieval triumph was ultimately a failure. And the reason for its failure was that mankind is intrinsically imperfect, endowed with original sin.

Here, however, Eliot and Berdyaev differ. While both agree that original sin has vitiated man's spiritual nature, that "modern history can . . . be understood as a metaphysical tragedy," and that we are living on the threshold of a new Dark Age,[3] Berdyaev is far more optimistic than Eliot. Despite the terrible shocks of contemporary history, Berdyaev continued throughout his mature years to believe that man would be able to change the structure of his consciousness, to help God create the Age of the Spirit, and eventually to abolish the temporal process and return to eternity. Eliot, on the other hand, spurned optimistic apocalyptic prognostications and usually described the relations between "the Enduring and the Changing" as being "permanent." He eschewed teleological eschatology in favor of mystical revelation and insisted that "all times are corrupt."[4] But "corrupt" only in the sense that all human beings in all times and places are endowed with original sin. The equal distribution of man's primordial guilt does not exclude one period from being "better" than another. Thus, although Eliot believed that every age was infected with Adam's curse, he appears to have thought that the thirteenth and the seventeenth centuries were better than his own. Hence, while his conception of history acknowledged decline, it rarely demonstrated any hope for significant improvement.

Perhaps the discrepancy between Eliot's image of man and Berdyaev's optimistic forecast of human potentialities can be partially explained in terms of personality differences. Berdyaev was expansive and impetuous, subject to moments of ecstasy and profound depression. When provoked he could explode into paroxysms of rage, a flaw which he attributed to the

Cossack blood of his ancestors. He was an incomparable paradox, a compound of aristocrat and revolutionary, absolutist and impassioned anarchist. Berdyaev spent much of his life struggling to transform civilization by the sheer power of his will, trying to infuse other persons with enough enthusiasm to answer God's message and "create" eternity. He was, in his own words, "a Russian romantic of the early twentieth century."[5]

At first glance, Eliot presents the opposite picture. He was not mercurial like Berdyaev. And though (as his poetry demonstrates) he was an intensely passionate man, he incessantly fought to discipline his emotions—to achieve what he called the "unification of sensibility," the integration of the personality through the fusion of thought and feeling. But he was not always successful; his emotions often gained the upper hand and threatened to submerge his reason "In the general mess of imprecision of feeling." This danger demanded perpetual surveillance, a constant struggle against the power of "Undisciplined squads of emotion."[6] Thus, Eliot was not inclined to get caught up in the world of apocalyptic speculation; he avoided the excesses and raptures of the eschatological visionary. He advocated the Delphic precept "nothing in excess" in religion, just as he championed classical order and balance in politics. And if sometimes Eliot seems to have been overly severe, reserved, or ascetic in his attempt to maintain the unity of his sensibility, it is simply because the passionate elements of his personality demanded strict control. He wore an impassive mask (as Vernon Watkins once observed of Richard Hughes), not to curb the "natural eagerness and enthusiasm" of others, but "solely for" his "own benefit." It enabled him to resist his own exuberance and keep his own awareness under restraint.

One must consider more than personality factors, however, to properly understand the contrasting metaphysical positions of the two men. And, in fact, it is probably more important to realize that they approached the same basic problems from different religious traditions than it is to recognize the emotional and intellectual balance of Eliot and the romantic propensities of Berdyaev. Eliot, who combined "a Catholic cast of mind, a Calvinist heritage, and a Puritan temperament,"[7] represented a religious tradition that did not stress the Last Judgment to the extent Russian Orthodoxy did. Indeed, whereas such references are virtually inexhaustible in Berdyaev's works, it is extremely difficult to find an unambiguous reference to the historical end of time in any of Eliot's writings. Perhaps this deemphasis of the Last Judgment stems in part from Eliot's greater respect for ecclesiastical and political authority. Berdyaev was inclined toward anarchism before he became a Christian; but his acceptance of Russian Orthodoxy seems to have increased his messianic fervor and his desire to abolish the political, psychological, and ontological features of the objectivized world. Eliot, on the contrary, became more staunchly conservative after joining the Church of England than he had been before.

Whereas Berdyaev wished to eliminate the hierarchy of the Church (a sentiment which, although apparently implicit within elements of the Orthodox tradition itself, derives primarily from his anarchist and Marxist sympathies as well as from his dispute with Church officialdom in 1913), Eliot continued to regard the Church as one of the strongest defenses against the chaos of modern life. Eliot thought that the world could be rejuvenated only with the help of the Church and that its influence and assistance were absolutely necessary if the *Idea of a Christian Society* were ever to be more than a speculative possibility. Berdyaev, on the other hand, envisioned the destruction of ecclesiastical hierarchy as a vital step toward the "creation" of eternity; and his conception of Apocalypse necessarily entailed the abolition of clericalism. This sentiment lies behind his assertion of "the predominance [in himself] of *homo mysticus* over *homo religiosus.*"[8]

It would be inaccurate, however, to say the reverse of Eliot. For although he thought that salvation should be gained through the Church, he reserved his greatest admiration for the saints. And of course, like Berdyaev, Eliot was a mystic. He regarded "the unattended / Moment, the moment in and out of time," as the consummatory experience of his life.[9] Yet, unlike Berdyaev, Eliot emphasized only this temporary transcendence, or release from time, and did not discuss the final abolition of the temporal process.

While they may have differed on certain eschatological and ecclesiastical matters, Eliot and Berdyaev agreed that any attempt to organize human life that was not based on an allegiance to God was doomed to failure. They detested time-philosophies with the fervor of converts (Eliot had been a Bergsonist and Berdyaev, a Marxist). They refused to believe that human history culminated in social Utopia or that man's destiny was limited to time. They deplored the disruptive forces of industrial civilization and held these forces responsible for transforming society into a machine and human life into a series of mechanical functions. With a Janus face they looked into the past, where they saw the thirteenth century as an example of what the excellence of the human spirit could accomplish, and into the future, where they saw darkness swiftly descending over the world, the darkness of a catastrophic age, which would decide the fate of man. And they urgently called upon all men to ground their lives in God, to help save the world from suicide, and to redeem the time by preparing the foundations of a new and regenerate historical epoch.[10]

It is quite probable that the fathers of T. S. Eliot and Nicolas Berdyaev would have had different reactions had they lived to read the eloquent exhortations of their youngest sons. The elder Berdyaev would, no doubt, have been terribly disappointed. He was a former guards officer, a Russian aristocrat with an "enlightened" gentleman's suspicion of religion, who liked affecting a Herzen-tainted liberalism but who, in actuality, supported the tsarist regime. Henry Ware Eliot, Sr., on the other hand, would probably have responded sympathetically to his son's message. Of course, he might have disapproved of his son's Anglo-Catholicism, but undoubtedly he would have appreciated the sense of duty that compelled his son to bring his analysis of contemporary perplexities before the public.

A sense of duty, a devotion to public service, was part of the Eliot family ethos. This standard of conduct had been set by the poet's dynamic grandfather, William Greenleaf Eliot, who had left the comfort of Massachusetts and Harvard Divinity School in 1834 to become minister of the Unitarians in the primitive western city of St. Louis. Eliot commented on the lasting influence of his grandfather's personality in a centenary address to Washington University in 1953:

> The standard of conduct [of the Eliot family] was that which my grandfather had set; our moral judgments, our decisions between duty and self-indulgence, were taken as if, like Moses, he had brought down the tables of the Law, any deviation from which would be sinful. Not the least of these laws . . . was the law of Public Service . . . [which] operated especially in three areas: the Church, the City, and the University. . . . These were the symbols of Religion, the Community, and Education.[11]

Eliot never forgot the moral injunctions of his grandfather. And it is possible to observe the operation of the Law of Public Service in every phase of his work: in his social and literary criticism, in his poetry and plays, in his editorship of *The Criterion,* in his membership in the English Church Union, and in his activities as a publisher. When he stressed the role of the classics in education, the merits of classical aesthetics, the impossibility of building a secular civilization, or the importance of the idea of the Christian community, Eliot was following the precepts of his grandfather. Much of Eliot's prose even sounds as if it were delivered from the pulpit. As Cleanth Brooks has pointed out, his poetry (which necessarily lacks the obviousness of his essays) may be understood as a "Discourse to the Gentiles."[12]

The Law of Public Service also lies behind Eliot's admiration of the saints, the Thomas à Beckets and Celia Copplestones of the world, who are sacrificed "for the glory of God and for the salvation of men."[13] William

Greenleaf Eliot had compared the trials and exertions of the Christian in public service with the ordeals and sufferings of the saint and apparently "was tempted to the martyr's role" himself. "It is to the holy throng of apostles and martyrs, God's saints on earth," he said, "that all progress in wisdom and goodness, and all triumphs over evil, are due." "The blood of the martyr is the seed not only of the Church, but of truth and liberty."[14] Echoes of this view can be discovered in the "Commentaries" of *The Criterion,* and especially in the "Interlude" of *Murder in the Cathedral,* where Thomas à Becket insists that "a martyr, a saint, is always made by the design of God, for His love of men, to warn them and to lead them, to bring them back to His ways."[15] The idea of martyrdom became as essential a part of T. S. Eliot's theology as it had been of his grandfather's. But the grandson developed the notion further than the grandfather would have wished. For T. S. Eliot considered the saint's sacrifice analogous to the Incarnation (a concept unacceptable to the Unitarian minister) and to the mystic's apprehension of Reality—actions which he thought represented the "intersection of the timeless / With time."[16]

Nearly forty years would pass, however, before Eliot would take issue with his grandfather's Protestant rationalism. And in the meantime young Thomas inculcated the original Law of Public Service, absorbed the Socinian moonlight, and learned to respect the philosophies of Schleiermacher, Emerson, and Spencer. He studied at Smith Academy in St. Louis, an affiliate of Washington University (of which his grandfather had been a founder), and spent a year at Milton Academy in Massachusetts before entering Harvard in the autumn of 1906.

During his undergraduate years, Eliot read Greek and Latin; studied literature, history, and philosophy; and contributed some of his first poems to the Harvard *Advocate*. In 1908 Eliot discovered Arthur Symons's book *The Symbolist Movement in Literature*. This was an extremely important find, for it introduced him to the works of Rimbaud, Verlaine, Corbière, and, in particular, Jules Laforgue, the poet who, Eliot said in later years, "was the first to teach me how to speak, to teach me the poetic possibilities of my own idiom of speech."[17]

Eliot graduated from Harvard in the spring of 1909, and in the next term began work on a Master's degree in English literature, which he completed in the following year. In 1910 he visited Paris where he studied French under Jacques Rivière (editor of the *Nouvelle Revue Française*), enjoyed the adventures of Bubu of Montparnasse, and attended the lectures of Henri Bergson at the Sorbonne. The encounter with Bergson was as significant to Eliot as Berdyaev's encounter with Marx was to him. Bergson's philosophy made an overwhelming impression on the twenty-three-year-old poet, and, as he admitted in 1948, he underwent "a temporary conversion to Bergsonism"—the only conversion he ever experienced "by the deliberate influence of any individual."[18]

Eliot accepted Bergson's substitution of time for eternity—his equation of the temporal process with reality. And although Eliot later abandoned *durée réelle* in favor of an idealistic interpretation of time, he continued to use memory to destroy the chronological categories of the time-process. F. O. Matthiessen says that Eliot wrote an essay in the winter of 1911 in which he declared that Bergson's *durée réelle* was "simply not final."[19] But while the poet may have criticized the limitations of real duration, he had nothing to offer in its place, and he definitely continued to accept the French savant's time-philosophy until he began reading F. H. Bradley in 1911. *Durée réelle* probably appealed to Eliot because it presented him with a means of overcoming the past-present-future structure of linear time. But, of course, real duration (the continuously developing present which contains its own past) is still time. Indeed, in one sense, Bergson's philosophy represents a reaction against the Eleatic tendencies of the late nineteenth-century idealists, for it denies the reality of Platonic essences as well as spatialized duration and reasserts the overwhelming importance of Becoming. Yet, on the other hand, the concept of real duration provides a partial escape from time, from chronology, and it may very well have been this feature of the Frenchman's philosophy which appealed to the author of "Prufrock."

Eliot left France in the autumn of 1911 to return to Harvard, where he enrolled as a graduate student in philosophy. Shortly after his return, he purchased a copy of *Appearance and Reality* and soon began to explore the philosophy of Francis Herbert Bradley. If Eliot previously had not been entirely satisfied with Bergson's *durée réelle,* his reading of Bradley added further grounds for uneasiness. For the British philosopher presented Eliot with an extremely convincing argument against the reality of time. Time, to Bradley, is an "appearance," a characteristic of the phenomenal world which is essentially unreal. But although it "is not real as such," time is nevertheless "an appearance which belongs to a higher character in which its special quality is merged." In other words, time's "own temporal nature does not . . . cease wholly to exist" when it merges with this "higher character," but it "is thoroughly transmuted. It is counterbalanced and, as such, lost within an all-inclusive harmony." Bradley, then, achieves a reconciliation of time and eternity by assimilating time to "a higher character," a "character" which not only thoroughly alters the nature of the appearance of time, but virtually annihilates it ("time tries to commit suicide").[20] The "higher character," of course, which is responsible for achieving this paradoxical reconciliation, is what Bradley (here following Hegel) calls the Absolute, the totality of being; it somehow constitutes both Appearance and Reality.

Whether Eliot accepted this argument upon first reading is doubtful. Bradley's philosophy is monistic; it ultimately reduces the manifold world (and the discrepancy between the world of objects and the world of essences) to one all-encompassing principle: the Absolute. Eliot criticized this position in his 1916 article on Leibniz (published in a periodical appropriately called the *Monist*) and again in 1929, a year after announcing his conversion to Christianity. But by 1935 (or certainly by 1940) Eliot not only uses a monistic argument to transfigure the time-process into "a pattern / Of timeless moments," but employs Bradley's Absolute (which, in Eliot's poetry, is called the "dance") to reconcile the "still point" and "the turning world." Thus, Bradley's analysis of time provided Eliot with a philosophical statement of his own mystical experience, a discursive description of his own awareness of the "intersection of the timeless / With time," and a set of concepts which Eliot was able to transform into poetic symbols and to use in the *Four Quartets* to describe the relationship between time and eternity.

While at Harvard Graduate School, Eliot complemented his examination of Bradley's system with an exploration of another monist's philosophy, a system which, in many respects, represents the Eastern equivalent of Bradley's Absolutism. He spent "a year in the mazes of Pantanjali's metaphysics" (which left him "in a state of enlightened mystification") and two years studying Sanskrit.[21] Yet once again, as with Bradley, it is impossible to determine what immediate influence Patanjali may have exercised on Eliot. It is possible, however, to trace his appreciation of Indian thought in his poetry (in the third and fifth sections of *The Waste Land,* for example, and in the evocation of the *Bhagavad Gita* in the third movement of "The Dry Salvages"); and it is quite probable that Eliot recognized similarities between Bradley's and Patanjali's monism.

When Eliot left Harvard for Europe in June 1914, he had already decided to write his doctoral dissertation on Bradley's epistemology. Upon arriving on the Continent, he went to Marburg (an important center of the neo-Kantian movement) to read philosophy. But the outbreak of the First World War interrupted his studies, and he left Germany for England, where he went to Merton College to become a pupil of Bradley's closest disciple, Harold Joachim. When Eliot left Oxford in 1915, he decided not to go back to Harvard, but to earn his livelihood in England instead. He "did not, however, abandon immediately the intention of fulfilling the conditions for the doctor's degree. Harvard," as he wrote in 1964, had made it possible for me to go to Oxford for a year; and this return at least I owed to Harvard. So, amongst my other labours, I completed the first draft of my dissertation, and despatched it across the Atlantic for the judgement of the Harvard Department of Philosophy.[22]

The department approved his dissertation in 1916 ("Josiah Royce, the *doyen* of American philosophers, had spoken of it 'as the work of an expert' ");[23] but because Eliot did not return to Cambridge to defend his thesis, he never received his Ph.D.

When Eliot completed his dissertation he was a junior master, teaching a variety of subjects at the Highgate Junior School. The summer before he had assumed his duties at Highgate, Eliot had married Vivien Haigh-Wood and had already begun establishing himself in the literary life of London. The London that Eliot visited in the autumn of 1915, however, was far different from the city he had undoubtedly passed through on his way to Merton College the previous summer. The capital of the British Empire —the city whose name still invoked like a magic word the myth of the Pax Victoriana and the "White Man's Burden"—was in the throes of disillusion and reappraisal. The electric euphoria which had marked the early months of the war was wearing off, prematurely, like an inadequate dose of anaesthesia. The British could be happy that the Kaiser had been wrong; that although autumn had come, thousands of ghosts (and not jubilant and victorious troops) danced with the wind-swept leaves in the Lindenstrasse. But to many this was a small consolation for the prospect of an interminable war.

While the war raged on the Continent, Eliot had a crucial encounter in London: he met the redoubtable Ezra Pound. As the vigorous sponsor of several periodicals and self-appointed patron and paterfamilias of every literary artist he considered worthy of encouragement and assistance, Pound was preeminently suited to judge the merits of Eliot's poetry and to launch his literary career. Pound immediately plunged his latest "discovery" into the British capital's society of letters. Through him Eliot quickly met Ford Madox Ford, Violet Hunt, H. D., and Harriet Monroe, who (at Pound's insistence) published "The Love Song of J. Alfred Prufrock" in the April–September 1915 edition of *Poetry* magazine. Wyndham Lewis (whom Eliot had met at the Pounds' apartment) also published some of Eliot's work at this time in his periodical, *Blast;* and the two artists soon established what became a lifelong friendship. After World War I, they traveled through France together, where they met James Joyce in Paris.

During this sojourn on the Continent and afterwards in England,

Men against Time

Lewis and Eliot discovered that they were preoccupied with similar problems. Both disliked the impersonal and mechanistic characteristics of modern culture, and both deplored the excessive emphasis placed on the value of time and change in an industrial society. Eliot had already implied his distaste for the West's customary appreciation of time in his 1917 essay "Tradition and the Individual Talent." There, he had defended tradition against "progressivist aesthetics," against the notion that art is capable of improving or being judged in isolation from the past. He believed that works of art form a timeless "ideal order among themselves," an order which could be "modified" but not improved "by the introduction of the new (the really new) work of art among them." "The existing order," Eliot maintained, "is complete before the new work arrives." Thus, "for the order to persist after the supervention of novelty, the *whole* existing order must be . . . readjusted." When a writer is aware of the changing and yet eternal nature of this ideal order ("changing" because it can be modified by the "supervention of novelty" and "eternal" because it is imperishable), he possesses a "historical sense"—"a sense of the timeless as well as of the temporal and of the timeless and of the temporal together" —and can be called an artist.[24]

Eliot's criticism of progressivist aesthetics (which formed the basis for his subsequent denunciation of theological liberalism and his advocacy of a theory of history analogous to axiological eschatology) not only reflects his appreciation of tradition, of the organic continuity between past and present, but his passing acceptance of Bergson's real duration. For by 1917—a year after completing his doctoral dissertation on Bradley's epistemology—Eliot had rejected the French philosopher's doctrine of creative evolution in favor of an idealistic theory of art which stopped "at the frontier of metaphysics or mysticism."[25]

On first glance, Eliot's conception of tradition seems to involve the Bergsonian notion of a continuously developing present which contains its own past. The "historical sense" of a writer, for example, is said to involve "a perception, not only of the pastness of the past, but of its presence." It "compels a man to write not merely with his own generation in his bones, but with a feeling that the whole of the literature of Europe from Homer and within it the whole of the literature of his own country has a simultaneous existence and a simultaneous order."[26] Closer scrutiny, however, reveals that this simultaneous order is not involved in the river-like flow of duration. For while this ideal order may be augmented, it is intrinsically timeless—it forms a whole that lies outside of time, including nonchronological time, or real duration. Eliot derives this concept of order from Anglo-American idealism and, in particular, from his study of Bradley. In

[74]

contrast to Plato, Bradley had insisted that reality is not static but dynamic. It is dynamic because—to use the words of A. Seth Pringle-Pattison—"the time-process is retained in the Absolute and yet transcended."[27] In other words, when time (an appearance of existence) and reality are assimilated into the all-inclusive context of the Absolute, time is transfigured into a "pattern / Of timeless moments." Eliot translated this argument into aesthetic terms by asserting that his ideal order was timeless and yet susceptible to modification, that it was eternal and yet dynamic, responsive to "the supervention of novelty." And he further justified this contention by using the coherence criterion of truth to explain why the introduction of novelty into an eternal order of reality did not deprive that ideal order of its timelessness. "The existing order," Eliot insisted, "is complete before the new work arrives."[28] When the new work arrives, however, it does not destroy any constituent of the order. On the contrary, the new work simply changes the relation (and not the substance) of the order: all works are merely readjusted to incorporate the new work of art into the framework of the whole order.

Thus, by 1917, six years after he had converted to Bergsonism, Eliot had abandoned *durée réelle* for an idealistic interpretation of art. He had accepted a theory of creativity that rested on a conception of the relationship between time and eternity, appearance and reality. He eventually used this theory (in *Four Quartets*) to transfigure the temporal process into "a pattern / Of timeless moments."

When Eliot and Lewis met periodically (often at Eliot's London residence) during the interwar years, they must have discussed tradition and the relationship between time and timelessness (between what Wyndham Lewis later called *The Writer and the Absolute*) as well as the fallacies of Bergsonism and other popular time-philosophies. Perhaps these discussions even helped to inspire Lewis's book *Time and Western Man* (1927) in which he registered his (and Eliot's) scorn for the "time-obsession" of the twentieth century. Although Lewis's blast was principally aimed at the Bergsonist "Time-cult," which subsumed all of reality, he extended his charge to include anyone who endorsed *"chronological* philosophy." He condemned real duration, the theory of emergent evolution, and the idea of progress just as strongly as he deplored the economic emphasis placed upon the value of time in an industrialized society, the Hegelian theory of history, or life-philosophy. "There is Alexander, Gentile, Bergson, Croce, Wildon Carr," Lewis wrote. "In its very heart and at its roots, for all of them, *reality* is 'History,' or reality is 'time,' which is the same thing."[29]

Both Lewis and Eliot cooperated in defending tradition against those who would destroy the present's connection with the past, and they vigorously endorsed an idealistic metaphysic as a defense against the futility of contemporary history. They interpreted World War I as an overwhelming indictment of all time-philosophies—of Hegelianism, Bergsonism, Marxism, theological immanentism, and Victorian liberalism. They regarded philosophies that placed the goal of man within the historical process as symptoms of Western man's failure to comprehend the purpose and responsibilities of existence. And they insisted that human actions must always be judged in the light of eternal values—values which cannot change and are understood only by recognizing the proper and permanent relation between the timeless and time, the individual and the Absolute.

Eliot may have decided to stay in England before he met Wyndham Lewis. At any rate, he did not return to the United States after he completed his dissertation because he felt that Britain was a stronger and more venerable bastion of tradition than America. Like Henry James before him, Eliot seems to have abandoned the United States for England because his country lacked an ancient tradition and living past. Eliot yearned for the "sense of history" just as much as James sought *The Sense of the Past* —that sense of being integrated with a heritage that exists in the present but also subsists above time. Eliot longed for what the French mystic Simone Weil (whom Eliot regarded as "a potential saint")[30] called *L'Enracinement:* he felt a need for roots—traditional and aesthetic at first, and then metaphysical and religious. Yet the England to which Eliot moved after his brief residence at Marburg hardly seemed to be a venerable bastion of tradition. On the contrary, it (and the rest of Europe) acted as if it were the senescent destroyer of the past. This enormous catastrophe affected Eliot profoundly. In the early months of the war, he still possessed what Wyndham Lewis later called a "Gioconda smile." But the "Gioconda period" vanished once the initial shock of disbelief wore off and Eliot and his contemporaries realized that Europe was involved in a major war for the first time in a hundred years. Eliot became more taciturn, and as Lewis says, Eliot's

> saturnine vein was strongly fed with the harsh spectacle of the times. He was an American who was in flight from the same thing that kept Pound over here; and with what had he been delected, as soon as he had firmly settled himself upon this side of the water? The spectacle of Europe committing suicide—just that.[31]

The postwar years did not alleviate Eliot's maturing pessimism; they only accelerated his antipathy toward what he considered the alienating features of Western society. He continued his literary career in London, publishing poetry and critical essays and working (between 1919 and 1921) with Conrad Aiken, Aldous Huxley, and J. W. N. Sullivan on the staff of the *Athenaeum,* under the editorship of Middleton Murry. But although Eliot was extremely active in the years immediately following the war, he was also under enormous pressure, and the year after he left the *Athenaeum,* he suffered a "nervous breakdown." On the advice of his London physician, Eliot first went to Margate, where he expected to remain for a month recuperating from his illness, before taking up residence in "a small cottage with a verandah which Lady Rothermere has offered me, in the mountains back of Monte Carlo (La Tourbie)." When his health failed to improve, however, after a fortnight on the North Sea Coast, he left England for Switzerland on 18 November 1922 to seek the help of "a specialist in psychological troubles." His initial encounter with Dr. Roger Vittoz was encouraging: "I am satisfied, since being here, that my 'nerves' are a very mild affair, due not to overwork but to an aboulie and emotional derangement which has been a lifelong affliction. Nothing wrong with my mind—."[32] Upon termination of his convalescence, "Eliot returned to London, after spending a few days in Paris, where he submitted the manuscript of *The Waste Land* to Pound's maieutic skill."[33]

Pound thought Eliot looked better after his treatment; unfortunately, however, the diagnosis proved wrong. As Pound learned from Richard Aldington, Eliot was in grave psychological difficulty within three months of his stay in Lausanne. Pound tried to come to the rescue by rallying his fellow writers (including Ernest Hemingway and the Bloomsbury Group) to the cause: They offered to support Eliot "for an indefinite period" so that he could devote all of his time to poetry. Yet, "The uncertainty of guarantees beyond the first year (for which £ 300 had been promised), combined with Eliot's lack of enthusiasm, put an end to a generous conception."[34] While *Bel Esprit*—the name given to the plan to assist Eliot— failed, he did receive aid from his literary agent in New York, John Quinn, who also arranged for Eliot to receive the Dial Award for *The Waste Land* later the same year. But in spite of the efforts to improve his finances and raise his spirits, the mood of depression which accompanied Eliot's illness—a mood which is objectified in *The Waste Land*'s images of sterility and spiritual barrenness—seems to have remained an enduring element in the poet's life; it pervades his other famous poem of the period, *The Hollow Men* (1925).

Indeed, the tone of depression and despair begins to subside gradually only after Eliot's conversion to Christianity. He had been raised within the Unitarian fold, but even though he appreciated its social ethic, he apparently did not believe in God. In a letter written in December 1932 to Sister Mary James Power, Eliot confided that although he "was brought up

[77]

a Unitarian of the New England variety," he was "for many years . . . without any definite religious faith, or without any at all."[35] Yet he was not content to remain an atheist or agnostic, or for that matter, to accept a philosophical system such as Bergsonism or Bradleyan idealism in place of a theological interpretation of reality. But a will to believe cannot guarantee the possession of belief; and Eliot had to struggle for his religious faith, he had to fight for his belief until he had given up all hope of winning, he had to despair of ever achieving faith before he achieved it. It was extremely difficult for Eliot to discover faith mainly because he was exceptionally sceptical. But as he said in his essay "The *'Pensées'* of Pascal," scepticism can sometimes lead to faith.

> For every man who thinks and lives by thought must have his own scepticism, that which stops at the question, that which ends in denial, or that which leads to faith and which is somehow integrated into the faith and which transcends it.[36]

Eliot eventually succeeded in uniting "the profoundest scepticism with the deepest faith,"[37] and he joined the Church of England in 1927. Eliot described his conversion to Anglo-Catholicism in a declaration of faith published five years later in *The Listener:*

> Towards any profound conviction one is borne gradually, perhaps insensibly over a long period of time, by what Newman called "powerful and concurrent reasons". . . . At some moment or other, a kind of crystallization occurs, in which appears an element of *faith* not strictly definable from any reason or combination of reasons. . . . In my own case . . . that was simply the removal of any reason for believing in anything else, the erasure of a prejudice, the arrival at the scepticism which is the preface to conversion. . . . Among other things, the Christian scheme seemed the only possible scheme which found a place for values which I must maintain or perish. . . .[38]

Thus Eliot's conversion to Christianity took place slowly; it grew gradually (but not without intensive struggle and discipline) during the nine years following the First World War and culminated in a crystallization, a sudden clarification, or realization, of religious faith.

In 1928, four years before Eliot published his declaration of faith, he described other consequences of his conversion in the introduction to a book of essays entitled *For Lancelot Andrewes.* There he described the "general point of view" from which his essays were written as "classicist in literature, royalist in politics, and anglo-catholic in religion."[39] Although

Eliot later modified this position, he continued to be a conservative, an anti-romantic, and an Anglo-Catholic throughout his life.

He had first been convinced of the necessity of classicism in literature by his Harvard mentor, Irving Babbitt. "Babbitt's motive," Eliot wrote in 1937, "was awareness of, alarm at, the ills of the modern secular world; and his work as a whole constitutes the most complete and thorough diagnosis of the malady, as it shows itself in literature, in education, in politics and philosophy, that has been made."[40] But while Eliot appreciated Professor Babbitt's keen analysis of the modern malady and agreed with most of his proffered remedies, he could not accept "The Humanism of Irving Babbitt" as a substitute for religion. He did not think that "Five Foot Shelf Culture," or reason uninspired by supernatural revelation, could resolve the metaphysical tragedy of modern history. And, in the last analysis, he condemned Babbitt's humanism because it represented a secular substitute for religious faith.

Eliot continued to defend his credo in poetry, plays, and essays; in his editorship from 1922 to 1939 of *The Criterion,* in which he attempted to assist in the creation of an integrated European culture; and in his support of the English Church Union. He continued to insist on discipline in politics because, like Plato, he had witnessed the political consequences of mass hysteria. He continued to defend classicism in literature, in particular, and in art, in general, because he thought that it served as a check on contemporary irrationalism. And he continued to maintain that the West could be saved from disintegration and destruction only if it chose to re-create a universal Christian culture analogous to that of the high Middle Ages. Eliot traveled widely during and after the Second World War, lecturing in Europe and America, but he always remained an inveterate Londoner. In 1948 he was awarded the Nobel Prize for literature and the Order of Merit. He remained active throughout his later years. Indeed, at the age of sixty-two, he began a "second career" as a playwright, producing *The Cocktail Party* in 1950, *The Confidential Clerk* five years later, and *The Elder Statesman* in 1959. Eliot remarried in 1957 (his first wife had died ten years earlier), issued the final edition of his complete poems in 1964, and, that same year, published his doctoral dissertation. On 4 January 1965, the most controversial and discussed poet of the century died at the age of seventy-five. He had left us his own epitaph in his essay on Pascal:

> Above all, he was a man of strong passions; and his intellectual passion for truth was reinforced by his passionate dissatisfaction with human life unless a spiritual explanation could be found.[41]

Eliot believed that he had found a spiritual explanation for human life.

And in describing it in his poetry, he not only enriched the English language, but may have elevated the sensibility of mankind as well.

"The Waste Land"

During the decade prior to his 1927 conversion, Eliot's outlook was marked by an exceptionally "passionate dissatisfaction with human life"—a dissatisfaction that he constantly tried to overcome by discovering a "spiritual explanation" for existence. The first stage of his spiritual quest consisted of his repudiation of Bergsonism and the idea of progress and his acceptance of an idealistic aesthetic. In the second stage, he adopted the mythical method. And the third and final stage of his religious quest culminated in his conversion to Christianity and realization of mystical experience—his adoption of monism and, ultimately, his transfiguration of time into eternity.

The Mythical Method

Eliot's dissatisfaction with his own life was integrally related to his abhorrence of the conditions of contemporary existence—an abhorrence which he eventually described by associating "the medieval inferno and modern life."[42] Just as he observed disorder in his own sensibility, he noticed chaos and futility in the conditions of life in the modern world. And he felt that the correlation between his own *déracinement* and the contradictions of modern existence was not accidental. Indeed, they were intimately related: both were the cause and effect of each other. Dissociation of the psyche (not just Eliot's, but modern man's, in general) resulted from the secularization of society. And secularism itself derived from an aberration in the soul. Thus, any attempt to cure the illness of one's own soul necessarily involves an attempt to eliminate the spiritual sterility of modern life.

Eliot made a tentative attempt in this direction (an attempt consistent with and developed from his concept of tradition) when he formulated his notion of the mythical method. In a review of James Joyce's *Ulysses,* published in *The Dial* in 1923, Eliot declared that this new method, which used a myth or series of mythical allusions to manipulate "a continuous parallel between contemporaneity and antiquity," was "a way of controlling, of ordering, of giving a shape and a significance to the immense panorama of futility and anarchy which is contemporary history." And thus, it represented "a step towards making the modern world possible for art, towards . . . order and form."[43] Eliot thought that the timeless world of myth provided a coherent background upon which the artist could focus the bewildering kaleidoscope of contemporary events. Myth was stable, not affected by the accidents of change, and thus could be used by the poet or novelist not only to impose pattern upon the anarchy of current history, but to structure his own experience.

Eliot had often used the mythical method himself, and, a year before he reviewed *Ulysses,* he brought the method to perfection in what is perhaps the period's most famous poem in any language. Structurally, *The Waste Land* employs analogous myths to manipulate "a continuous parallel between contemporaneity and antiquity"—the initial prerequisite of the method. At first glance, however, this manipulation does not appear to give shape and "significance to the immense panorama of futility and anarchy which is contemporary history." On the contrary, it seems to contribute to the chaos of modern history by making ironic contrasts between the magnificence of the past and the sordidness of the present. For example, a line from Edmund Spenser's *Prothalamion* ("Sweet Thames, run softly, till I end my song"), invoking the beauty of the royal river during the Elizabethan age, is contrasted with the "testimony of summer nights," refuse ("empty bottles, sandwich papers, / Silk handkerchiefs, cardboard boxes, cigarette ends") which contaminates the river today.[44] Similarly, the tale of Actaeon and Diana, preceded by a line from Marvell's "To His Coy Mistress" and subsequently blended with a reminiscence of the ceremonial washing and purification of Anfortas, the Fisher King, is distorted and deprived of spiritual significance by its modern rendering:

> But at my back from time to time I hear
> The sound of horns and motors, which shall bring
> Sweeney to Mrs. Porter in the spring
> O the moon shone bright on Mrs. Porter
> And on her daughter
> They wash their feet in soda water
> *Et O ces voix d'enfants, chantant dans la coupole!*[45]

But it would be a mistake to think that the contrast between glorious past and barren present constitutes the central theme of *The Waste Land*. Actually, the element of ironic contrast, so striking upon first reading, operates only on a superficial level of the poem. For instead of believing that the past is ontologically superior to the present, Eliot consistently insisted (before and after his Christian conversion) that all eras are the same in the sense that they are equally corrupt—a sentiment he emphatically confirmed in the conclusion of "Thoughts after Lambeth": "I do not mean that our times are particularly corrupt; all times are corrupt."[46] Thus, the concept of the moral equality of all times (which was first noticed by

Cleanth Brooks and subsequently discussed at length by Staffan Bergsten) reduces the qualitative barrier between past and present (superficially confirmed by the ironic contrasts) and asserts the sterility of all temporal civilization.[47]

Up to this point, Eliot's use of the mythical method does not appear to have imposed any order on the anarchy of contemporary history. Instead, by advocating the unity of all times and the corruption of all epochs, he seems to have precluded any discovery or creation of order and to have resigned himself to the futility of modern life. Those of Eliot's contemporaries who read *The Waste Land* in the 1920s thought as much, for they read into it their own despair and disillusionment—disillusionment caused initially by the First World War and, of course, later by the Great Depression. But Eliot would have none of this, for as he remarked in 1931:

> When I wrote a poem called *The Waste Land* some of the more approving critics said that I had expressed the "disillusionment of a generation," which is nonsense. I may have expressed for them their own illusion of being disillusioned, but that did not form part of my intention.[48]

Eliot's criticism, however, is somewhat unfair, for it rests on the Pickwickian sense of "disillusionment" contained in the "Catholic philosophy of disillusion,"[49] a philosophy which divests the believer of the illusion that terrestrial accomplishments are meaningful in and for themselves—that is, divorced from God. Be that as it may, it is incontestable that most of Eliot's contemporaries who were acquainted with *The Waste Land* interpreted it as a correlative of their own despair, the despair of the "Lost Generation." And it is equally incontestable that Eliot himself felt profoundly the despair and pessimism of the postwar generation. But while the terror of modern history and the degeneracy of Western civilization often paralyzed his contemporaries, they merely accelerated Eliot's personal search for meaning. And it is within this context that the full significance of Eliot's adoption of the mythical method becomes apparent.

In a lecture to the Concord Academy in 1947, Eliot stated (but unfortunately did not elaborate) that he "wrote the 'Waste Land' simply to relieve my own feelings"[50]—feelings which he had obviously had long before his "nervous breakdown," but which he was able to objectify poetically only during his convalescence in Switzerland in 1922. Hence, taking *The Waste Land* as an expression of those feelings, it is possible to distinguish, beyond the use of superficial ironic contrasts and the notion of the unity and corruptness of all times, an additional complex of ideas in the poem: namely, a yearning for order and pattern, a search for a spiritual explanation of life, and a desire to transcend time. And Eliot expresses all of these ideas with the assistance of the mythical method, and specifically with the help of the myth of the eternal return. Thus, he fulfills another criterion of the method; the imposition of order upon "the immense panorama of futility and anarchy which is contemporary history"—and hence, by implication, upon the experience of the poet himself.

The Myth of the Eternal Return

In his memorable book *Cosmos and History,* Mircea Eliade notes "that the work of two of the most significant writers of our day—T. S. Eliot and James Joyce—is saturated with the nostalgia for the myth of eternal repetition and, in the last analysis, for the abolition of time."[51] While this statement is not applicable to all of Eliot's creative work (or even to his later poetry where, for example, he does not associate the myth of eternal recurrence with the abolition of time), Eliade's characterization is especially relevant to *The Waste Land.* For whereas Eliot eventually succeeded in transcending time through mystical experience, in 1922—that is, five years before his conversion and perhaps thirteen years before his first mystical experience—he attempted to structure the fortuitousness of events and to express his desire to escape time with the assistance of the myth of the eternal return.

The concept of cyclical recurrence was preeminently suited to Eliot's purpose, for instead of imparting a value to the unique occurrences of secular history, the archaic notion of time (or the myth of eternal repetition) denies the "reality" of particular, everyday events. In fact, it does not consider any of the objects in the external world, or any human action or temporal occurrence, "real" unless it participates in an archetypal event, or paradigmatical gesture, executed by a god, culture hero, or venerated ancestor in that mythical time during, or just after, creation of the cosmos. According to this view, the unique events the contemporary historian deals with would not have an ontic status. The mere succession of events is meaningless to a preliterate person because, to him, "true history" records only those exemplary events or actions performed outside "profane" time, in that "sacred" or timeless time when the world was created and when, for a short period, mankind enjoyed a paradisal existence.[52]

Archaic man believed that he could return to the sacred time of the beginnings by periodically abolishing profane time. And he thought that he could accomplish this task by reenacting the original act of cosmic creation during his New Year's rites. By repeating the paradigm of the cosmogony, primitive man not only succeeded in destroying the profane cycle of the temporal process, but achieved a total regeneration of time and, consequently, a renewal of every form of life. At the end of the year, as the current temporal cycle drew to a close, a series of rites was executed that signified a reversion to the primordial chaos from which a "new world," purged of contamination and pestilence, would be symbolically "created" to inaugurate a fresh cycle. Archaic man believed that he was sympathetically contemporaneous with the original creation—projected back, as it were, into the mythical moment when the gods defeated the forces of "chaos." He thought that the celebration of this ritual provisionally suspended the flow of "profane" time and cut off the ordinary tempo of "non-categorical" events (i.e., those events which did not conform to an archetype, or mythical category).

As it appears in *The Waste Land,* the myth of eternal recurrence is represented by two intertwining motifs: the quest for the Holy Grail and the vegetation ceremonies of archaic and classical societies. Eliot derived the plan, title, and much of the symbolism of the poem from Jessie L. Weston's essay on the Grail legend, *From Ritual to Romance.*[53] According to Weston, the Grail legend, with its motif of the stricken King, the devastated realm, and the subsequent regeneration of the wasteland, is nothing less than a transparent description of an ancient vegetation ritual. In the New Year's rite of a traditional society, the New King supplants the Old King (who is usually killed) during the reenactment of the cos- mogonic scenario (i.e., that ceremony in which archaic man destroys pro- fane time, returns to the Eternal Now of the Beginnings, and regenerates the cosmos by inaugurating a new time-cycle). The predominant symbols, the Cup and the Lance, originally had nothing to do with the Christian story; they are patent fertility symbols, depicting the respective generative organs of the sexes. This ancient ritual, whose "ultimate object" was "the initiation into the secret of the sources of Life, physical and spiritual," was eventually adopted and sublimated—given an "esoteric" as well as an "ex- oteric" meaning—by the mystery religions (e.g., the cults of Attis and Mithra) of antiquity and was, according to Weston, exported to Great Britain where it was "wedded . . . to the Arthurian legend" sometime after the Conquest.[54]

Weston discovered her skeleton key to the Grail legend in the other major source of *The Waste Land, The Golden Bough* of Sir James George Frazer. (Weston was especially interested, it appears, in the same volumes that interested Eliot—viz., those on dying and reviving gods such as Adonis, Attis, and Osiris.) Together the works of Weston and Frazer provided Eliot with an "'objective correlative'; in other words, a set of objects, a situation, a chain of events"[55] with which he could express his desire to discover the spiritual sources of life—to arrive at a center of being beyond the manifold appearances and changes of the phenomenal universe.

Eliot used the Grail legend and, consequently, the myth of eternal recurrence—the concept of time contained in all vegetation rituals and archaic cosmogonic myths—to structure his poem. Just as Joyce imposed Vico's cycle on the "nightmare of history" in *Finnegan's Wake,* just as Spengler, Sorokin, and Toynbee revolted against Rankean historicism by employing cycles and spirals to pattern the temporal process, Eliot revolted against "the immense panorama of futility and anarchy which is contemporary history" by stamping a circle on the time-process. He used the myth of eternal repetition to objectify his highest aspirations because it enabled him both to control and order the anarchy of modern history and to express his desire to penetrate into another dimension—into the sacred time or durationless moment of the eternal now.

Was he successful? In 1922 did Eliot believe that he had established contact with nontemporal reality? Did he think that he had created an order in his own soul, or psyche, that was analogous to the order described in the myth of cyclic repetition—a pattern of repetition which he also employed to connote the cycle of death and rebirth, the abandonment of materialism, and the acceptance of spiritual values? The answer is obviously no. For although he found the symbols he borrowed from the Grail legend and the vegetation rituals meaningful and extremely helpful in expressing his spiritual desires (as well as in enabling him to create art in the traditionless wasteland of the twentieth century), Eliot did not believe that he had fulfilled his spiritual quest. There is an approximation of the mystical experience in the sequence of the hyacinth garden in Part I:

"You gave me hyacinths first a year ago;
"They called me the hyacinth girl."
—Yet when we came back, late, from the Hyacinth garden,
Your arms full, and your hair wet, I could not
Speak, and my eyes failed, I was neither
Living nor dead, and I knew nothing,
Looking into the heart of light, the silence.[56]

Although this passage prefigures Eliot's later use of the images of the garden, of silence, and of light as objective correlatives for his experience of timelessness, it is an isolated episode in *The Waste Land,* a brief description of a moment of ecstasy, exceptional in the modern world, where such experiences are quickly replaced by a sense of monotonous desolation, a sensation suggested by Wagner's "desolate and empty sea" (*Oed' und leer das Meer*), which terminates the passage. More frequently, however, *The*

Waste Land presents a world in which spiritual values (represented by the Grail legend and the rites of the vegetation and mystery religions) are debased and parodied. For example, the Tarot pack (which includes among its designs the Grail and the Lance), which was once used to describe the relationship between the divine and the human, is now employed by a disreputable clairvoyant, Madame Sosostris, to titillate her rich clients. The "drowned Phoenician Sailor"[57] (symbolizing the possibility of spiritual rebirth), "the man with three staves" (the Fisher King), "the Wheel" (an image of cyclical recurrence), and "The Hanged Man" (the Hanged God described by Frazer, as well as the resurrected Christ at Emmaus)—once, and actually still, symbols of authentic religious experience—are all relegated to Madame Sosostris's "wicked pack of cards." And "Mr. Eugenides, the Smyrna merchant" (who, had he been living in ancient Turkey and not the modern world, would have been exporting the mystery religions as well as currants), is described as inviting the protagonist "To luncheon at the Cannon Street Hotel / Followed by a weekend at the Metropole" instead of attempting to initiate him into the rites of Attis or Mithra.

Yet the fact that traditional religious values are grotesquely parodied by an unregenerate world does not eliminate the desirability of regaining the spiritual heritage of the past. Thus, it is not only valid but necessary for every man to set out on the quest for the Holy Grail—to attempt to cure the Fisher King or his own soul and restore the "heap of broken images" that is the modern world. We "who turn the wheel,"[58] or are involved in the cycle of time, ought to examine the fate of Phlebas the Phoenician because he died by water—a precondition of spiritual rebirth. For if we could regenerate our souls, if we could discover the source of our being, we should be able to restore the wasteland of modern history and escape the devouring futility of time.

With *The Waste Land* Eliot took a further step away from atheism or agnosticism toward religion. He decided to die "With a little patience," to dismantle the sterility of his life in hopeful anticipation that he could then construct or discover a spiritual explanation for existence. He reached the Chapel Perilous in "The awful daring of a moment's surrender," and although he did not succeed in restoring the wasteland of his own life, he took a significant step in that direction. The Fisher King may have been left "Fishing, with the arid plane behind" him in the closing section of the poem; Eliot may still have asked himself when or whether he would transcend the death-in-life of modern existence; and he may have also wondered at the apparent futility of shoring up "fragments . . . against" his "ruins" at the conclusion of *The Waste Land*. But his exploration, his pursuit of the sacred Grail or the spiritual sources of life, had at least re-sulted "In a flash of lightning" and "a damp gust / Bringing rain."[59]

At first glance, Eliot seems to be employing two unrelated concepts of time in *The Waste Land,* a practice that may even appear contradictory at first. For while the notion of the corruptness of all periods stresses the continuity between past and present, the archaic notion of time denies the existence of a historical past. The unity of all times entails a superficial distinction between past and present (preserved in the poem by the ironic contrasts). But although the stress upon the ubiquity of corruption tends to de-emphasize the chronological distinction between past and present, the distinction remains. For the proposition "all times are corrupt" does not entail the notion that all times are necessarily the same in every respect. It only implies that all epochs are morally identical. Thus, historical change is still considered a primary actuality of existence. There are fundamental differences between certain types of events; and, therefore, there is a past and a present, as well as a future. Or, to put it another way, although all periods possess the same moral resemblance, the Middle Ages and the twentieth century, while sharing certain common characteristics because of the permanence and homogeneity of human nature, are not ontologically synonymous.

The archaic notion of time, on the other hand, is totally antihistorical; it refuses "to preserve the memory of the past, even of the immediate past."[60] And it denies the existence of a future—it deprives events of direction—by repeatedly destroying and regenerating the temporal process.

While these ideas of time may initially seem incompatible, it is possible to reconcile them by interpreting them as examples of "sacred" and "profane" time (concepts of time which are implied in the poem by Eliot's use of the myth of the eternal return). It will be recalled that the archaic notion of time involves a cycle of secular or profane events, and an eternal present, the sacred (nontemporal) time of the beginning. For a person living in a pre-literate society, profane time (or the unique and unrepeatable events that do not participate in archetypes) is essentially unreal; whereas sacred time, which is synonymous with eternity,[61] is preeminently real: it is the Great Time or Eternal Now, which is reached by periodically annulling time.

Given this distinction, then, it is possible to say that the notion of the unity of all times is a concept of profane time; for although it stresses the unregenerate nature of all periods, it acknowledges the distinction between past and present. Eliot's use of the myth of eternal recurrence, on the other hand, may be taken as an example of sacred time. For while the cycle itself is profane (and, therefore, may be associated with the concept of the corruptness of all time), its function (and the result of its function) is not.

In other words, the cycle assimilates contingent occurrences to a circular form, thus imposing a rhythmic pattern on events that permits a periodic cessation of time and the physical and spiritual regeneration of life.

Thus, these two types of time (which to the preliterate person are characteristics of two related but different modes of being) are not only related, they are reconcilable. This is clearly demonstrated by preliterate man's "paradoxical desire to attain an historic existence," on the one hand, and "to be able to live only in sacred time," on the other. He attempts to resolve this paradoxical desire by "transforming . . . succession into 'eternity,' " by transfiguring "successive time into a single eternal moment."[62]

It is amazing how closely primitive man's reconciliation of profane and sacred time parallels Eliot's own resolution of the time-eternity problem. Whether Eliot recognized the implicit possibilities for achieving such a resolution within the myth of eternal recurrence itself is impossible to say. But—and this point is worth emphasizing—Eliot's use of the myth of eternal repetition in *The Waste Land* is consistent both with his discussion of time and the ideal order of art in "Tradition and the Individual Talent" and with his subsequent use of Bradleyan idealism to describe the relationship between time and eternity in *Four Quartets*—a relationship which he equated with the Christian concept of Incarnation and with his own mystical experience. Just as Eliot said in 1917 that a new work of art created in time could be assimilated (and, hence, transmuted) by an eternal ideal order of art, just as he later insisted in *Four Quartets* that one could transcend the temporal process by perceiving the transfiguration of time into "a pattern / Of timeless moments," so he implied in 1922 (by his use of the myth of eternal recurrence) that two parallel types of time (sacred and profane) could be reconciled "by transforming successive time into a single eternal moment."[63]

Eliot may not have recognized the consistency in his approach to the time-eternity problem. And indeed, he apparently did not even believe in eternity in 1922. He was still arrested "at the frontier of metaphysics or mysticism." But *The Waste Land* proves how desperately Eliot wished to cross that frontier, how fervently he wished to transcend the corrupt and profane time of history. And thus, his use of the myth of the eternal return is not simply an artistic device; it is not merely a poetic conceit which makes "the modern world possible for art,"[64] it is a spiritual confession.

The Rose Garden

After completing "one of the most important 19 pages in English," Eliot did not publish another poem for three years. When *The Hollow*

T. S. Eliot

Men eventually did appear (perhaps delayed by his physical illness), it revealed that the poet was still struggling to transcend "the frontier of metaphysics or mysticism," struggling without success to glimpse the "multifoliate rose" of paradise while standing on the "beach of the tumid river" of the modern inferno.[65] Beginning in 1927, however, when he converted to Anglo-Catholicism and composed Part II of what eventually became "Ash Wednesday," T. S. Eliot gradually began to fill the hollowness of his own life with spiritual meaning—he slowly began to transform the wasteland into a rose garden, to transfigure time into eternity.

The Dark Night of the Soul

His success in discovering a spiritual explanation of life was not achieved without difficulty. Eliot had to work and suffer for his belief, and he only conquered "the demon of doubt" after he had submitted himself to an arduous exercise in self-discipline and self-surrender. Since Eliot believed that the highest goal a Christian can attain under the aspect of time is an experience of timelessness, the aspiring believer must strive for the consciousness of the mystic. But even though time can be conquered or transcended only through mystical consciousness, it is extremely difficult to approximate the vision of the saint. And yet by retreating to the innermost depths of one's spirit, by enduring what the sixteenth-century Spanish mystic St. John of the Cross called *The Dark Night of the Soul*—"an essential stage," as Eliot recognized, "in the progress of the Christian mystic"[66]—it may be possible for the determined believer to transcend time and commune with Reality.

Between 1927 and 1929, when Eliot was writing *Ash Wednesday,* he considered himself a novice in religious matters. Although he had succeeded in transforming his previous scepticism into religious belief, he was still plagued by a feeling of anxiety, by a sense of despair, which (as he implies in his essay "The *'Pensées'* of Pascal") he only later realized was "a necessary prelude to, and element in, the joy of faith." Just where or when he first read the Spanish mystic cannot be determined. But it is abundantly clear that he developed a profound and lasting appreciation for the saint. And as he states in his essay on Pascal, Eliot was fully aware that the works of "great mystics, like St. John of the Cross, are primarily for readers with a special determination of purpose"—readers, like Eliot himself, who wish to advance beyond the condition of elementary belief by seeking to eliminate time through mystical revelation.[67]

While the goal of the *Dark Night* may be easily anticipated, it is extremely difficult to realize. Indeed, it can only be gained through constant sacrifice and renunciation. The cardinal sacrifice demanded by the negative system of purgation can be described as a paradoxical synthesis of desire and despair. Though the novice may yearn for revelation, he must abandon all hope of achieving it—he must "be still, and wait without hope" before he can perceive Reality. He must abandon the hope of turning toward God and "sit still," waiting "in darkness," until the free gift of God's grace dispels the darkness with the light of divine illumination.[68] Eliot summarized St. John's definition of this paradoxical method of approaching reality in "East Coker":

> In order to arrive there,
> To arrive where you are, to get where you are not,
>   You must go by a way wherein there is no ecstasy.
> In order to arrive at what you do not know
>   You must go by a way which is the way of ignorance.
> In order to possess what you do not possess
>   You must go by the way of dispossession.
> In order to arrive at what you are not
>   You must go through the way in which you are not.
> And what you do not know is the only thing you know
> And what you own is what you do not own
> And where you are is where you are not.[69]

Thus, before the aspiring mystic can even contemplate the possibility of experiencing religious ecstasy, of transcending time and participating in Reality, he must renounce the possibility of achieving divine illumination. Not only that: he must also detach himself from things, from the objects of this world and their attendant pleasures; he must transcend the cravings and revulsions, the desires and aversions of his ego before he can become a person worthy of God's grace. He must

> Descend lower, descend only
> Into the world of perpetual solitude,
> World not world, but that which is not world.
> Internal darkness, deprivation
> And destitution of all property,
> Desiccation of the world of sense,
> Evacuation of the world of fancy,
> Inoperancy of the world of spirit.[70]

When these conditions have been fulfilled, when the spirit has died so that it can be born again (a conception objectified in *Ash Wednesday* by the dismemberment and implied reconstitution of the protagonist's body under the "Juniper tree"), the soul can begin its climb upward out of darkness toward the light of timeless Reality.

Kristian Smidt has said that Eliot's poetry can be divided into sections which correspond to the divisions of Dante's *Divine Comedy*. Thus, the poems from *Prufrock* to *The Waste Land* represent Eliot's *Inferno,* while *Ash Wednesday* and the poems preceding *Four Quartets* (which are themselves analogous to Dante's *Paradiso*) parallel the spiritual development of the *Purgatorio*—a parallel explicitly drawn by Eliot himself in the third section of *Ash Wednesday.* Eliot originally published the third section of his first Christian poem separately under the title of *Som de l'Escalina* (1929), summit of the stairway, a title which he derived from a line of Arnaut Daniel's famous speech in the *Purgatorio:*

> "And so I pray you, by that Virtue which leads you to the topmost
> of the stair—be mindful in due time of my pain." Then dived he
> back into that fire which refines them.[71]

Eliot's allusion to the Provençal poet is particularly appropriate, for, like Arnaut, he was striving to refine his spirit. But whereas Arnaut was doomed to remain in purgatory for many centuries, doomed to remain at the bottom of the stairway, Eliot was able to begin his climb through the three stages of Dante's *Purgatorio.* "At the first turning of the second stair," Eliot perceived and escaped "the devil of the stairs" (an image reminiscent of "the demon of doubt" of the Pascal essay) "who wears / The deceitful face of hope and of despair,"[72] the simultaneous hope and despair of transcending scepticism and discovering a religious explanation of life. "At the second turning of the second stair," "the devil of the stairs" vanished from the poet's sight, "and the stair was dark"—filled with the darkness of the *Dark Night,* the purgatorial darkness which presages revelation and which Eliot himself could only discover after his realization of faith.

> At the first turning of the third stair
> Was a slotted window bellied like the fig's fruit
> And beyond the hawthorn blossom and a pasture scene
> The broadbacked figure drest in blue and green
> Enchanted the maytime with an antique flute.
> Blown hair is sweet, brown hair over the mouth blown,
> Lilac and brown hair;
> Distraction, music of the flute, stops and steps of the wind over the
>   third stair,
> Fading, fading; strength beyond hope and despair
> Climbing the third stair.[73]

At the first turning of the last stair, the poet is tempted by a vision of earthly love (symbolized by "the fig's fruit" and the garden god, Priapus), but he transcends the temptation and continues to climb to the summit of the helicoid stairway of purgatory. The invocation of the earthly lady ("Blown hair is sweet, brown hair over the mouth blown, / Lilac and brown hair") is fused in Parts II, IV, and V with an image of the Virgin Mary walking in a rose garden. This image symbolizes the transformation of terrestrial love into divine love, the transition from the *Dark Night* to a state of spiritual illumination, and, consequently, the poet's vision of timelessness in time.

Eliot appears to have derived his image of the rose garden from several sources.[74] But undoubtedly the most important and direct literary source of the symbol is Lewis Carroll's *Alice in Wonderland*—a point emphasized in private conversation by Eliot himself.[75] It will be recalled that at the commencement of her journey, Alice sees a little door at the end of a long corridor. After some difficulty, she succeeds in opening the little door, which reveals a beautiful garden graced by a white rose tree. But, to her great displeasure, she quickly discovers that she is too large to enter the garden. And it is only after many adventures in Wonderland that she succeeds (with the assistance of a magic elixir) in entering the lovely garden.

Eliot heightens the meaning of this delightful story by transforming it into an allegory of man's spiritual odyssey, by translating it into an image of his quest for redemption and communion with eternity. It is impossible for natural, unregenerate man, man endowed with original sin, to enter the door of the rose garden—to have a direct experience of reality—until he acknowledges his imperfection and voluntarily turns toward God. Most human beings are incapable of seeking God because they are obsessed with time. They care nothing for spiritual values and are content to equate goodness with utility, time with money, and history with technological progress. In other words, unregenerate man is capable of understanding only external events. He cannot comprehend

what has happened.
And people to whom nothing has ever happened
Cannot understand the unimportance of events.[76]

The inhabitants of the modern wasteland may "have heard the key / Turn in the door once and turn once only,"[77] but they are unwilling to renounce the sterility of their own lives; they are unwilling to make the sacrifice necessary to be able to turn the key themselves and open the door to reality.

Eliot underscores this point in his second play, *The Family Reunion,* by describing the spiritual emancipation of Harry, Lord Monchensey.

Harry, who has evidently murdered his wife, eventually admits his guilt and resolves to serve God by becoming a missionary. By his violent act Harry sought "a momentary rest on the burning wheel" of time. But instead of achieving release from the "continual impact / Of external events,"[78] he only succeeded in tormenting himself with a pathological sense of guilt (symbolized in the play by the Furies). Yet by accepting his guilt not simply as a crime but as a sin, Harry discovers expiation and commences his spiritual odyssey. In Scene II, he catches a fleeting glimpse of spiritual reality:

> You bring me news
> Of a door that opens at the end of a corridor,
> Sunlight and singing; when I had felt sure
> That every corridor only led to another,
> Or to a blank wall. . . .[79]

But he still cannot open the door, for while he admits pushing his wife over the railing of the ocean liner, he still does not realize that his crime is a sin. After his long conversation with Agatha, however, Harry understands the metaphysical significance of what he did. And thus, he is able to achieve redemption. Not only that; he is able to open the little door and enter the rose garden. In their re-creation of an imaginary encounter, Agatha tells Harry that she

> only looked through the little door
> When the sun was shining on the rose-garden:
> And heard in the distance tiny voices
> And then a black raven flew over.
> And then I was only my own feet walking
> Away, down a concrete corridor
> In a dead air.[80]

Like Alice, Agatha fails in her first attempt to enter the rose garden. But eventually both she and Harry are able to penetrate its precincts. For after the dark night, after "a lifetime's march" "across a whole Thibet of broken stones / That lie, fang up,"

> The chain breaks,
> The wheel stops, and the noise of machinery,
> And the desert is cleared, under the judicial sun
> Of the final eye, and the awful evacuation
> Cleanses.
> I was not there, you were not there, only our phantasms

And what did not happen is as true as what did happen,
O my dear, and you walked through the little door
And I ran to meet you in the rose-garden.[81]

The Re-creation of Eternity

Eliot's readers have been frequently puzzled by his use of symbols such as the rose garden. The meanings of his images have often seemed obscure, if not impenetrable. But the obscurity of his poems is only apparent; it is only a superficial quality of his work, necessitated by his method of presentation. As Cleanth Brooks points out, "Eliot's poetry, from the very beginning, is conceived in terms of the following problem: how is revealed truth to be mediated to the gentiles?" Eliot's answer: the method of indirection. It not only permits the mystic poet to translate "that which is by definition ineffable . . . into words,"[82] it enables the Christian artist to communicate religious verities to a secular society in a new guise. Or, as F. R. Leavis (here, borrowing a notion of D. W. Harding's) puts it, it allows a poet like Eliot to re-create "the concept of 'eternity.' "[83]

But do eternity-images like the rose garden really represent "re-creations" of the concept of timelessness? They do if "re-creation" is interpreted as implying the reexperience of previous mental acts, for the expression of the concept of eternity in the symbolic form of a garden has ancient precedents. And actually T. S. Eliot's rose garden is merely a variation on an immemorial theme: it is a representation of the notion of "sacred space." Archaic man believed that certain geographical areas (e.g., temple gardens, woodland groves, sacred mountains, the precincts of sanctuaries), certain physical objects (*omphalos* stones, thunderstones), and certain architectural structures (temples, altars) were ontologically different from the objects and the environment of everyday activity. When an individual came into contact with these holy places or objects, he impinged upon or entered a transcendent space, a dimension of being qualitatively different from his ordinary mode of existence. He penetrated a "mystical space . . . quite different in nature from profane space," a space in which the diurnal flux of events ceased to exist. He projected himself into the center of timeless reality. For, as Mircea Eliade observes, "Every 'construction,' and every contact with a 'centre' involves doing away with profane time, and entering the mythical *illud tempus* of creation." Hence, it is possible to see that preliterate man's "wish to be always and naturally in a sacred place . . . corresponds" to his "wish to live always in eternity by means of repeating archetypal actions." Eliot himself expresses these two interrelated desires in *The Waste Land* (by his use of the myth of eternal repetition) and in

T. S. Eliot

Ash Wednesday (by his objectification of his experience of eternity in the image of the rose garden). The man of archaic societies felt a " 'nostalgia for eternity,' " a longing "for a concrete paradise," that "can be won *here, on earth, and now,* in the present moment."[84] He tried to realize his desire through the imitation of mythical paradigms, just as Eliot (and, in a sense, the axiological eschatologists) sought to transcend time through concrete mystical experience.

Thus, Eliot's "re-creation of eternity" is really a representation of the concept of timelessness in the form of ancient religious symbols—symbols which, since they have been forgotten by our secular society, present the Christian message in a new light. Like Thomas Mann in his *Joseph* novels, Eliot dredged the "time-coulisse" of past religious experience to maintain a fresh and revitalized discourse to the gentiles. He sought "new symbols for the central experiences" of Christianity; and he tried "to reconstitute the old symbols" by "reclaiming them, redeeming them, setting them in contexts which" would "force us to once again confront their Christian meanings."[85]

T. S. Eliot's attempt to reshape the Christian message, to present spiritual realities in a new symbolic form, is not unique in the history of twentieth-century English literature. In fact, there are many other contemporary authors writing in the English language—W. H. Auden, W. B. Yeats, Lawrence Durrell, Charles Williams, and C. S. Lewis—who have sought to "re-create eternity," who have tried to construct new images of timelessness. W. H. Auden, for example (who, as a left-wing poet of the thirties, criticized the idea of a Christian society until he converted to Anglicanism shortly before the Second World War), developed a complex of "new" symbols to represent the Christian message—a set of images which, on many occasions, is virtually identical with Eliot's. Like Eliot, Auden uses the image of the garden, quite often the rose garden, to represent the concept of eternal reality. He describes "gardens that time is for ever outside," gardens where "The Devil in the clock"—i.e., "Time that tires of everyone"—is abolished and transcended.[86] In *The Door,* Auden makes an explicit reference to the chief source of Eliot's rose garden, *Alice in Wonderland:*

> We pile our all against it [the door] when afraid,
> And beat upon its panels when we die:
> By happening to be open once, it made
>
> Enormous Alice see a wonderland
> That waited for her in the sunshine, and
> Simply by being tiny, made her cry.[87]

[95]

Just as Agatha and Harry could not enter the rose garden until they achieved redemption, just as Eliot himself could not perceive the garden of *Ash Wednesday* until he endured the dark night of the soul, so "Enormous Alice," the unregenerate self, cannot penetrate the sacred precincts of Reality, for she has not redeemed herself through spiritual catharsis.

Although it is impossible to say whether Auden, like Eliot, had mystical experiences, his poetry occasionally bears the mark of mystics such as St. John of the Cross. And while Auden prefers Kierkegaard's formulation of man's experience of the awful chasm separating the divine from the human, he evidently believes that the individual in search of "the Great Good Place"[88] must practice spiritual exercises analogous to those described by the Spanish mystic. In "East Coker" Eliot makes a direct reference to the *Dark Night* by insisting that

> We must be still and still moving
> Into another intensity
> For a further union, a deeper communion
> Through the dark cold and the empty desolation.[89]

Auden echoes the same conviction in *The Sea and the Mirror* ("we have only to learn to sit still") and represents it more specifically in *The Labyrinth*:

> My problem is how *not* to will;
> They move most quickly who stand still;
> I'm only lost until I see
> I'm lost because I want to be.[90]

After an individual has purged himself of desire, of attachment to physical objects, and has learned to "stand still," he may momentarily leave the "alienated land" of time and perceive reality. In Part III of *New Year Letter* (1 January 1940), Auden describes the result or final cause of purgation, an experience of liberation that strongly resembles a personal record of mystical revelation:

> Yet anytime, how casually,
> Out of his organised distress
> An accidental happiness,
> Catching man off his guard, will blow him
> Out of his life in time to show him
> The field of Being where he may,
> Unconscious of Becoming, play
> With the Eternal Innocence
> In unimpeded utterance.[91]

When, Auden says elsewhere, you have "nowhere to go on to, your existence is indeed free at last to choose its own meaning, that is, to plunge headlong into despair and fall through silence" until you are humbly aware of God and the gulf that separates you from Him. But "that Wholly Other Life from which we are separated by an essential emphatic gulf"[92] can be bridged if we renounce pride, temporal desire, and "the shadow cast by language upon truth."[93] If we abandon the hope of apprehending God through logical categories and purge our selves of earthly cravings and revulsions, we will suddenly realize that "we / In fact live in eternity"; we will be able to see "the field of Being" and know the "Good Place." Or, as Auden puts it in another section of the *New Year Letter,* Part III, "Though compasses and stars cannot / Direct to that magnetic spot, / Nor Will nor willing-not-to-will," we may enter "the *temenos'* small wicket" and perceive "the well of life" "shining at the centre."[94]

Whether or not Auden's use of "new" eternity-images (viz., the "rose-garden," the "Good Place," the *"temenos,"* the timeless "centre," the "motionless rose") indicates that he feels he has succeeded in transcending time through mystical experience, it does reveal his obvious desire to bridge the gulf separating man from God. In his poetry, Auden frequently seems to say that it is impossible to achieve reunion with Reality. And yet he continually stresses the fact that we already live in eternity, that if we could teach ourselves to see properly, we would "wake, a child in the rose-garden" of timeless Being.[95] He persistently softens Kierkegaard's terrifying message by expressing his own desire for communion with God—a desire which he, like Eliot, often objectifies in symbolic forms of sacred space. Like Caliban, in the poet's commentary on Shakespeare's *The Tempest,* Auden prays to be translated

> from this hell of inert and ailing matter . . . to that blessed realm
> . . . that Heaven of the Really General Case where, tortured no
> longer by three dimensions and immune from temporal vertigo, Life
> turns into Light, absorbed for good into the permanently stationary,
> completely self-sufficient, absolutely reasonable One.[96]

William Butler Yeats, who died in 1939, a year after Auden had composed *The Sea and the Mirror,* shared his younger contemporary's desire to eradicate "temporal vertigo." Prior to the publication of *A Vision,* Yeats expressed his yearning for wholeness, for union with timeless being, in symbols that are analogous to the eternity-images used by Eliot and Auden. Although Yeats was not a Christian, he believed in supratemporal reality and wished to transcend contingency in "a fiery moment" of mystical illumination.[97] In his play *The Shadowy Waters* (1911), Yeats employs the symbol of the rose to describe the state of wholeness that arises when one experiences the "fiery moment" of liberation. "I can see nothing plain," Forgael says:

> all's mystery.
> Yet sometimes there's a torch inside my head
> That makes all clear, but when the light is gone
> I have but images, analogies,
> The mystic bread, the sacramental wine.
> The red rose where the two shafts of the cross,
> Body and soul, waking and sleeping, death, life,
> Whatever meaning ancient allegorists
> Have settled on, are mixed into one joy.[98]

Mystical illumination, the torch burning inside Forgael's head, dispels the mystery of existence and floods the mind with the light of the truth. But "when the light is gone," when the brief moment in which the soul escapes time has lapsed, "I have but images" or "analogies" of the mystical experience. These images, however, are extremely significant; for, unlike the sensory data of ordinary consciousness, they possess an intrinsic connection with reality—they are a step closer to timeless Being than the symbols which organize our everyday experience.

Yeats believed that special images like the "red rose" originate in the "Great Memory," in that part of the mind which Carl Jung would call the "collective unconscious." Although these images are inherent in everyone's mind, it requires "a fiery moment" of illumination or—as Yeats puts it elsewhere—a "trance" to release them. But once they have been released, once the imagination has been freed from the intellect and the will, the images of the Great Memory integrate the personality and effect a reconciliation between individual existence and Being, between time and eternity. In the "marmorean stillness" following a "fiery moment" of illumination, the mind's "red rose opens at the meeting of the two eye beams of the cross, and at the trysting-place of mortal and immortal, time and eternity."[99] The opposites of the fragmented self are reconciled by the symbol of the "red rose," and existence is reconciled with immortal being. "Life," as Auden would say, is turned "into Light" at the meeting place of time and eternity.

Unlike Eliot, Yeats, and Auden, Lawrence Durrell does not employ the image of the "rose," "the trysting-place," or the "rose-garden" to express his concept of timelessness. But like them, he uses a symbolic equivalent of sacred space, a concrete spatial image, to objectify his experience of abolishing time. In a letter to Henry Miller written in the fall of 1936, Durrell informs the American novelist that he is quietly laying the founda-

tion of a "HERALDIC UNIVERSE"—i.e., a universe in which space alone exists—
and that "I AM SLOWLY BUT VERY CAREFULLY AND WITHOUT CONSCIOUS THOUGHT
DESTROYING TIME." For

> I have discovered that the idea of duration is false. We have in-
> vented it as a philosophical jack up to the idea of physical disinte-
> gration. THERE IS ONLY SPACE. A solid object has only three dimen-
> sions. Time, that old appendix, I've lopped off. So it needs a new
> attitude. An attitude without memory. A spatial existence in terms
> of the paper I'm writing on now at this moment.[100]

Durrell is in revolt against the use of Bergsonian duration and Proustian
memory—a point which he also emphasizes in the Preface to *Balthazar,* the
second novel in the *Alexandria Quartet*—for he wishes to establish the
structure of the modern novel on the foundation of "space-time" (i.e., his
interpretation of relativity theory). But his concept of the heraldic universe
appears to be more than a morphological device. As he admitted in another
letter to Henry Miller (written that same fall): "I am beginning to inhabit
this curious HERALDIC UNIVERSE when I write," a universe in which "time as
concept does not exist," although it still seems to be "an attribute of matter—
decay, growth, etc." Durrell continued, "If it seems a bit precocious of me to
be trying to invent my own private element to swim in, it can't be helped."[101]
What seems to be a concrete example of the conditions of Durrell's heraldic
universe appears in his novel *The Dark Labyrinth.* Two of the major
characters who pass through the dark labyrinth, and eventually succeed in
adapting themselves to their new "shangri-la" environment, eliminate the
concept of chronological time from their consciousnesses. They do not
eradicate *"l'ordre du temps"* as Swann did in *A la Recherche du Temps
Perdu* by the grace of memory, but by living a "spatial existence" in which
the concept of time vanishes. Time is still a characteristic of matter—indeed
the characters in the novel grow older—but the notion of time is no longer
relevant. To Elsie Truman and her husband, for example, measurable
time is utterly meaningless: "There was no sense of calendar time left in
either of them."[102]

Durrell's heraldic universe (which, in concrete terms, refers to a utopian
community of self-sufficient individuals living a "spatial" existence—that is,
an existence that is not conscious of chronological time) bears some similarity
to Charles Williams's Arthurian kingdom. Williams purposely returned
to the principal source of Eliot's *Waste Land,* the Grail legend, to forge a
mythical or "indirect" representation of the Christian drama. By using
themes from the Arthurian romances (which he discovered primarily in
the writings of Chrétien de Troyes and Sir Thomas Mallory), Williams

developed a complex set of symbols that permitted him not only to describe the rise and fall of a civilization (Arthurian Britain and, by implication, any civilization without a spiritual ethos), but to present the major tenets of the Christian message (original sin, the Fall, redemption) in a new symbolic form.

To Williams, Arthurian Britain represents the perfect civilization. It is harmoniously ordered, a microcosmic reflection of God's own order and perfection. Human beings love each other, not for themselves, but as images or concrete manifestations of Divine Love. Arthurian Logres is nothing less than the garden of paradise before man's fall and the actual beginning of the historical process. It represents an intersection of eternity and time, a temporal civilization based on eternal values, an incarnation of divine truth analogous to the Incarnation itself.

But Logres cannot endure forever, and the Dolorous Blow (the wounding of the Fisher King, symbolizing man's Fall) eventually initiates the disruption of the Kingdom. People no longer love each other on the basis of Substitution or Exchange—that is, as images of Divine Love—they love themselves. And their spiritual incest, their egotistical cravings and revulsions, destroy the ethos that unified Logres. The quest for the Holy Grail in the wood of Broceliande is ultimately a failure; and the perfection of temporal civilization (portrayed by the circle of the Round Table) is broken. But not irreparably, for although Williams (and his friend C. S. Lewis, who culminates his trilogy of novels *Out of the Silent Planet, Perelandra,* and *That Hideous Strength* with a similiar analysis of the Grail legend) thinks that man has fallen into time, he believes that human beings can be redeemed. In fact, the Grail legend itself offers us a paradigm for achieving reunion with God. As Williams says in *Arthurian Torso,* the Grail quest is "the tale of Galahad; it is the tale of the mystical way" to salvation.[103]

Following Dionysius the Areopagite,[104] Williams says that there are two (mystical) ways to God: the Way of Affirmation (which resembles St. John of the Cross's *Ascent*) and the Way of Rejection (the way of negation, described by the Spanish mystic in the *Dark Night*).

> The Way of Affirmation was to develop great art and romantic love and marriage and philosophy and social justice; the Way of Rejection was to break out continually in the profound mystical documents of the soul.[105]

Actually, the Way of Affirmation begins only when an individual has a "Romantic experience—a moment of vision, in which some image of the created universe is seen as embodying the transcendent Good."[106] This experience is analogous to Dante's recognition of Beatrice as an image of Divine Love, and it leads the individual on to other visionary experiences, eventually culminating in a direct experience of supernatural Reality.

Like Eliot, Williams had mystical experiences. But whereas Eliot usually seems to have preferred the negative way of approaching God, Williams was always, as Dorothy Sayers writes, the "Master of the Affirmations." As Eliot pointed out in 1946, Williams was "a man who was always able to live in the material and the spiritual world at once, a man to whom the two worlds were equally real because they are one world." And Williams had the ability to describe (especially in his novels) his experience of living in both worlds at once. He was able to "describe, with extraordinary precision, the kind of unexplainable experience which many of us have had, once or twice in our lives and been unable to put into words."[107] And just as he was able to express his own experience of transcending time and communing with reality (in such prose works as *Descent into Hell* and *All Hallow's Eve*), Williams was equally capable of representing (in his poetic works *Taliessin through Logres* and *The Region of the Summer Stars*) the experience of man's Fall from Grace, the disunity of contemporary civilization, and the desire of men like himself and his friend T. S. Eliot to reestablish society on the spiritual foundations of Christianity. Like C. S. Lewis, J. R. R. Tolkien, Nicolas Berdyaev, and C. G. Jung, Williams may have believed that "myth in general is . . . a real though unfocussed gleam of divine truth falling on human imagination."[108] At any rate, both he and Lewis used the Arthurian romances and the Grail legend to conduct their respective discourses to the gentiles—to insist on transcending what Eliot calls the "lower dream" of the modern world—to reassert the spiritual message of history and the potential spiritual dignity of man.

"Four Quartets": The Final Vision

The Unattended Moment

Five years after the publication of *Ash Wednesday*, T. S. Eliot had an experience that gave him his final vision of Reality and that inspired his last and most magnificent poetic discourse to the gentiles: *Four Quartets*. According to his friend the literary critic and historian John Hayward, Eliot visited the uninhabited country estate of Burnt Norton during the summer of 1934. At some point in his visit, Eliot entered the garden of Burnt Norton,[109] and there, "in the autumn heat" of late summer, experienced a moment of ecstasy, an unexpected revelation of spiritual reality.[110]

[101]

Like Nicolas Berdyaev (who walked into the garden of his country house in the summer of 1907 and felt a "burning light" flare "up in my soul"), like St. Augustine of Hippo (who resolved his spiritual crisis by converting to Christianity in the garden of a friend's house), Eliot entered the garden of Burnt Norton and "felt a moment of inexplicable joy, a moment of release, like the moment Agatha speaks of when she looked 'through the little door, when the sun was shining on the rose-garden.'"[111]

In his essay on John Marston, Eliot provides us with a description of what it is like to have an unexpected perception of reality. Discussing Marston's *Sophonisba,* Eliot remarks that

> in spite of the tumultuousness of the action, and the ferocity and horror of certain parts of the play, there is an underlying serenity; and as we familiarize ourselves with the play we perceive a pattern behind the pattern into which the characters deliberately involve themselves; the kind of pattern which we perceive in our own lives only at rare moments of inattention and detachment, drowsing in sunlight.[112]

Eliot often employs the symbol of sunlight to depict the phenomenon of mystical illumination. Perhaps it is not too exaggerated to conjure up an image of the poet himself strolling "inattentively" in the sunlight "Along the empty alley, into the box circle, / To look down into the drained pool" of the garden of Burnt Norton—walking in a drowsy state of detachment just before his rare moment of illumination, his unexpected perception of "a pattern behind the pattern." The pool that the poet first sees is dry, "dry concrete, brown edged." But, then, suddenly

> . . . the pool was filled with water out of sunlight,
> And the lotos rose, quietly, quietly,
> The surface glittered out of heart of light, . . .
> Then a cloud passed, and the pool was empty.[113]

For an instant, an "intense moment / Isolated, with no before and after," an "unattended / Moment . . . in and out of time," Eliot experienced a rare moment of illumination.[114]

Whether he actually saw the lotos floating at the center of the pool, or whether he chose it as an objective correlative of his experience, is immaterial within the present context: the significance of the symbol is the same in either case. The lotos at the center of the pool symbolizes (in the iconography of Hindu art) the state of wholeness or integration enjoyed by the spiritually enlightened soul. It is a graphic representation of the reconciliation of opposites, in the personality and the cosmos; and it depicts the stillness felt by the individual who has succeeded in transcending the illusion of temporal multiplicity. The lotos is what Yeats would call a "red rose" or Carl Jung, a "Golden Flower," or *mandala*—an archetypal symbol of the integrated personality. And, in Eliot's poetry, it is analogous to the rose garden of *Ash Wednesday* and to the "still point" and "turning world" of the second section of the first *Quartet*.

In an interview with Kristian Smidt, Eliot indirectly verified the significance of his experience in the garden of Burnt Norton. When asked, were you "seeking a spiritual revelation in the *Four Quartets?*" Eliot replied that "he was not seeking a revelation when writing them, but that he was *'seeking verbal equivalents for small experiences he had had, and for knowledge derived from reading.'*" Such "small experiences," Smidt adds, "may not be comparable to the ecstasies of the saints, but they are what, for most of us, come closest to the beatific vision."[115] Eliot sums up this position in the closing lines of "The Dry Salvages":

> to apprehend
> The point of intersection of the timeless
> With time, is an occupation for the saint—
> No occupation either, but something given
> And taken, in a lifetime's death in love,
> Ardour and selflessness and self-surrender.
> For most of us, there is only the unattended
> Moment, the moment in and out of time,
> The distraction fit, lost in a shaft of sunlight.[116]

Evidently Eliot believed that "A martyr, a saint is always made by the design of God,"[117] and although he, like his grandfather, may have been occasionally tempted by the martyr's vocation, he realized that he (as opposed, for example, to someone like Simone Weil) was not a potential saint. And yet Eliot definitely believed in the validity of his own mystical experience. Even though he recognized that he did not, like the saint, have constant access to eternity, to "The point of intersection of the timeless / With time," Eliot felt that, on several occasions during his life, he had transcended time by perceiving Reality.

Yet the difference between Eliot's vision and the saint's is only one of degree, and it can be reconciled by a reference to Catholic theology. For Eliot's "unattended moment" (like Auden's "accidental happiness") seems to be "in the nature of what Catholic theologians call a 'gratuitous grace.'" To quote Aldous Huxley: "One may have a gratuitous grace . . . while in a state of mortal sin, and the gift is neither necessary to, nor sufficient for, salvation."[118] But such an unexpected experience of timeless reality may be extremely meaningful to the subject receiving it; it may be the source, the inspiration, for further spiritual exercises and investigations. Eliot makes this point himself in his third *Quartet:*

> the unattended
> Moment, the moment in and out of time
> The distraction fit, lost in a shaft of sunlight
> The wild thyme unseen, or the winter lightning
> Or the waterfall, or music heard so deeply
> That it is not heard at all, but you are the music
> While the music lasts . . . these are only hints and guesses,
> Hints followed by guesses; and the rest
> Is prayer, observance, discipline, thought and action.[119]

After the "intense moment / Isolated, with no before and after," the individual who has not been made a saint "by the design of God" must, if he wishes to pursue the full meaning of his "accidental happiness," continue to struggle to understand the "hints and guesses" provided by his experience. Eliot, of course, fulfilled this requirement (his own, as well as the Catholic theologian's, requirement for continued spiritual development) by "seeking verbal equivalents" for the "small experiences" or gratuitous graces he had had. These "verbal equivalents" eventually became the poems of the *Four Quartets,* poems in which he explored the significance and dimensions of his unexpected happiness. Thus, Eliot's momentary awareness of "the intersection of the timeless moment" did not diminish his metaphysical curiosity. On the contrary, it reinforced his resolution to observe the spiritual disciplines of St. John of the Cross—to follow the Way of Rejection or "detachment / From self and from things and from persons." It compelled him to continue to admonish his soul to "be still, and let the dark come upon you"—the dark night—which "shall be the darkness of God" and to interpret his "small experiences" within the framework of his own "lifetime's death in love, / Ardour and selflessness and self-surrender."[120]

Monism

When Eliot described his experience of timeless reality in *Ash Wednesday,* he believed that the material and spiritual worlds were radically different. In 1929, for example, the year the *Ash Wednesday* poems were completed, he defended Paul Elmer More's conception of Christian dualism in the *Times Literary Supplement.* In 1933, when he published his essay on Pascal, Eliot recommended the French savant's doctrine of "the *three orders,*" i.e., "the order of nature, the order of mind, and the order of charity"—orders of being which "are *discontinuous*," for "the higher is not implicit in the lower as in an evolutionary doctrine it would be."[121]

But by 1934 and 1935, when he began to describe and analyze his "unexpected happiness" in "Burnt Norton" (and subsequently in the other *Quartets*), Eliot had renounced dualism in favor of monism. By adopting a monistic interpretation of reality, Eliot reestablished the connection between his own thought and the philosophy of Francis Herbert Bradley. As a Bergsonist prior to the First World War, Eliot accepted the French philosopher's sharp distinction between "matter" and "memory"—a position Eliot subsequently reversed when he defended an idealistic aesthetic in "Tradition and the Individual Talent" (1917). Some ten or twelve years later, Eliot once again reversed himself by defending Christian dualism—a position he then rejected (evidently for the last time) in favor of Bradleyan idealism when he composed the *Four Quartets*.

The monistic philosophy found in *Four Quartets* is usually not discovered in Eliot's prose works. Perhaps this is because he realized that monism is unacceptable to some Catholic theologians. In any case, it is undeniable that Eliot not only believed that Bradleyan idealism assisted him in comprehending his vision of timeless reality, but that it accurately translated the knowledge he gained during his mystical experience into words. This point is indirectly substantiated by Eliot's B.B.C. lecture on Charles Williams, in which he said (obviously speaking for himself as well as the dead author) that Williams was "a man who was always able to live in the material and the spiritual world at once, a man to whom the two worlds were equally real because they are one world."[122]

But if Eliot is a monist, does he (like the Hindu mystic) accept the view that the personality is annihilated during mystical experience? Does his reduction of the multiplicity of the phenomenal world and his repudiation of ontological dualism lead him to deny the reality of the individual soul? The answer is no. For although he accepts Bradley's reconciliation of appearance and reality, Eliot still believes in the Christian concept of the soul. His mysticism (to follow Professor Zaehner's terminology) is theistic even though he believes, with Williams, that "the two worlds . . . are one world." In fact, Eliot's mysticism is quite similar to that of Nicolas Berdyaev. For while the Russian's mysticism is active or ecstatic (that is, comparable to St. John of the Cross's *Ascent* or Williams's Way of Affirmation) and Eliot's mysticism is usually passive or negative, both agree that the mystic communes with Reality, that he establishes a personal relationship with God, and that consequently the soul's identity is preserved during revelation.

Men against Time

Three Types of Time

Eliot's "personalist" interpretation of monistic metaphysics is further illustrated by his solution of the time-eternity problem in the *Four Quartets*. According to Eliot, there are essentially three types of time: chronological, nonchronological, and cyclical. Chronological time is linear, a succession of unrepeatable events. It provides the temporal structure for what man calls "history" and, from the vantage point of the present, is divisible into a past and a future. Eliot's attitude toward linear time (symbolized by the river in "The Dry Salvages") is extremely hostile. For while it may be the basis of the Christian philosophy of history, linear time is also the foundation of modern secular eschatologies—concepts of human destiny which Eliot deplored. Today "Men's curiosity searches past and future / And clings to that dimension"[123] because "Secularism" has virtually destroyed the concept of eternity. Twentieth-century man is principally interested in creating or anticipating terrestrial Utopias (finite substitutions for eternity) because he is no longer concerned with his own salvation or redemption.

> the enchainment of past and future
> Woven in the weakness of the changing body,
> Protects mankind from heaven and damnation
> Which flesh cannot endure.[124]

But a disregard for spiritual reality is characteristic not only of our age: "It is difficult to conceive of an age (of many ages) when human beings cared somewhat about the salvation of the 'soul.'" It is indisputable that "human kind / Cannot bear very much reality."[125] And yet, because modern man is accustomed to find meaning in origins rather than "*final causes*," because he thinks historically and seeks to resolve all of his problems in and through history, Eliot believes that we are justified in regarding twentieth-century history as "a metaphysical tragedy."[126]

The concept of nonchronological time is a vestige of Eliot's loyalty to Bergsonism. It is what the French philosopher called *durée réelle,* nonspatialized time, and it is represented in the *Four Quartets* by the sea. The river, which "Is a strong brown god—sullen, untamed and intractable," is the pulse of "time past and time future." It represents the chronological rhythm of historical events. But when the river flows into the sea, it is transformed and absorbed into infinite and unmeasurable time. On the sea

> The tolling bell
> Measures time not our time, rung by the unhurried
> Ground swell, a time
> Older than the time of chronometers, older

Than time counted by anxious worried women
Lying awake calculating the future,
Trying to unweave, unwind, unravel
And piece together the past and future.[127]

When one perceives nonchronological time ("the ground swell, that is and was from the beginning"), "time stops and time is never ending"—chronological duration ceases to exist, and time appears to extend forever.[128]

In contrast to real duration, cyclical time is divisible into repetitive categories; and, since it is symbolized by the circle, it is representative of what Bergson called "spatialized time." Eliot describes his concept of cyclical time at length in "East Coker":

In that open field

If you do not come too close, if you do not come too close,
On a Summer midnight, you can hear the music
Of the weak pipe and the little drum
And see them dancing around the bonfire
The association of man and woman
In daunsinge, signifying matrimonie—
A dignified and commodious sacrament.
Two and two, necessarye coniunction,
Holding eche other by the hand or the arm
Whiche betokeneth concorde. Round and round the fire
Leaping through the flames, or joined in circles, . . .

Keeping time,

Keeping the rhythm in their dancing
As in their living in the living seasons
The time of the seasons and the constellations
The time of milking and the time of harvest
The time of the coupling of man and woman
And that of beasts. Feet rising and falling.
Eating and drinking. Dung and death.[129]

The myth of eternal recurrence, which Eliot used in *The Waste Land* to control, order, and give "a shape and significance to the immense panorama of futility and anarchy which is contemporary history," reappears in *Four Quartets* as the circular round of what Harry (in *The Family Reunion*) called "external events." In the passage quoted above, the life-cycle of man, as well as "The time of the seasons and the constellations," is described as the cyclical rhythm of an endless dance. But although the symbol of the circle may organize and clarify the realities of biological and astronomical time, it does not (as Eliot had previously implied) allow the individual to control the temporal process. For

> Only
> The fool, fixed in his folly, may think
> He can turn the wheel on which he turns.[130]

Cyclical time is inexorable; it cannot be governed by man. And, as Eliot points out in *Murder in the Cathedral,* it is a cruel irony of existence that everything in time perishes while time itself endures: "nothing lasts, but the wheel turns."[131] Or, as Sir Philip Sidney puts it in his *Arcadia:*

> Time, ever old and young, is still revolved
> Within it selfe, and never tasteth end.
> But mankind is from age to nought resolved.[132]

All of human experience seems to be reducible to the revolving pattern of cyclical time. Even linear or historical time, "time past and time future," appears to vanish, to be abolished by the circular dance of cosmic time.

> We do not know very much of the future
> Except that from generation to generation
> The same things happen again and again.[133]

Thus, even the river of "The Dry Salvages" is more than a symbol for "the time of chronometers." For "the river," which "is within us," also has his "rhythm" or repetitive phases—"his seasons and rages."[134] This paradox exemplifies Eliot's apparent unwillingness to accept the reality of pure, unrepeatable succession. He recognizes the existence of linear time in the opening passage of "Burnt Norton":

> Time present and time past
> Are both perhaps present in time future,
> And time future contained in time past.[135]

But he denies the existence of novelty in (secular) history in *Murder in the Cathedral:* "from generation to generation / The same things happen again and again."

And yet Eliot seems to establish a compromise between "the time of chronometers" and the time of "the living seasons." "Men," he admits, may "learn little from others' experience. / But in the life of one man, never / The same time returns."[136] Thus, the lifetime of each individual is unique. Still, this does not mean that all time is linear. It is true, for example, that the Middle Ages are past, that a gulf of time separates the twentieth century from the age of Dante. But because human nature is unregenerate and endowed with Original Sin, man's behavior is predictable. Hence, even though there have been and always will be superficial differences between historical epochs, "the same things" will often "happen again and again." Specific moments in time, such as the individual's life-experience, cannot be repeated; but since human nature is homogeneous, the Life-Experience of Man in General will continue to conform to a basic pattern. W. H. Auden summarizes this idea in *For the Time Being:*

> As events which belong to the natural world where
> The occupation of space is the real and final fact
> And time turns round itself in an obedient circle,
> They occur again and again but only to pass
> Again and again into their formal opposites,
> From sword to ploughshare, coffin to cradle, war to work,
> So that, taking the bad with the good, the pattern composed
> By the ten thousand odd things that can possibly happen
> Is permanent in a general average way.[137]

But "permanent in a general average way" does not mean that everything always repeats itself in exactly the same way. And thus for Auden, as for Eliot, it would be more accurate to describe time's "obedient circle" as a spiral.

At any rate, although Eliot tended to reduce terrestrial history to a continual repetition of the same—a concept which he probably derived from his notion of the corruptness of all periods—he still recognized the existence of chronological sequence. Superficiality notwithstanding, "ages" are different from one another, not only in terms of the relation of succession, but because the lifetime of each individual cannot be repeated. From a historical point of view, then, time remains linear; from the perspective of nature or morality, however, it remains cyclical. But when both history and the cycle of external events are considered simultaneously, their synthesis may best be described as a spiral.

The Still Point and the Turning World

Eliot minimized the significance of linear time because (in contrast to the liberal or the Marxist) he did not believe in the redemptive value of history. As he wrote in 1932 in *The Criterion,* however man "is improved by social and economic re-organization, by eugenics, and by other external means possible to the science of the intellect," he "will still only be the natural man, at an infinite remove from perfection."[138] Yet, Eliot had another reason for minimizing the existence of linear sequence: it enabled him to make a sharp distinction between (and an eventual reconciliation of) time and eternity. By using the cycle to stand for time in general and by describing eternity as the point (or center) of the temporal cycle, Eliot was able to establish a relationship between the time-process and timeless reality—a relationship which he then sought to reconcile by using the image of the dance to symbolize the transfiguration of temporal motion into "a pattern / Of timeless moments."[139]

Eliot had used the image of the "still point" before he composed *Four Quartets*. It is described, for example, in *Coriolan*:

O hidden under the dove's wing, hidden in the turtle's breast,
Under the palmtree at noon, under the running water
At the still point of the turning world. O hidden.[140]

It is also referred to in "Choruses from 'The Rock'":

O perpetual revolution of configured stars,
O perpetual recurrence of determined seasons,
O world of spring and autumn, birth and dying!
The endless cycle of idea and action,
Endless invention, endless experiment,
Brings knowledge of motion, but not of stillness.[141]

But the most detailed discussion of the "still point" is found in "Burnt Norton":

At the still point of the turning world. Neither flesh nor fleshless;
Neither from nor towards; at the still point, there the dance is,
But neither arrest nor movement. And do not call it fixity,
Where past and future are gathered. Neither movement from nor
    towards,
Neither ascent nor decline. Except for the point, the still point,
There would be no dance, and there is only the dance.
I can only say, *there* we have been: but I cannot say where.
And I cannot say, how long, for that is to place it in time.[142]

The "still point" is Eliot's symbol for eternal reality—it is neither in space nor in time. We "can only say, *there* we have been." In other words (to quote Aldous Huxley), the divine "Ground can be denoted as being *there,* but not defined as having qualities." For that would be to describe it in spatial and temporal terms. But while Reality is timeless—completely above and beyond temporality—it is not static. It knows "neither arrest nor movement," and yet it serves (like Aristotle's unmoving Mover) as the "Timeless" "cause and end of movement."[143] Reality is not a profane or

T. S. Eliot

secular system of temporal events, but a divine "pattern / Of timeless moments." Thus the appearance of time (which in this case is synonymous with cyclical motion and change) is ultimately unreal. But, as Bradley would say, its "temporal nature"[144] is not totally absent from the eternal dimension: that is, while Eliot believes that Reality transcends time (and space), he does not believe that it is static (Eleatic or Platonic)—"do not call it fixity." Consequently, he employs the metaphor of the dance to describe the paradoxical "unmoving movement" of timeless Reality.

This view is similar to the contention of Pringle-Pattison, mentioned above, "that the time-process is retained in the Absolute and yet transcended." According to the Edinburgh idealist, "Time (and space) are to be regarded . . . as the forms of finite individuation, but as somehow transcended in the ultimate Experience on which we depend."[145] This is essentially Eliot's position. But the poet, of course, interprets his conception of the time-eternity relationship within the framework of Christian theology. Time and space are ontological characteristics of existence (even though they are intrinsically unreal), attributes of a sinful human nature and a fallen world ("The whole earth is our hospital / Endowed by the ruined millionaire," Adam).

For most of us, space and time are characteristics of the "real" world. The saint and the mystic, however, are capable of rising above this common and erroneous illusion. They are capable of transcending time and space, of apprehending the "still point," "The point of intersection of the timeless / With time," where temporal history is "transfigured, in another pattern"—"a pattern / Of timeless moments."[146] They are capable of seeing the light of Reality ("a white light still and moving"), of perceiving the dance which reconciles the "turning world" with the "still point"—"the centre of the silent Word" with "the unstilled world"—and of participating in "the stillness of God" which is "the dancing" of timeless moments.[147]

As mentioned above, the recognition of the unity of the material and spiritual worlds, the transfiguration of time into the unmoving movement of eternity, enhances (and does not destroy) the consciousness of the individual. The mystic's personality may be transfigured by his experience, but it is not eclipsed. And actually, communing with reality, participating in divine (as opposed to secular) history, is a precondition for achieving consciousness. For not only is it true that since "history is a pattern / Of timeless moments," "A people without history / Is not redeemed from time," but that "To be conscious is not to be in time." Thus, it can be said that our ordinary temporal existence (which most moderns interpret as being final)—existence governed exclusively by the "metalled ways / Of time past and time future"—is "unconscious," divorced from Reality like

[111]

the shadows of Plato's cave. Yet the mystic whose consciousness is enhanced by experiencing a "sudden illumination," by momentarily transcending and participating in timeless reality, does not escape time permanently.[148] As Berdyaev said:

> There are such things as moments of communion with eternity. These moments pass, and again I lapse into time. Yet it is not that moment which passes, but I in my fallen temporality: the moment indeed remains in eternity.[149]

Similarly, Eliot recognized the brevity of the "unattended moment, the moment in and out of time," but his acknowledgment of the ephemerality of "consciousness" ("supraconsciousness" in Berdyaev's terminology) did not encourage him to construct an apocalyptic philosophy of history. And on occasion, Eliot even stressed the necessity of remaining in time in order to conquer time:

> Time past and time future
> Allow but a little consciousness.
> To be conscious is not to be in time
> But only in time can the moment in the rose-garden,
> The moment in the arbour where the rain beat,
> The moment in the draughty church at smokefall
> Be remembered; involved with past and future.
> Only through time time is conquered.[150]

This passage contains an allusion to yet another way of transcending time. For while Eliot believed that gratuitous graces enabled the subject to penetrate into the "sacred time" of eternity—to perceive "the intersection of the timeless moment" (a moment which is analogous to the Incarnation, i.e., "the impossible union" in which "the past and future / Are conquered, and reconciled")—he continued to believe in "the use of memory: / For liberation."[151] He continued, in spite of his repudiation of Bergsonism, to believe that the remembrance of an unattended moment could bring momentary release from the pressures of the temporal process. By remembering "the moment in the rose garden," by recapturing a moment of past happiness in the present, the poet believed that he regained "consciousness," that he restored the meaning of the original experience. And, like Berdyaev, Eliot believed that it was possible to reestablish contact with the original moment "of communion with eternity" because "the moment" itself "remains in eternity."

T. S. Eliot

"The Idea of a Christian Society"

Although Eliot regarded his sudden illuminations (and his remembrances of unattended moments) as the consummatory experiences of his life, he insisted that the mystic must put his knowledge to practical use. For, as he pointed out in *Essays Ancient and Modern,* "even the most exalted mystic must return to the world, and use his reason to employ the results of his experience in daily life."[152] Thus, even after his own experiences of timeless reality, Eliot continued to observe his grandfather's Law of Public Service. He continued to occupy himself with the mundane affairs of an imperfect civilization. And, like Nicolas Berdyaev, Eliot made mysticism (and religious conversion) a basis for social revolution and ideological reform. "In a society like ours," he wrote in 1934, "worm-eaten with Liberalism, the only thing for a person with strong convictions is to state a point of view and leave it at that."[153] But Eliot did more than "state a point of view." He actively sought to change men's minds, to convince them of the hollowness of modern secularism and persuade them to reestablish society on Christian principles.

Since the seventeenth century, Eliot argued, Western civilization has been in decline: in that century "a dissociation of sensibility set in, from which we have never recovered." The unity of sensibility, exemplified by the Thomistic synthesis of faith and reason (and here Eliot follows Gilson and Maritain), has been destroyed; men no longer "feel their thought as immediately as the odour of a rose" because their emotions are dissociated and detached from their thoughts.[154] In the modern world, human beings do not perceive their environment in terms of an "I-Thou" relationship; they differentiate between subject and object and tend to regard other persons as "Its" instead of "Thous."

Science and technology are largely responsible for this disruption of sensibility—not only, however, for the fragmentation of the self but, in a broader sense, for the fragmentation and destruction of continuity in the history of the modern world itself. Scientific reasoning has anchored man's mind in the external world (and, thus, deprived him of his belief in eternity). But, Eliot continues, instead of integrating man with his environment, science has alienated him from nature. Industrialization has annihilated the organic unity of nature, just as it has made man a slave of the clock. It has destroyed the continuity of natural time by dividing the temporal process into a series of discrete and irrevocable events measured and evaluated in terms of quantitative utility. Hence, today men "concern themselves only with changes of a temporal, material, and external nature; they concern themselves with morals only of a collective nature." And they preoccupy

[113]

themselves with Utopia-building. But "all ambitions of an earthly paradise are informed by low ideals," for even if an ideal secular society could be created, it would "be at best a smooth running machine without a purpose, an efficient bureaucracy with no meaning."[155]

Yet, if temporal change is not intrinsically important, must we give up all hope of transforming the wasteland of modern history? Eliot says no, for, "There are, surely, ways of reorganizing the mechanisms of this world, which in bringing about a greater degree of justice and peace on that plane will also facilitate the development of the Christian life and the salvation of souls." Yet, would it be possible to reshape liberalism to meet this demand for social reorganization? Again, the answer is no: "The attitudes and beliefs of Liberalism are destined to disappear, are already disappearing." But, then, "If . . . Liberalism disappears from the philosophy of life of a people, what positive is left?" The answer to this question is as obvious to Eliot as it is to Arnold Toynbee: "The only hopeful course for a society which would thrive and continue its creative activity in the arts of civilization, is to become Christian."[156] This may seem impossible or undesirable, but when we realize that "our present-day ruin is the external sign of a world religious crisis," when we recognize that "modern history can also be understood as a metaphysical tragedy," we will also realize that we can only redeem the time and "save the World from suicide" by revolutionizing the structure of contemporary civilization—by re-creating the idea of a Christian society.[157]

It should be obvious, then, that the ultimate purpose of society is not to be found in the future or in time itself. A society ought "to allow every individual the opportunity to develop his full humanity," for "every man is ultimately responsible for his own salvation or damnation." But "Unless this humanity is considered always in relation to God," Eliot continues, "we may expect to find an excessive love of created beings, in other words humanitarianism, leading to a genuine oppression of human beings in what is conceived by other human beings to be their interest." Thus, Eliot warns, society must not coerce the individual—that is, "The conception of individual liberty . . . must be based upon the unique importance of every single soul."[158] Society must act as a catalyst, facilitating the individual's attempt to save his own soul, to become conscious of timeless reality. Hence, if society's goal is to create conditions favorable to spiritual development, it must establish conditions which allow individuals to receive gratuitous graces and in which new saints may be born.[159] The most significant achievement realizable in time is man's transcendence of time. And thus, the society that best enables the individual to attain his End (i.e., redemption and a direct perception of reality) is obviously the most perfect—in Eliot's view, a Christian society.

CHAPTER 4

Aldous Huxley and the
Illusion of Time

Men achieve their Final End in a timeless
moment of conscious experience.
—*Collected Essays*

The Journey to the East

In Shakespeare's *Henry IV* "the dying Hotspur casually summarizes an epistemology, an ethic and a metaphysic"—a concept of life and moral action which brilliantly epitomizes Aldous Huxley's Perennial Philosophy:

> But thought's the slave of life, and life's time's fool,
> And time that takes survey of all the world,
> Must have a stop.[1]

The entire meaning, import, or guiding purpose which unified the various strands of Huxley's mature thought—which drove him to reiterate and develop the same message again and again with increasing urgency and tenacity in his novels, biographies, and essays—is captured in these three brief lines. For Huxley (as he insisted in his 1944 novel), *Time Must Have a Stop* and does have a stop in the timeless vision of the mystic or "theocentric" saint. And because Huxley hoped everyman would aspire to transcend time and participate in Reality, because he believed that mankind could only survive if it changed the structure of its own consciousness, he advocated the universal adoption of the Perennial Philosophy. Since he believed that "men achieve their Final End in a timeless moment of conscious experience" and since he thought that mysticism—the nonpersonal monistic mysticism championed by the Perennial Philosophy—was the only effective method which has been discovered "for the radical and permanent transformation of personality," Huxley spent nearly thirty years of his life cajoling and admonishing his fellow men to ground their lives in eternity.[2]

Huxley believed that only by opening the doors of our perception (with or without the assistance of drugs), only by expanding our awareness of

[115]

the mind's dimensions, can we hope to escape the suffocating limitations of the ego and unite ourselves with the divine Ground of all being. War, murder, psychological and physical torture—all could be ended, all would be abolished, if only mankind would cast off the strait jacket of its collective ego and gain the time-shattering vision of the saint, the mystic, the authentic hero of history who has hitherto "saved the civilized world from total self-destruction."[3]

There are—to borrow Eliot's terminology (a terminology which Huxley may have known and, in any case, would have undoubtedly admired)—two dreams competing for the allegiance of men's minds: a higher dream and a lower dream. Those who follow the lower dream believe that the world of time is intrinsically real, that nothing is higher than man, for he is the measure of all things. Those who follow the higher dream, on the other hand, believe that the world of time is a nightmare, or phantasmagoria of deception—a dimension of infernal darkness that deprives human beings of the light of eternal Reality. We must choose our dream. And, Huxley would say, if we choose to read the "unread vision of the higher dream," we eventually will be able not only to transcend time, but to reconcile and surmount the apparently unbridgeable gap separating time from eternity. For by uniting ourselves with the divine Ground, we will necessarily realize that time is an illusion, that paradoxically time and eternity (samsara and nirvana) are really One and the same: Reality is an eternal process, an unmoving dance of timeless moments.

The emphasis that Huxley placed on sainthood or mysticism—his belief that mystical experience represents the purpose and highest goal of society as well as the sole method for transforming human nature (and social institutions)—is indicative of the view which he shared with Eliot as well as Berdyaev that contemporary man is living in a time of crisis, a dark age. In his early work, Huxley often alluded to the analogy between twentieth-century events and the "Dark Age" of the medieval period. In his 1936 novel *Eyeless in Gaza,* he made the allusion specific. During a conversation at an evening party, Beppo Bowles insists that Mark Staithes is "barbarous" for excoriating the Weimar Republic. To which the imperturbable Staithes (who on this occasion speaks for Huxley) replies:

> As one should be if one lives in the Dark Ages. You people —you're survivors from the Age of the Antonines. . . . Imagining you're still in the first volume of Gibbon. Whereas we're well on in the third.[4]

Huxley continued to regard the twentieth century as a Dark Age or, in more optimistic moments, a time of crucial transition that (given its acceptance of his diagnosis of the modern malady) would *possibly* result in a better world—even (to use Berdyaev's words) "a new heaven and a new earth." The solution to the problems besetting the twentieth century, however, is not (as many contemporary intellectuals think) to be found in an emulation, or reconstruction, of medieval society. As Huxley pointed out in his 1958 *Brave New World Revisited:* "The lyrical accounts of the Middle Ages with which many contemporary theorists of social relations adorn their works" are "romantically misleading." They not only ignore the fact that the Middle Ages produced "an enormous amount of chronic frustration, acute unhappiness and a passionate resentment against the rigid hierarchical system," but the resurrection of the medieval system—its contemporary use to confront "the impersonal forces of over-population and over-organization"—could only result in a society comparable to that of *Brave New World* or *1984.*[5]

Yet while he is unalterably opposed to the integrated or neo-medieval society advocated by T. S. Eliot and other contemporary intellectuals, Huxley seems to share Berdyaev's and Eliot's nostalgia for an earlier period of Western history. Eliot and Berdyaev, of course, admired the integrated culture of the Age of Dante, or mystic Italy, and they agreed that the modern epoch began with the disintegration of the medieval ethos—with the advent of the Renaissance and the "dissociation of sensibility." In contrast, however, Huxley's position is somewhat paradoxical; for while he obviously deplores the social and political structure of the Middle Ages, he seems to appreciate the medieval synthesis of faith and reason. And when accounting for the development of present problems, he (like Eliot and Berdyaev) invariably deprecates the secularization of modern life: "We are living to-day," Huxley writes, "in what is probably the most irreligious epoch of all history."[6] The process began with the Scientific Revolution, in general, and "the decline of mysticism at the end of the seventeenth century," in particular.[7]

Huxley recognized the eugenic values of many scientific discoveries, but he nevertheless held science partially responsible for the devastating uses of technology in the twentieth century. "We are living now," he wrote in *Ends and Means* (1937),

> not in the delicious intoxication induced by the early successes of science, but in a rather grisly morning-after, when it has become apparent that what triumphant science has done hitherto is to improve the means for achieving unimproved or actually deteriorated ends.[8]

When this attitude toward science is united with Huxley's corollary notion of a decline of mysticism in the seventeenth century and contrasted both with Berdyaev's explanation of the origins of dehumanization and Godforsakenness and with Eliot's account of the development of secularism and the dissociation of sensibility in the age of the metaphysical poets, one can see that Berdyaev, Eliot, and Huxley are endorsing a similar philosophy of history.

All three regarded the history of the West from the high Middle Ages, or the seventeenth century, to the present as a process of decline. On occasion, Huxley and Eliot tended to view this process as one of almost inevitable decay—a process which was slowed only by the grace of saints ("theocentric saints are the salt which preserves the social world from breaking down into irremediable decay").[9] Berdyaev, on the other hand, while accepting Spengler's analysis of the decline of Western culture (its transformation into civilization and its eventual fossilization), never entertained the notion that the world would destroy itself before the conclusion of the aeon of existential time. This is because Berdyaev structured his philosophy of history on a progressive linear pattern. Although he realized that there might be a Third World War, he still looked to a future resolution of the contradictions of the historical process and a return to eternity.

Eliot and Huxley, however, usually described the historical process in cyclical terms. And while they, like Berdyaev, considered human nature to be homogeneous,[10] they interpreted this fact to assert the circularity of events, to deny contemporary claims of progress or human improvement, and generally to discount the possibility of a future transformation of human nature and society. Instead of viewing the future with the apocalyptic hope of Berdyaev, they remained sceptical of man's ability to establish a viable religious society. They usually thought, as Eliot puts it in *Choruses from "The Rock,"* that "The cycles of Heaven in twenty centuries" have brought "us farther from God and nearer to the Dust."[11]

These differences are important, but they must not be allowed to obscure the fundamental identity of Berdyaev's, Eliot's, and Huxley's common attitude toward modern history—their antagonistic attitude toward the development of secular civilization in the West and their hostility toward time itself. All were unanimous in regarding the progress of contemporary history as a psychological, or spiritual, disease which had its roots in the dawn of the modern era. For even though they believed the development of a money economy, the growth of technology, and the Scientific Revolution influenced the development of the West's materialistic culture, the gradual erosion of religion, and the foundation of the "temporal orientation" of Western civilization—even though they thought all of these factors interacted and helped give modern European culture a definite shape, or character—they did not believe that these factors caused the modern period. And, therefore, they agreed that these developments per se were not ultimately responsible for the devastating course taken by European history in the late Middle Ages and the seventeenth century.

In other words, environmental determinism is an inadequate hypothesis: at best, it offers a superficial and incomplete theory of historical explanation. History is not simply a mechanical process; events cannot be explained entirely in quantitative terms. For events have an inside as well as an outside; there is a difference between internal happenings and external events, between the inner and outer occurrences of the historical process.[12] This concept of history is quite similar to R. G. Collingwood's *Idea of History,* but with one important exception: Huxley, Berdyaev, and Eliot interpret the inside of events in a religious sense. They regard the internal process of history as a divine-human drama, as man's struggle for salvation and temporal transcendence; and consequently they consider external events—for example, the development of modern civilization—as symptoms of mankind's spiritual struggle.[13]

Western man's obsession with time is itself one of the major symptoms of the course of soteriological history—a symptom which, in the opinion of Berdyaev, Eliot, and Huxley, has currently assumed the characteristics of a contagious disease. And it is in their individual responses to this urgent problem, in their attempts "to preserve men and women from the temptation to idolatrous worship of things in time—church-worship, state-worship, revolutionary future-worship, humanistic self-worship,"[14] that Berdyaev, Eliot, and Huxley demonstrate their uniqueness as well as their similarities. All three oppose "the apocalyptic religion of Inevitable Progress" (as well as other substitutes or surrogates for religion);[15] all three demand an end to Godless humanism and a universal restoration of religious values; and all three agree that man's destiny lies outside time—that his final cause is a "timeless moment of conscious experience," or the apocalyptic "creation of eternity." Yet Berdyaev is primarily an apocalyptist and secondarily a mystic, whereas Eliot and Huxley are primarily mystics who de-emphasize or ignore eschatology in favor of a realization of eternity here and now. But their differences are not resolved so easily; for although Berdyaev stresses an eschatological message, he also emphasizes the importance of theistic mysticism. And, in this sense at least, Berdyaev is much closer to Eliot than he is to Huxley. Huxley advocates a monistic and impersonal variety of Eastern mysticism: he calls upon men to transcend the personalist mysticism of the West and take (to borrow a phrase of Hermann Hesse's) what he believed was the higher, more exalted, and arduous "Journey to the East."

Yet, however desirable and rewarding, mystical experience (of any variety) is not easily achieved. This fact is borne out just as clearly by Huxley's life-history as by Eliot's. Born at Godalming, Surrey, on 26 July 1894, Aldous Leonard Huxley entered life as a member of one of the most distinguished families of England. He was the third son of the journalist and biographer Leonard Huxley and the grandson of "Darwin's Bull Dog," T. H. Huxley, and Julia Arnold, who was the niece of the famous Victorian critic and poet Mathew Arnold. Like his brother, the biologist Sir Julian Huxley, and his half-brother, Andrew (who won the Nobel Prize for physiology in 1963), Aldous wished to pursue a career in science. He apparently decided to become a physician while attending Eton, but his subsequent studies at Balliol College, Oxford, were interrupted in 1911 by keratitis, an eye affliction which left him temporarily blind.

Perhaps this first encounter with blindness helps explain the origins of Huxley's introspective character, for while he insisted that he was "congenitally an intellectual"[16] and maintained that temperament has an inherited and somatic basis, his early bouts with blindness (and the enforced solitude which accompanied them) probably encouraged his self-reliance and introversion. Not that Huxley was completely isolated during his first attack of keratitis. Indeed, during these two years he continued to study (with the aid of private tutors and the assistance of Braille) and, after having partially regained his eyesight, went to Oxford in 1913 (the year before T. S. Eliot arrived in Oxbridge to read philosophy under Harold Joachim).

Huxley's illness, however, forced him to abandon his plan to study medicine, and he decided to read English literature instead. In later years, Huxley said that he regretted very much "the scientific training which my blindness made me miss. . . . It is ludicrous to live in the 20th century equipped with an elegant literary training suitable to the 17th."[17] Yet if Huxley was disappointed when he began his "elegant literary training" in 1913, he did not hesitate to make peremptory use of his literary talent. And he published his first book of poetry *(The Burning Wheel)*—a collection of poems which reflects his wartime despair—before he left Oxford in 1916 to fulfill his alternative war service on the farm of Philip and Lady Ottoline Morrell.

Huxley had begun to read the works of Jakob Boehme and William Blake in 1913. It is difficult to say whether his interest in mystical literature was stimulated by the death of his mother in 1908 or by the suicide of his brother Trevenen in 1914 or by the tragic spectacle of the atrocities of war ("The West has plucked its flowers and has thrown / Them fading on the night").[18] Yet whatever the motive, the grandson of the scientist who coined the term "agnostic" to describe his own religious disbelief was immersed in the writings of the mystics at the age of twenty-one:

Aldous Huxley

I was always interested in the descriptions and philosophies of the mystical life . . . I read a fair amount [about it] at the time— with a mixture of admiration and hostility . . . a good deal of scepticism. And with a good deal of fascinated interest.[19]

Following this initial encounter with the literature of mysticism, Huxley devoted much of the time he did not spend teaching students at Eton to writing poetry. He had become a master in the college shortly after the war, but, while he tried to make the most of it, he found the work unsatisfactory and was thus delighted when in April 1919 he was offered a job on the editorial staff of the *Athenaeum*. During his stint with the *Athenaeum* (whose staff included not only Middleton Murry—whom Huxley later satirized as Burlap in his *roman à clef Point Counter Point*—but T. S. Eliot and the Beethoven expert J. W. N. Sullivan), Huxley married Maria Nys, whom he had first met at Garsington in 1916 when she was a refugee from her native Belgium. In 1920 Huxley published his first collection of short stories, *Limbo,* and in the following year he brought out his second novel, *Crome Yellow,*[20] which soon became a best seller.

Upon first reading, *Crome Yellow* appears to be nothing more than a clever satire of upper-class English country life, written by a young man who obviously delights in shaping ironic (and even cynical) caricatures of his subjects' temperaments, mores, and ideas. Yet when examined with hindsight—when placed within the context of Huxley's subsequent novels —it is possible to see that the arduous struggle (a struggle which was only resolved with the 1936 publication of *Eyeless in Gaza*) between Huxley's "this-worldliness" and "other-worldliness," between the materialistic and mystical sides of his character, is already well under way.[21] This point is extremely important, for although at this stage of his career, Huxley displays a bemused legerdemain in dealing with the highest spiritual aspirations of mankind, he nevertheless betrays a compelling desire to find a supernatural explanation of life. Indeed, after tracing his spiritual odyssey through the corpus of his work, it is obvious that the seeds of Aldous Huxley's mysticism (and consequently his negative attitude toward time) exist in his earliest work. He may still have been, as D. H. Lawrence once observed, very much the agnostic *Enkel* of T. H. Huxley during the 1920s. As an acquaintance of the Bloomsbury Group and the author of *Eminent Victorians,* he may have continued to exhibit a youthful irreverence toward religion throughout "the lost generation." But beneath the superficial exterior of *Jesting Pilate,* behind the "amused" mask of the "Pyrrhonic aesthete,"[22] one discovers a perplexity of spirit and a profound concern for metaphysical questions.

Undoubtedly much of Huxley's uneasiness—his perplexity and sense of deracination—had been caused by the Great War. Prior to the war he not only believed in the possibility of progress, he was thoroughly convinced that mankind had already transcended the Darwinian struggle for existence. As he said in 1958:

> Fifty years ago, when I was a boy, it seemed completely self-evident that the bad old days were over, that torture and massacre, slavery, and the persecution of heretics, were things of the past. Among people who wore top hats, traveled in trains, and took a bath every morning such horrors were simply out of the question. After all, we were living in the twentieth century.[23]

Yet this optimistic self-confidence—this innermost conviction, as Tennyson puts it in *Locksley Hall,* that mankind was living in a time when "the war-drums throbb'd no longer, and the battle flags were furl'd"—was not to last. And some six years later the enlightened and civilized "people who took daily baths and went to church in top hats" began committing "atrocities on a scale undreamed of by the benighted Africans and Asiatics."[24] The war shattered Huxley's belief in time-philosophy, his faith in what he subsequently called "the apocalyptic religion of Inevitable Progress," and left him with a feeling of abandonment, rootlessness, and uncertainty from which only his ironical sense of humor could defend him. For however hard he tried, Huxley could not immunize himself from the despair of the postwar years. And he is undoubtedly speaking of himself when in his third novel, *Those Barren Leaves* (1925), he has Mr. Cardan insist that

> you made a mistake in so timing your entry into the world that the period of your youth coincided with the war and your early maturity with this horribly insecure and unprosperous peace. How incomparably better I managed my existence! I made my entry in the late fifties—almost a twin to The *Origin of Species.* . . . I was brought up in the simple faith of nineteenth-century materialism; a faith untroubled by doubts and as yet unsophisticated by that disquieting scientific modernism which is now turning the staunchest mathematical physicists into mystics. We were all wonderfully optimistic then; believed in progress and the ultimate explicability of everything in terms of physics and chemistry, believed in Mr. Gladstone and our own moral and intellectual superiority over every other age.[25]

But if Huxley felt a nostalgia for "the simple faith of nineteenth-century materialism," he did not, as one critic maintains, "revolt into meaningless-

Aldous Huxley

ness."²⁶ He revolted against the narcissistic Victorian image of man; he enjoyed ridiculing any cherished dogma of the Establishment; but he did not abandon himself to nihilism. And *Crome Yellow,* his first published novel, establishes unequivocally that Huxley's imputed "revolt into meaninglessness" really marked the beginning of a search for transcendental meaning and a method of overcoming time.

In the fourth chapter of *Crome Yellow,* Denis confesses that he has "to invent an excuse, a justification for everything that's delightful," whether it be "beauty, pleasure, art, women."

> Otherwise I can't enjoy it with an easy conscience. I make up a little story about beauty and pretend that it has something to do with truth and goodness. I have to say that art is the process by which one reconstructs the divine reality out of chaos. Pleasure is one of the mystical roads to union with the infinite—the ecstasies of drinking, dancing, love-making. . . . And to think that I'm only just beginning to see through the silliness of the whole thing!²⁷

While this passage prefigures Huxley's later infatuation with D. H. Lawrence's life-worship, it is also a further revelation of his acquaintance with the literature of mysticism (in addition to Blake and Boehme, he had evidently also read St. John of the Cross at Oxford)²⁸ and his desire "to see through the silliness" of his rationalizations, cravings, and revulsions. By itself, however, Denis's self-analysis would not be sufficient to establish Huxley's early interest in discovering a religious explanation of life. In a subsequent conversation, however, between Scogan (Huxley's other principal mouthpiece in *Crome Yellow*) and Anne, the young novelist makes his religious aspirations quite clear. As a young man, Scogan explains, he wanted to feel religiously, and thus he tried to take a holiday from himself. He recognized that he possessed "the mathematical faculty" but did not have "religious emotions"—a condition which he found insufferable. And yet, however hard he struggled to transcend the limitations of his personality and his discursive intellect—however hard he "tried to take holidays, to get away from myself, my own boring nature, my insufferable mental surroundings!"—he continually failed to achieve success. But he kept "striving—how hard!—to feel religiously," and thus he "read the works of the mystics." Unfortunately, however, he could not feel "what the authors felt when they were writing."²⁹ He could not penetrate their verbal descriptions and reach the inexpressible experience upon which their doctrines were founded. For mystical experience is ineffable, and it is futile to try to understand mysticism without first having experienced mystical emotions. But although he had failed to become a mystic, Scogan continued to respect the mystic's ability to transcend the suffocating limitations of selfhood. And yet, he was forced to admit, while he recognized the value of mystical experience (and still possessed a wistful desire to become a mystic himself), he could not (however much he may have wished to) regard mysticism as a supratemporal mode of experience.

Recognition of Scogan's ambivalent attitude toward mysticism—his appreciation of religious emotions, on the one hand, and his inability to accept mystical experience as anything more than "a rich feeling in the pit of his stomach," on the other[30]—as well as Huxley's early interest "in the description and philosophies of mystical life," should not only establish his ultimate concern, but also the tension between his "this-worldliness" and "other-worldliness," between his agnosticism and his own desire to transcend time. In his second published novel, *Antic Hay* (1923), Huxley continued to express a desire for mystical experience; but once again his subterranean interest in overcoming time and personality is masked by the superficial irreverence of the Pyrrhonic aesthete.

Antic Hay is usually viewed as the work of a passionately honest and masterful "mouthpiece of a lost age, the age of the 'modern temper.'"[31] And certainly, when it appeared, *Antic Hay* received the same enthusiastic response as *The Waste Land* (1922), for it also seemed to express the disillusionment of the lost generation. Yet while this appraisal may be justified, contemporary critics failed to see that *Antic Hay*'s spiritually sterile landscape is underscored by the author's fervent desire to be delivered from the futility of history and, ultimately, from time itself. In *Crome Yellow* Huxley's growing interest in mysticism dovetailed with his increasing interest in the problem of time. And in his portrait of Henry Wimbush, master of Crome, distinguished authority on the antiquity of the plumbing of Crome, and self-esteemed author of the *Crome Journal,* Huxley registered his first attack on historical time, in general, and man's obsessive preoccupation with the past, in particular. Huxley eventually employed this attack against Proust, for he equated the French novelist's "remembrance of things past" with man's enslavement in time. In *After Many a Summer Dies the Swan* (1939), he described Proust's as a revolt against "evil at a distance."[32]

Huxley pursued his war against time in *Antic Hay,* expressing in the several passages describing the ephemeral romance of Emily and Gumbril, Jr., his own desire to be delivered from time. "There are," Gumbril is made to say, "quiet places . . . in the mind. But we build bandstands and factories on them. Deliberately—to put a stop to the quietness. We don't like the quietness" because it forces us to come to grips with our shallow selves; it makes us painfully aware of a reality beyond man and time. Yet the thought of abandoning ourselves to another world, another reality—a world of silence and timelessness—is "too terrifying," for "it's too painful to die" and become a new person. Thus, we do our best to think of any diversion that will "break the silence, smash the crystal to pieces."[33]

This description of quietness (which resembles Eliot's description of silence and the still point in the *Four Quartets* and which is also strikingly similar to passages in Max Picard's famous work *The World of Silence*) clearly shows that Huxley used a religious vocabulary to express his intimations of another dimension of reality in a novel which his contemporaries hailed as an intrepid manifesto of the lost generation. Of course Huxley had not yet converted to mysticism. As he admits, his fear of being transformed by contact with another realm of being prevented him from transcending the limitations of his own personality. Nevertheless, he obviously wished he could establish contact—permanent contact—with the "quiet places . . . in the mind." And when, in subsequent passages, Huxley describes Gumbril's and Emily's momentary transcendence of time (in which "the past is forgotten, the future abolished; there is only this dark and everlasting moment," an "endless present"),[34] it is possible to see that in 1923 Huxley employs virtually the same metaphors to describe his religious aspirations as he would in 1936 to express his newly gained mystical convictions.

Huxley continued to explore the possibilities of achieving mystical experience in his third novel, *Those Barren Leaves* (1925)—a work that provides a dramatic view of the growing tension between the sceptical and mystical sides of his personality. Francis Chelifer (who represents Huxley's agnostic mask) condemns the aspirations of the mystic, while Calamy, the novel's hero, defends mysticism and the contemplative life. Chelifer bases his indictment of mysticism on his contention that it represents "an escape into mere fancy" because it "does not prevent facts from going on; it is a disregarding of the facts." Mr. Cardan, a vestigial remnant from the Pax Victoriana (who resembles Scogan, and Eustace Barnack of *Time Must Have a Stop*), continues Chelifer's argument against mysticism by directly engaging Calamy in debate. Cardan opposes the notion that we all have "to live on lettuces and look at our navels." And he insists that mysticism loses its validity because it "doesn't in any way mitigate the disagreeableness of slowly becoming *gaga,* dying and being eaten by worms." But Cardan's wit and mockery do not prevent Calamy from insisting that "there *is* a reality which is totally different" from the phenomenal world, a world "which a change in our physical environment, a removal of our bodily limitations would enable us to get nearer to." And, Calamy continues, when you do get "beyond the limitations of ordinary existence . . . you see that everything that seems real is in fact entirely illusory—*maya,* in fact, the cosmic illusion. Behind it you catch a glimpse of reality." After having defended his belief in a timeless and spaceless reality, Calamy discloses his intention of discovering it, of experiencing it directly. For lately, he admits, "I begin to find in myself a certain aptitude for meditation which seems to me worth cultivating."[35] Nor is it foolish to do so, for

> It's not fools who turn mystics. It takes a certain amount of intelli-
> gence and imagination to realize the extraordinary queerness and
> mysteriousness of the world in which we live. The fools, the in-
> numerable fools, take it all for granted, skate about cheerfully on
> the surface and never think of inquiring what's underneath.[36]

But, Cardan answers, the cultivation of one's aptitude for medita-
tion—"protracted omphaloskepsis"—cannot possibly lead to self-knowledge "because you can't know yourself except in relation to other people." Calamy agrees that "part of yourself you can certainly get to know only in relation to what is outside." But, "On the other hand, there is a whole universe within me, unknown and waiting to be explored." Cardan and Chelifer make further protestations but Calamy remains adamant, and the novel closes with Calamy remaining in his mountain refuge. "Perhaps," he admits, "he had been a fool." But looking at the shining peak of the mountain, "he was somehow reassured."[37]

Sean O'Faoláin has criticized *Those Barren Leaves* (and Huxley's early novels as a whole) for not possessing "general conclusions."[38] But, as O'Faoláin himself recognizes, Huxley had not yet reached a permanent metaphysical position of his own. He was still groping for general conclu-
sions, for a resolution of the struggle between the agnostic and mystical sides of his character. The closing scene of *Those Barren Leaves* may have appeared to put an end to this struggle. But as Huxley's next work, *Jesting Pilate* (1926)—a travelogue of Aldous and Maria Huxley's visit to the Far East—reveals, Calamy's reassurance was only temporary. Indeed, Huxley takes mysticism to task in *Jesting Pilate* for inhibiting the progress of Eastern, and particularly Indian, civilization. "Admirers of India," he tells us,

> are unanimous in praising Hindu "spirituality." I cannot agree with
> them. To my mind "spirituality" (ultimately, I suppose, the product
> of the climate) is the primal curse of India and the cause of all her
> misfortunes. . . .
> It is for its "materialism," that our Western civilisation is
> generally blamed. Wrongly, I think. For materialism—if ma-
> terialism means a pre-occupation with the actual world in which
> we live—is something wholly admirable. If Western civilisation is

unsatisfactory, that is not because we are interested in the actual world; it is because . . . we are not materialistic enough. . . . We do not interest ourselves in a sufficiency of this marvellous world of ours.[39]

Instead of appreciating change and scorning fixity, instead of involving ourselves in the rich and variegated events of the manifold world, Huxley continues,

for some inexplicable reason, most of us prefer to spend our leisure and our surplus energies in elaborately, brainlessly, and expensively murdering time. Our lives are consequently barren and uninteresting. . . . The remedy is more materialism and not, as false prophets from the East assert, more "spirituality"—more interest in this world, not in the other. The Other World—the world of metaphysics and religion—can never possibly be as interesting as this world, and for an obvious reason. The Other World is an invention of the human fancy and shares the limitations of its creator.[40]

This statement, a sarcastic criticism of beliefs that Huxley later cherished, is amazing in itself. But followed as it is both by the suggestion that "an Atheist Mission" be established to cure India of its spiritual illness and eventually by the confession that "Ford seems a greater man than Buddha," it is remarkable that Aldous Huxley ever reversed his materialistic position and became a mystic. The critical denunciations of *Jesting Pilate,* however, conceal Huxley's continued preoccupation with mysticism. He may say (like Francis Chelifer) that "murdering time" is futile and wasteful and that spirituality and the Other World are fictitious products of the imagination, but he can also inform us with equal (and, evidently to his mind, not inconsistent) facility that he transcended time in a self-induced trance on the way to Ajmere, that "the automobile has placed the whole world at the mercy of the machine," and that mysticism is good for the health[41]—a position he restated in *Proper Studies* (1927).

But while Huxley stressed the "conduct value" of mysticism—while he continued to yearn for the serenity Calamy experienced in his mountain retreat, looking into the setting light of the late summer sun—he failed to become a mystic or, for that matter, a convinced materialist. He could not accept the agnostic heritage of his grandfather any more than he could yield himself to his evolving religious feelings. Any attempt to resolve this dichotomy by emphasizing one metaphysical position over the other invariably met with failure.

This stalemate was further complicated on Huxley's return from Asia in 1926. In 1925, while still in India, he received a letter from D. H. Lawrence. The two authors had first met in 1915, but after a brief flirtation with the idea of establishing a type of pantisocratic society in Florida (Bertrand Russell, a mutual friend, was also invited to join), the two parted company and did not see each other regularly for nearly ten years. When Huxley returned from the Orient, however, he decided to join Lawrence in Italy, and the two men soon became fast friends. Huxley was extremely impressed with Lawrence. He wrote in his diary (27 December 1927) that he regarded Lawrence as "one of the few people I feel real respect and admiration for." Huxley continued, "Of most other eminent people I have met I feel that at any rate I belong to the same species as they do. But this man has something different and superior in kind, not degree."[42]

Huxley restated this enthusiastic estimation in his sympathetic portrait of Lawrence (i.e., Mark Rampion) in his fourth novel, *Point Counter Point,* published in 1928. This novel represents the apogee of Lawrence's influence over Huxley, for Huxley seems to have believed that Lawrence's life-worship offered him a means of synthesizing his own contradictory proclivities for mysticism and materialism. Still, Lawrence's position was not ultimately satisfactory; and Huxley realized that even though it possessed a certain irresistibility, it could not solve his dilemma. Life-worship merely complicated and intensified the severity of his identity crisis.

Huxley examined the dimensions of his own dilemma through his portrait of Philip Quarles, a central character in *Point Counter Point,* generally accepted to be Huxley himself. Like Huxley, Quarles has returned from a trip to the Orient only to find himself more perplexed than ever. Who is he? What are his beliefs? Is he a mystic, sceptic, or a Lawrencian? Unfortunately, Quarles admitted, he could not decide. For

> this question of identity was precisely one of [his] chronic problems. It was so easy for him to be almost anybody, theoretically and with his intelligence. He had such a power of assimilation that he was often in danger of being unable to distinguish the assimilator from the assimilated, of not knowing among the multiplicity of his rôles who was the actor.[43]

This amoebic personality led him, "at different times in his life and even at the same moment," to fill "the most various moulds. He had been a cynic and also a mystic, a humanitarian and also a contemptuous misanthrope. . . . The choice of moulds depended at any given moment on the books he was reading, the people he was associated with." When, for example, he was associated with Burlap (Middleton Murry), he rediscovered the works of Jakob Boehme and became a mystic; when he read Pascal's

Pensées, he momentarily became an enthusiastic Catholic; when he joined the company of Carlyle or Whitman or Browning, he believed in strenuous living. And finally, when he spent a few hours with Mark Rampion (Lawrence), "he really believed in noble savagery."

> But always, whatever he might do, he knew quite well in the secret depths of his being that he wasn't a Catholic, or a strenuous liver, or a mystic, or a noble savage. And though he sometimes nostalgically wished he were one or the other of these beings, or all of them at once, he was secretly glad to be none of them and at liberty, even though his liberty was in a strange paradoxical way a handicap and a confinement to his spirit.[44]

Quarles, like his creator, had not yet discovered his "metaphysical" identity: he remained neutral—checkmated by the hypersensitive suggestibility of an omniverous intellect. But, as he hints in the last lines of this passage, he did not find his "liberty" totally satisfactory. Nor, as he soon demonstrated, did the author of *Point Counter Point.* Huxley could not content himself with the suspended judgment of Philip Quarles—a fact he implied in the closing sections of *Point Counter Point* in describing Spandrel's attempt to deduce the existence of God from Beethoven's later quartets, a fact he subsequently made explicit in *Music at Night* (1931) and in *Eyeless in Gaza.*[45]

With the publication of *Eyeless in Gaza,* Thomas Henry Huxley's grandson permanently abandoned his agnosticism and finally resolved his identity crisis by becoming a convert to the Perennial Philosophy. This book marks the resolution of the conflict between Huxley's "this-worldliness" and "other-worldliness," the reconciliation between the mystical and materialistic facets of his temperament. This resolution, however—this acceptance of mysticism, of the belief that "men achieve their Final End in a timeless moment of conscious experience"—did not transform Aldous Huxley into an eremitic escapist. On the contrary, it forced him to become a serious social critic—an extremely effective advocate of spiritual (and economic) revolution—who demanded the total reorientation of Western history, culture, and civilization. Like his brother Sir Julian, Aldous Huxley stressed the importance of ecology, warned the world of the dangers of overpopulation, and argued that the complexity of modern society—the increasing rationalization, or systematization, of every aspect of contemporary life—would probably lead to totalitarianism.

Huxley was a pragmatic prophet: he diagnosed the ills besetting the twentieth century, offered nostrums, and prognosticated the future. If, he maintained, the world adopted spiritual values (especially the Perennial

Philosophy's principles of "non-attachment"), if mankind abandoned the egotistical and idolatrous worship of things in time and selflessly tried to solve the gigantic problems (ecological and genetic, social and political) confronting modern civilization, then there would not only be a chance of survival, but a possibility for creating a regenerate society. If, on the other hand, Huxley insisted, the world failed to alter its current course of action, human beings would destroy themselves in a nuclear war or become the termites of a Brave New World.

After the publication of *Eyeless in Gaza,* Huxley settled in southern California, where he soon associated himself with the Vedantist movement, centered in Los Angeles. He remained on the West Coast where he continued to champion the tenets of the Perennial Philosophy in his novels, essays, and lectures until his death in 1963. He called upon all men to build a better world, to realize a higher destiny, by giving full expression to their spiritual potentialities. For although Huxley was a mystic, he loved this world because he realized that time and eternity, Becoming and Being, were actually the same.

It is possible to gain a partial appreciation of this paradoxical perception of reality by studying his life-history—by catching a glimpse, for example, of Aldous Huxley and Igor Stravinsky enjoying an outing at Disneyland; by imagining Huxley on a picnic with Bertrand Russell, Charlie Chaplin, Paulette Goddard, Anita Loos, and a coterie of Indian Theosophists; by picturing him greeting an incredulous Brazilian anthropologist in the depths of the Amazon jungle ("'Uxley—Uxley . . . *Contrapunto.*' The two men embraced. Aldous, too, was moved");[46] or by reading his vivid description of his experience under mescaline sedation or his pessimistic forecasts of human history in *Ape and Essence* and *Island.* Huxley possessed a redemptive sense of humor as well as a hypersensitive and articulate awareness of the difficulties of the human condition. Yet, instead of remaining self-satisfied with a static set of preconceptions, he continued to explore new dimensions of experience and persisted in seeking new solutions to the perennial problems facing man. This flexibility of character is best illustrated in Huxley's own words. In the early 1950s, he won a blue ribbon and three dollars for a drawing he entered in the Lancaster Alfalfa Festival. Commenting on his triumph, Huxley recalled another drawing

> in another gallery, a long way from Lancaster . . . for which the
> author received neither prize nor blue ribbon. It represents an
> ancient man hobbling along on two sticks, and underneath in
> Goya's strong, beautiful handwriting, is a brief caption: "aun
> aprendo." It means "I'm still learning." If ours were still the age

of heraldry, those words and the accompanying image would be my crest and motto: An old codger, rampant, but still learning.[47]

If this is Aldous Huxley's epitaph, it is also his legacy; it is a motto for every man: *aun aprendo.*

"The Perennial Philosophy"

The Minimum Working Hypothesis

Eyeless in Gaza assumes the same importance in Huxley's works as *Ash Wednesday* does in Eliot's—that is, it marks the culmination of Huxley's struggle with what Eliot called the "demon of doubt"—but it does not represent the final phase of Huxley's religious development. Indeed, it may be more accurate to say that *Eyeless in Gaza* represents a new, or second, beginning of Huxley's quest for timeless Reality. Aldous Huxley's conversion, like that of T. S. Eliot, failed to breed the self-righteous complacency of the true believer; it failed to stifle, or coagulate, his inventive metaphysical curiosity. And yet, conversion gave Huxley a direction, a path to follow. It accelerated his journey to the East, for it compelled him to explore the dimensions and ramifications of the Perennial Philosophy.

But what is the Perennial Philosophy? What are its presuppositions, its motive concepts, its claims to truth? The phrase *philosophia perennis* was

> coined by Leibniz; but the thing—the metaphysic that recognizes a divine Reality substantial to the world of things and lives and minds; the psychology that finds in the soul something similar to, or even identical with, divine Reality; the ethic that places man's final end in the knowledge of the immanent and transcendent Ground of all being—the thing is immemorial and universal.[48]

Ingredients of the Perennial Philosophy are found on every cultural level: in the myths of primitive societies, in the beliefs of classical civilizations, and in the theologies of all the higher religions. As such, the Perennial Philosophy represents a lingua franca of man's religious experience. It is a universal language of the spirit, based on traditional wisdom, but unfortunately unknown or forgotten by Western man. The Perennial Philosophy supports the notion of the unity of truth—a doctrine which is itself derived from the belief "that mystical aspiration is a genuine part of human nature" which "assumes the same general form wherever it is developed."[49]

This belief represents the raison d'être of Huxley's anthology *The*

Perennial Philosophy. He wished to present the (true) statements discovered in the works of Eastern and Western religious philosophers which
exhibited the tenets of the *philosophia perennis*. He intended to describe
and analyze the "Minimum Working Hypothesis" of a "scientific religion"
(i.e., the hypothesis that there is a timeless reality beyond the multiplicity
of the phenomenal world which can be known through nonpersonal mystical
experience).[50] Such a religion is founded on research: "Research by means
of pure intellectual intuition into non-sensuous, non-psychic, purely spiritual
reality," which eventually descends "to rational theories about its results and
to appropriate moral action in the light of such theories."[51] The course of
religious research, like that of scientific research, begins with, and derives
its validity from, experience.

The Perennial Philosophy is an "empirical theology" and as such is
analogous to "empirical astronomy"—that is, it is "based upon the experience of naked-eye observers." Of course, empirical astronomy establishes
its claims to validity on public experience, while the empirical theologian
justifies his beliefs on the pure, brute facts of private (mystical) experience.
But the subjectivity of mystical experience does not diminish its validity;
on the contrary, Huxley argues, there is nothing so overwhelmingly convincing as "the self-validating certainty of direct awareness" of Reality. In
Huxley's view, if the sceptic is not satisfied with this contention, he will
nevertheless find it extremely difficult to deny the ubiquitous and immemorial testimony of mystics, theologians, and philosophers whose writings contain the essential principles of the Perennial Philosophy, thus (in-
tentionally or unintentionally) lending support to the notion of the unity
of truth.

The Truth of the Perennial Philosophy, therefore, can be recognized
either by studying the works of those who have been "capable of a more
than merely human kind and amount of knowledge" and/or by mystical
experience.[52] When an individual achieves the vision of the mystic, he
experiences a direct awareness of timeless reality in which he not only
transcends the limitations of his own ego, but surmounts the destructive
power of time itself. Indeed, the transcendence of time is the basic theme
of the Perennial Philosophy. For, as Huxley insists, "True religion concerns itself with the givenness of the timeless. An idolatrous religion is
one in which time is substituted for eternity—either past time, in the form
of a rigid tradition, or future time, in the form of Progress towards Utopia."
Huxley stressed this point over and over again because he believed time-
philosophy, or religion, necessarily demands "human sacrifice on an enormous scale. Spanish Catholicism," for example, "was a typical idolatry of

past time." And "Nationalism, Communism, Fascism, all the social pseudo-religions of the twentieth century, are idolatries of future time."[53]

The only way to avoid the man-made horrors of history is for man himself to become a pacifist, which requires disavowing the cravings and revulsions of his own ego. But how can this be accomplished? Only, Huxley assures us, through the unitive knowledge of timeless Reality. Man is selfish because he hates, or desires, things in time. He becomes aggressive, or bellicose, because he allows his behavior to be shaped according to the dictates of a hedonistic calculus. Hobbes, Helvetius, and Bentham appear to have achieved a profound insight into the nature of man when they reduced his codes of behavior to the activities of pleasure and pain. But, Huxley argues, man acts like a Utilitarian or Pavlovian dog only insofar as he allows himself to be determined by time. Human beings respond positively to the promises of idolatrous religions because they wish to satisfy the unlimited desires of their narcissistic egos. Thus, if men could be shown—could be convinced—that their destinies lie outside of time, that there is another and all-important Reality beyond the multiplicity of the phenomenal world which should command their allegiance, they would no longer possess an avidity for temporal gratifications. They would become pacific, and there would be an end to war; for human beings would then realize that "their Final End" is found not in time, but "in a timeless moment of conscious experience." Hence, "The only hope for the world of time lies in being constantly drenched by that which lies beyond time."[54]

Huxley's detestation of the temporal process, in general, and the time-consciousness of Western man, in particular, is sharply delineated in his attack on Christian eschatology—especially as described by Reinhold Niebuhr in *Faith and History*. While Huxley agrees with the Union Seminary theologian "that, in itself, history is not, and cannot be, a redemptive process," he chides Niebuhr for dismissing "the age-old revelation that man's Final End is the unitive knowledge of God here and now, at any time and in any place." In place of this immemorial doctrine of the Perennial Philosophy, Niebuhr "proclaims" (and here Huxley believes the theologian contradicts himself) "that, though history is not redemptive in any ordinary sense of the word, it is yet supremely important for salvation in some Pickwickian sense—because of the General Resurrection and the Last Judgment." Thus, Huxley concludes, "So far as I am able to understand him, Dr. Niebuhr seems to imply that the meaning of life will be clarified only in the future, through a history culminating in 'the end of history, in which historical existence will be transfigured.'" Huxley condemns this eschatological interpretation of historical time with the same argument he used against reactionary traditionalism and the pseudo-religion of Progress. For what

Niebuhr and all teleological eschatologists—whether immanentists, non-immanentists, or apocalyptists—seem to imply is "that all persons living in the past, present and pre-millennial future are in some sort mere means and instruments, and that their redemption depends, not upon a personal relationship, here and now, with the divine Spirit, but upon future events in which it is impossible for them to participate."[55]

Ironically enough, this is also Berdyaev's argument. And this attitude also helps to explain the Russian's advocacy "of a universal mystical experience and a universal spirituality which cannot be described in terms of confessional differences."[56] Yet, however much Berdyaev stressed personal communion with eternity here and now, he remained committed to an apocalyptic interpretation of the historical process. And on this point he parts company with Huxley—and with Eliot, for Eliot also appears to have viewed the relationship between time and eternity as permanent, not subject to a redemptive resolution at some time in the future. Huxley and Eliot can be compared with the axiological eschatologists—theologians such as Dean Inge, the early Paul Althaus, or (prior to the First World War) Karl Barth—who emphasized an "upward-looking" eschatology and the realization of eternity here and now in a personal confrontation with God.

Yet, here again Huxley divorces himself from traditional Christianity. He is bitterly opposed to the Christian emphasis on "personality" as "the highest form of reality with which we are acquainted." He urges us to divest the term "personality" of its undeserved reverential connotations by replacing it with the unpretentious Saxon word "selfness"—much as we substitute "belch" for the euphemistic Latin "eructation." Casting aside the mask of *Jesting Pilate,* Huxley explains that he is opposed to Christian personalism because, as an exponent of the Perennial Philosophy, he has "constantly insisted" that "man's obsessive consciousness of, and insistence on being, a separate self is the final and most formidable obstacle to the unitive knowledge of God." Praising the self is as absurd as "worshipping 'the personality of Jesus.'" Both attitudes are "God-eclipsing" because they focus on finite entities: under the aspect of eternity, there is no such thing as an ego, a personality, or a self.[57] The individual self is not essentially "individual" or "particular." It is really an indissoluble part of the single Self and Absolute Reality of the universe—the divine Ground. Appearances to the contrary are created by man's illusion of separateness, of finite individuation, an illusion generated by the cravings and revulsions of the time-bound ego. Thus, "all personality is a prison" because it prevents man from transcending time.

When an individual claims to be serving an ideal—say, "the artist's ideal of beauty, or the scientists' ideal of truth, or the humanitarian's ideal of what currently passes for goodness," or "the Western theologian's ideal of personality"—"he's not serving God; he's serving a magnified aspect of himself." For an ideal—whatever it may be—"is merely the projection, on an enormously enlarged scale, of some aspect of personality."[58] And as such it is an obstacle in the way of Truth. The contemporary personalist's ideal—the ideal of such men (mentioned by Huxley) as Emmanuel Mounier, Nicolas Berdyaev, Martin Buber, Jacques Maritain, and Paul Tillich—however admirable it may appear, however highly motivated it may be, is nevertheless just as culpable of egotism as historical Christianity (how many people have been killed in the name of the personal Christian God?) or Soviet propaganda (with its perduring "cult of personality").[59]

Huxley's detestation of personality is also reflected in his distaste for systematic theology—especially of the Western variety. He regards the verbalizations of theologians or metaphysicians with the same contempt as he does their ideals. For, "The overvaluation of words and formulae may be regarded as a special case of" the "overvaluation of things in time"—a feature, by the by, "which is so fatally characteristic of historic Christianity." Discursive representations of Reality are necessarily distortions, Huxley argues, for words are divisive as well as temporal. But "God . . . is not a thing or event in time," and it should be obvious that "the time-bound words which cannot do justice even to temporal matters are even more inadequate to the intrinsic nature and our own unitive experience of that which belongs to an incommensurably different order."[60]

Scholastic formulae, like ideals, are nothing but reifications of the personality. And the anthropomorphic or personal deities described with painstaking meticulousness by theologians—whether they hail from East or West—are merely hypostatizations, reflections, or projections of the ego. Thus, to paraphrase Marx, a society's ideals (religious as well as secular) compose a superstructure which mirrors the egotistical desires and aversions of its members. In other words, the theologian's concept of God and the patriot's notion of country are nothing less than the frustrations of time-bound egos writ large.

In opposition to theologies which stress eschatology, personality, and discursive analysis, Huxley proposes a philosophy based, paradoxically, on the ideal of the "non-attached" man.

> Non-attached to his bodily sensations and lusts. Non-attached to his craving for power and possessions. Non-attached to the objects of these various desires. Non-attached to his anger and hatred; non-attached to his exclusive loves. Non-attached to wealth, fame, social position. Non-attached even to science, art, speculation, philan-

thropy. Yes, non-attached even to these. For, like patriotism, in Nurse Cavell's phrase, "they are not enough."[61]

It may be contradictory to advocate an "ideal" after having denounced all ideals as reifications of personal desires. But Huxley would no doubt respond by pointing out that his ideal involves a thorough repudiation of what people usually consider to be ideal. His defense of non-attachment represents a negation of the basic psychological and historical conditions of our lives:

> Non-attachment to self and to what are called "the things of this world" has always been associated in the teachings of the philosophers and the founders of religions with attachment to an ultimate reality greater and more significant than even the best things that this world has to offer. . . . The ethic of non-attachment has always been correlated with cosmologies that affirm the existence of a spiritual reality underlying the phenomenal world and imparting to it whatever value or significance it possesses.[62]

Huxley formulates his ideal of human conduct by looking at the world under the aspect of eternity, not, as is normally done, by looking at eternity under the aspect of time. He chooses to view life from the perspective of eternity because he believes that our diurnal psychology makes us myopic and prevents us from seeing and, consequently, participating in Reality. Reality is not divisive: it is a harmonious Whole—the totality of Being— which cannot be grasped by minds obsessed with petty, mundane affairs. Terrestrial desires and aversions confine us to a three-dimensional world, and the words we employ to formulate our experience distort our visions of reality. But Reality cannot be segmented; it cannot be analyzed into subjects and predicates. Nor can it be categorized in terms of temporal relations; there is no before or after, change or succession, in eternity. Reality is timeless and spaceless, an all-inclusive unity of spirit, something an individual can get to know only by pursuing the ideal of non-attachment. Only then will he realize, in "a non-personal experience of timeless peace,"[63] that his self is not really a separate entity but a part of the universal Self which is indistinguishable from the Absolute and divine Ground of all being.

Huxley derived his conception of Reality from Hindu and Buddhist sources.[64] Like Eliot, he was a monist, but in a far more rigid way than Eliot. Huxley does not shirk at following the reductionist logic of spiritual monism to its inevitable conclusion: Reality is Spirit, and Spirit "is identical with the Absolute."[65] Thus, to Huxley, the notion of an individual, or personal, soul is utterly untenable, for there can be no distinctions in

Reality. Every thing is really One and the same, absolutely identical and synonymous. Language and our own egos create the illusion of separateness—of time and space, causality and individuality. Few people, Huxley argued, ever realize that "analytical thought is fatal to the intuitions of integral thinking"; few people ever understand that "potential evil is *in* time" and that "actual good is outside time"; and fewer still ever perceive that their own egos, personalities, identities, are not real.[66] "Why should this be so? We do not know. It is just one of those facts which we have to accept, whether we like them or not and however implausible and unlikely they may seem."[67] But we do know—from the testimony of the saints and avatars, from the mystics of all ages—that our own personalities are illusions, that "we" are actually "one" with the divine and absolute Ground of all being.

Does this mean that there is no personal immortality? no personal communion with God? Yes, for the genuinely emancipated mystic, it does. To a Christian—to Eliot and Berdyaev, Charles Williams and W. H. Auden—this message is untenable. It represents a repudiation of one of the most cherished convictions of Christianity, the denial of a hope which, by the way, has always been present in the vast majority of Western religions. To a Freudian, the Perennial Philosopher's destruction of the ego probably represents a manifestation of *thanatos*—an example of a self-directed or suicidal death wish—while the ideal of non-attachment undoubtedly signifies a rationalization for the cultivation of psychosis. But to Huxley it represents a tough-minded acceptance of Reality, a belief born of "naked-eye" experience, a conviction founded on the perennial message, the true statements, of mystical philosophers from every age and clime. If accepted by the vast multitudes, this belief would endow mankind with an ethic founded on charity and the spontaneous compassion of love, with a faith that would lead every man out of the sorrow of time and into the peace of eternity. For

> Sorrow is the unregenerate individual's life in time, the life of craving and aversion, pleasure and pain, organic growth and decay. The ending of sorrow is the awareness of eternity—a knowledge that liberates the knower and transfigures the temporal world of his or her experience. Every individual exists within the fields of a particular history, culture and society. Sorrow exists within all fields and can be ended within all fields.[68]

It can be ended by an acceptance of the Perennial Philosophy.

While Huxley maintains, in Berdyaev's words, that the Perennial Philosophy is derived from "a universal mystical experience and a universal spirituality which cannot be described in terms of confessional differences,"[69] it is obvious that the Perennial Philosophy has been significantly shaped by the religious thought of the East. Huxley's conception of Reality, for example, is derived from the Hindu (nondualist Vedanta) equation of Atman and Brahman. Atman represents "the spiritual principle in us," the universal Spirit of the cosmos in which we participate (even though our illusion of separateness, which divorces us from Reality, gives us an individual consciousness), while Brahman designates the Absolute. Atman and Brahman are identical; together they form the One and all-encompassing Reality. In the more familiar terminology of Western philosophy, it may be said that Atman and Brahman are equivalent (or at least analogous) to Bradley's conception of Appearance and Reality, which, it will be recalled, are identified and united in the Absolute. Huxley recognized this formal similarity (as, no doubt, Eliot recognized the similarity between the monistic philosophies of Patanjali and Bradley) but was unwilling to attribute the same importance to Bradley's metaphysics as to, for example, Sankara's.[70]

This is quite typical of Huxley: whenever it comes to choosing between an Eastern or Western mystic or religious philosopher, Huxley invariably chooses the former. And it is here that R. C. Zaehner's hypothesis seems valid. Huxley's background and surely his grandfather's influence appear to have made him a congenital anti-Christian—or at least an early and tenacious opponent of "the aberrations of organized Christianity."[71] It was only natural, then, that after his conversion Huxley should prefer a non-Western or, at least, non-Christian religion. And yet Huxley's catholicity automatically counteracted any tendency toward parochialism. Indeed, the universalism of his outlook not only helps to explain why he was attracted to a "perennial" and purportedly cosmopolitan religion, but also why he published a compendium of Eastern and Western mystical literature. Yet, after making this qualification—after insisting upon Huxley's desire to see East and West meet in an affirmation of the perennial message of mystical philosophy—it is impossible to discount the predominantly Eastern features of his thought.

Huxley is one of many contemporary Western intellectuals who have found a panacea for the chaos of modern history in the wisdom of the Orient. Like René Guénon, Christopher Isherwood, and, more recently, Frithjof Schuon, Huxley has based his "discourse to the gentiles" and to every man on a common religious language which he finds most fully developed in the philosophies of India. If at times, as Professor Zaehner argues, Huxley distorts the individual differences among the varieties of mysticism, it is only because he believes that parochial differences (especially religious and ideological differences) have been a source of super-fluous acrimony and violence. Nevertheless, it would be misleading to say that Huxley's religious allegiance did not ultimately belong to the East. Like the renowned Indologian Heinrich Zimmer, Aldous Huxley joined "in the world-reverberating jungle roar of India's wisdom."[72]

Three Modes of Liberation

Huxley's preference for Indian thought is also reflected in his "psychology." But just as his presentation of the Perennial Philosophy draws (and in fact is established on) significant parallels between Eastern and Western religious thought, so his psychology relies upon a Western psychology—namely, the somatic theory of personality formation advanced by the American psychologist William Sheldon.

According to Sheldon, human temperament is relative to one's physical constitution. Thus, if an individual is fat (endomorphic), his temperament will be "viscerotonic"—that is, he will be extroverted and jovial, endowed like Pickwick with an appreciation of gastronomy. If, on the other hand, a human being is "middle sized" (mesomorphic), he will naturally be "somatotonic"—aggressive and energetic, a veritable Hotspur. If an individual has the lean and hungry look of Cassius or Hamlet, his character will be "cerebrotonic"—intellectual, introspective, and (in Huxley's opinion) "almost insanely sexual."[73] Now according to Huxley (and Hindu philosophy) there are three modes of "liberation from time," or union with the divine Ground: liberation through devotion, works, or knowledge.[74] And "these three ways of deliverance are" themselves "precisely correlated with the three categories, in terms of which Sheldon has worked out [his] classification of human differences." Hence, an endomorph will seek "liberation through action with attachment"; a mesomorph will strive for "liberation through action without attachment"; and an ectomorph will seek "liberation through knowledge of the Self and the Absolute Ground of all being with which it is identical." It is interesting to note that Huxley insists that "knowledge is a function of being" and that an individual "*is* an individual with one particular kind of constitution and temperament and therefore capable of knowing only according to the mode of his own being."[75] It is interesting because it gives the "insanely sexual" cerebrotonic ectomorphs of the world a virtual monopoly of genuine mystical experience.

Huxley dodges the issue of whether a fat person or a muscular mesomorph will be perpetually deprived of the Beatific Vision by stating that man is a mixture of Sheldon's three coordinates and that, "So far as the achievement of man's final end is concerned, it is as much of a handicap to be an extreme cerebrotonic or an extreme viscerotonic as it is to be an extreme somatotonic."[76] Nevertheless, he continues to draw metaphysical conclusions from Sheldon's "tri-polar system." Just as there are three personality types (based on three fundamental somatic structures), so there are three modes of grace (animal, human, and spiritual), three orders of being (Nature, Man, and Charity—shades of Pascal and Eliot), three aspects of human nature (body, mind or psyche, and spirit), and finally, three forms of consciousness (subconsciousness, consciousness, and superconsciousness). Like Berdyaev, Huxley maintains that temporal transcendence is achieved through the superconscious. But unlike Berdyaev, he not only believes that mystical contemplation is "imageless," but that "the way to superconsciousness is through the subconscious."[77]

It is amazing to see Huxley advocate a method of transcending time that he once ridiculed mercilessly. This view—that the unique consciousness of mystical experience is attained by plunging into the depths of the unconscious—is virtually identical with that held by Mr. Barbecue-Smith, a minor (and satirical) character in *Crome Yellow*. Mr. Barbecue-Smith maintains that it is possible to get in touch with eternity through the subconscious, an opinion based on personal experience and described in his "little book, *Pipe-Lines to the Infinite*."[78]

This conception of the role played by the subconscious in attaining timeless experience is quite similar to Jung's, and one which Huxley vigorously defends in *Heaven and Hell*. On the basis of his own experience, Huxley believed "that we live on the border-line between two worlds, the temporal and the eternal, the physical-vital human and the divine," and that it is possible to reach eternity through the psyche, or mind, which lies between the animal world and the divine. The psyche itself (and here Huxley follows Jung) is composed of a personal conscious, personal subconscious, and a collective unconscious. By activating, or getting into contact with, the unconscious layers of our minds, we gradually approach the threshold of eternity; we allow ourselves to cross the frontier of the collective unconscious and enter "the world of Visionary Experience." That is, we begin to escape the confines of our own personalities; we begin to impinge upon the world of our own spirits (i.e., the third facet in our tripartite natures), which may eventually lead us on to a full-fledged awareness, or Beatific Vision, of Spirit or Mind at Large (Atman, which is also Brahman).

The world of Visionary Experience momentarily permits us to transcend time, but it is not synonymous with the world of Beatific Experience. At "the limits of the visionary world, we are confronted by facts which . . . are independent of man," which "are manifestations of the essential givenness, the non-human otherness of the universe."[79] These "facts" are indeed nontemporal, but our awareness of them still occurs in the contingent world of opposites. Nevertheless, Huxley argues, visionary experience at the antipodes of the mind is equivalent to "what Catholic theologians call 'a gratuitous grace,' not necessary to salvation but potentially helpful and to be accepted thankfully, if made available." It allows us "to be shown for a few timeless hours the outer and the inner world, not as they appear to an animal obsessed with survival or to a human being obsessed with words and notions, but as they are apprehended, directly and unconditionally, by Mind at Large."[80] Visionary Experience represents perhaps the second most effective way of conquering time.

"Time Must Have a Stop"

Barring the Beatific Vision (which is the supreme mode of deliverance) and the gratuitous grace, the third most efficacious manner of transcending the temporal process is achieved by imposing a pattern, or symbolic order, upon contingent events that will transfigure the time-process (and here Eliot's terminology is appropriate) into "a pattern / Of timeless moments."

Time the Destroyer

Even before his conversion, Huxley had begun to explore the possibility of discovering a nontemporal pattern in the time-process. He was particularly interested in the success of this venture because he was hypersensitively aware of the annihilating power of time. During the Second World War, Huxley described "Time"—which is nothing else but the "personification of Nature"—as "the devourer of its own offspring," "the Destroyer" that imparts "enormous evils" to mankind.[81] Although he wrote this indictment after his conversion, it nevertheless reflects a perduring and antagonistic attitude toward time which can be traced in his earliest works. In his second novel, for example, Huxley described the ephemerality of life in terms of passing time:

> Grief doesn't kill, love doesn't kill; but time kills everything, kills desire, kills sorrow, kills in the end the mind that feels them; wrinkles and softens the body while it still lives, rots it like a medlar, kills it too at last.[82]

Time is man's most intractable enemy. Indeed, "The most intractable of our experiences is the experience of Time—the intuition of duration, combined with the thought of perpetual perishing." For "life is short, and time flows staunchlessly, like blood from a mortal wound."[83] Huxley often used the metaphor of a bleeding wound to express his revulsion at the notion of "perpetual perishing." He employed it first in *Antic Hay* as a counterpoint to the "endless present" of Gumbril's and Emily's moment of love: "Time passed, time passed flowing in a dark stream, staunchlessly, as though from some profound mysterious wound in the world's side, bleeding, bleeding for ever." And he used it in *Jesting Pilate,* in *Music at Night,* and in *The Genius and the Goddess:* "The clock had struck, time was bleeding away and even the living are utterly alone."[84]

Huxley's fear of ephemerality, his equation of time with death, and his subsequent protest against perpetual perishing is reminiscent of the poet's immemorial war against "Mutability." The tradition is a noble one: it extends into the remote past (perhaps even to the shamans of archaic societies) and includes the *carpe diem* tradition (exemplified, for example, by Mimnermus), the Elizabethan and metaphysical poets, and, more recently, the protests of Edwin Muir and Dylan Thomas. The sentiment is always the same: "By merely elapsing time makes nonsense of all life's conscious planning and scheming." The passage of time ensures that everything significant a man has done will "vanish the way everything [else] vanishes and changes." According to Huxley, the sorrow and suffering created by the temporal process makes time "nightmarish in itself—intrinsically nightmarish," and inimical. For "time is evil"; it is "the medium in which evil . . . lives and outside of which it dies." Time, symbolized by the clock—"Time for its own sake. Always imperiously time, categorically time," the time kept by "one's watch"—is itself categorically evil.[85]

Thus, after his conversion to the Perennial Philosophy, Huxley concluded that "a temporal act can never be more than potentially good, with a potentiality, what's more, that can't be actualized except out of time." In other words, present time is just as evil as past time and future time. History—that is, "past time"—"is only evil at a distance; and, of course, the study of past time is itself a process in time." It is a study of fossil time, a "cataloguing" process which records "bits of fossil evil [that] can never be more than an *ersatz* for the experience of eternity."[86] The historian can no more transcend the evil of time by studying the past than Bergson or Proust could ultimately surmount the temporal process through memory. "No, the life of the spirit is life out of time"; and if one wishes to participate in eternity, "memory must be lived down and finally died to." Thus *la recherche du temps perdu* is never successful in abolishing time. For in the last analysis, it is undeniable that "Time Regained is Paradise Lost, and Time Lost is Paradise Regained." ("God isn't the son of Memory; He's the son of Immediate Experience.")[87]

Future time, the time of "Industrial man"—that "sentient reciprocating engine having a fluctuating output, coupled to an iron wheel revolving with uniform velocity"—is equally as evil as past time, for it sacrifices "millions of lives to an opium smoker's dream of Utopia." And it precludes man's escape from the temporal process. But time—past or future, present, natural or historical—Time the Destroyer, must have a stop. For as the dying Hotspur says, as he "casually summarizes an epistemology, an ethic and a metaphysic,"

> But thought's the slave of life, and life's time's fool,
> And time, that takes survey of all the world,
> Must have a stop.[88]

Patterning Time and the Philosophy of History

Huxley assures us, of course, that time not only must but does have a stop in the unitive knowledge of the divine Ground. But there are other ways of stopping time, ways which, at the very least, permit a perception of eternity analogous to that of a gratuitous grace. There are ways, in other words, of imposing patterns upon time, patterns which transfigure duration "into something intrinsically significant," which transform "time into the symbol, *into the very fact,* of a more than human life!"[89]

What are these patterns? How are they perceived and created? They are the "insights and inspirations of genius"—insights which together form a supratemporal order, inspirations which are "perfectly independent of the kind of events . . . described in the works of philosophical or non-philosophical historians." "Talent" may exist "within a particular cultural and social framework, but" it nevertheless "belongs to realms outside the pales of culture and society." Every individual, it is true, "occupies a certain position in time," "lives surrounded by history," and participates in a certain culture, civilization, or society. Every individual (whether or not he realizes it) occupies a position in "Objective time" (although the *Zeitgeist* may not be the same for him as for someone else). But it is also true that an individual is never completely determined by historical time or totally conditioned by his "cultural curve."[90] When, for example, he is asleep or is sick or dies or has a mystical experience or creates art, he necessarily escapes the temporal process.

This view is quite similar to that of Berdyaev and Eliot—especially as it pertains to the notion of creativity. For like Eliot and Berdyaev (Croce and Collingwood), Huxley believes that the creative act transcends time, that artistic expression possesses an "internal logic" which is not affected by "merely historical events."[91] The creative act itself is unconditioned by the temporal process, whereas the work of art—the material embodiment of the artist's idea—is subject to (and exists in) time. Nevertheless, it is possible for the perceiver to recapture the artist's original expression (and to transcend time) by recreating the work of art in his own mind. When we listen to a piece of music, for example, we are capable of participating in the transfiguring pattern, or actual inspiration, of the artist—a pattern which permits us "to discover a coherence in the flux of events, to impose an order on the chaos of experience." As Huxley observes,

> Music is a device for working directly upon the experience of Time. The composer takes a piece of raw, undifferentiated duration and extracts from it, as the sculptor extracts the statue from his marble, a complex pattern of tones and silences, of harmonic sequences and contrapuntal interweavings. *For the number of minutes it takes to play or listen to his composition, duration is transformed into something intrinsically significant,* something held together by the internal logics of style and temperament, of personal feelings interacting with an artistic tradition, of creative insights expressing themselves within and beyond some given technical convention. This Fantasia [of Bach], for example—*with what a tireless persistence it drills its way through time! How effectively . . . it transfigures the mortal lapse through time into the symbol, into the very fact, of a more than human life!*[92]

T. S. Eliot expressed the same conviction in the first poem of his *Four Quartets,* "Burnt Norton":

> Words move, music moves
> Only in time; but that which is only living
> Can only die. Words, after speech, reach
> Into the silence. Only by the form, the pattern,
> Can words or music reach
> The stillness, as a Chinese jar still
> Moves perpetually in its stillness.[93]

Music and poetry impose a pattern on the raw material of our temporal experience, a pattern which transfigures that experience and allows us to reach the stillness of eternity. Imposing a significant pattern upon time transforms our experience of time into an experience of timelessness. Successful poetry or music is actually "transparent"; for after it imposes a significant form upon the flux of events, it seems to vanish, leaving us with an experience of eternal peace. Words and music move only in time, but they allow us to get beyond time. Eliot early set himself the task "To get *beyond poetry,* as Beethoven, in his later works, strove to get *beyond music.*" And

Huxley, perhaps even earlier than Eliot, began to experiment with the notion that music (for example, Beethoven's later quartets) proves the existence of God.[94] In an essay on "Water Music," for example, published in *On the Margin* (1923), he observed that

> If I could understand this wandering music [i.e., the sound of dripping water], if I could detect in it a sequence, if I could force it to some conclusion—the diapason closing full in God, in mind, I hardly care what, so long as it closes in something definite—then, I feel, I should understand the whole incomprehensible machine, from the gaps between the stars to the policy of the Allies.[95]

A year before he wrote *Brave New World*—that is, five years before his conversion—Huxley expressed his belief that a composition of music or a painting helps us perceive "for a few brief moments" that there is "a certain blessedness lying at the heart of things, a mysterious blessedness," "like some exquisite soft harmony apprehended by another sense."[96] He continued to augment and develop this idea for the rest of his life.

Thus, after his acceptance of the Perennial Philosophy, Huxley described the "insights and aspirations of genius" as "gratuitous graces";[97] and he located the source of these gratuitous graces at the crossroads between the psyche and the spirit, time and eternity, in the realm of nontemporal Visionary Experience. The inspiration for a work of art, therefore, lies outside of time, in what Berdyaev would call "existential time." Each artistic insight forms a transfiguring pattern by which time is transformed into eternity; each creative act participates in a nontemporal history—a history which transcends "objective time" (the *Zeitgeist*). The history of creativity is a history of gratuitous graces (of the "insideness" of events) and as such constitutes, in Eliot's phrase, "a pattern / Of timeless moments."

If, as Huxley insists, there is a timeless "history" of creative acts, is there not also a meaningful pattern to (temporal) history in general—a pattern which imparts a universal significance and order to the course of both material and spiritual events? It is extremely difficult to pin Huxley down on this question. He can be extremely evasive. In his essay "Maine de Biran: The Philosopher in History," he remarks that "History-as-something-experienced" is virtually "unwritable," for it can never be fully recorded. Thus, we

> must perforce be content with history-as-something-in-the-minds-of-historians. This last is of two kinds: the short-range history of tragedies and catastrophes, political ups and downs, social and

economic revolutions; and the long-range, philosophical history of those very long durations and very large numbers in which it is possible to observe meaningful regularities, recurrent and developing patterns.[98]

But unfortunately both short-range and long-range historians differ among themselves. They seem quite incapable of achieving unanimity on either micro- or macroscopic subjects: *Everyman His Own Historian,* as Carl Becker put it. History appears to be totally relative and subjective.

If this is the case, is it impossible to construct an objective metaphysics of history? Must we renounce the attempt to explain why the historical process has and is occurring? Huxley's answer seems to be cautiously, no; it is possible to discover a meaning for the historical process. Huxley draws his answer from Buddhist and Hindu sources (while frequently adding his own speculative footnotes or variations). He accepts the notion that time—i.e., human history as well as the events of the material universe—began with "the incomprehensible passage from the unmanifested One into the manifest multiplicity of nature." The creation of time, in other words, represents the Fall, the first Fall. For while "creation is the beginning of the Fall," "the consummation of the Fall takes place when creatures seek to intensify their separateness beyond the limits prescribed by the law of their being." This "urge-to-separateness," this "accentuation of division" which is equivalent to "evil," is consummated on the biological as well as the human level.[99] "Pain and evil are inseparable from individual existence in a world of time."[100]

Specialization represents the sin of nonhuman life, for all living matter, "Every species, except the human, chose immediate, short-range success by means of specialization" "at one time or another during its biological career." Huxley notes, however, that "specialization always leads into blind alleys" because it precludes the biological generalization necessary for the creation of intelligent life.[101] Thus, nonhuman forms of life are permanently debarred from achieving knowledge of the divine Ground. Human beings, on the other hand, who are unspecialized enough to gain unitive knowledge, rarely succeed in achieving it because of their arrogant predilection for self-assertion. We humans originally fell from God's grace because of our voluntary urge to be separate selves. And now, it is impossible for us to perceive eternity unless we modify the conditions of our consciousness, an extremely difficult task, and one which the majority of us will not strive to attain.

But will mankind ever return to eternity—ever be reunited, perhaps permanently, with the divine Ground? If this ever were to occur, history would come to an end, time would be abolished, and the illusion of the phenomenal world would vanish like dew before the dawn. But—and here is the rub—"the nature of humanity remains unaltered" throughout time. Thus, the conditions of human life—"the substance that underlies" the institutions and philosophies of mankind—remain "indestructible." Just as Thucydides derived his circular theory of history from his belief in an immutable and greedy human nature, so Huxley accounted for the "cyclic insanity" of history as the outcome of man's apparently unredeemable, egotistical nature.[102] Yet must this regrettable state of affairs always exist? Can it not be transcended? Is there not some way to end the nightmare of history once and for all? There is, but only when "every sentient being in all the worlds"—Huxley cites Weizsäcker to postulate the existence of a plurality of worlds—"shall have won to deliverance out of time into eternal Suchness or Buddhahood." And, of course, this final consummation of the temporal process is "inconceivably remote."[103] Yet, it represents a hope. For although the world has seen few saints, and while the same temporal cycle seems to repeat itself again and again, eventually it may be possible for all living matter, human and nonhuman, to be reintegrated and transfigured in a final consummation of history.

The Reconciliation of Time and Eternity: The Still Point, the Cone, and the Dance

In order to achieve this inconceivably remote consummation of history, it is necessary for human beings to become aware of the paradoxical truth that "Samsara and Nirvana, time and eternity, are one and the same." This momentous task can be achieved only if all men eventually gain Enlightenment, direct unitive experience of the divine Ground. And when and if this colossal spiritual transformation occurs, men will not only immediately realize that "time and eternity, the phenomenal and the Real, are essentially one,"[104] they will also formulate and describe their experience of transcendence in a basic vocabulary of nondiscursive symbols. This vocabulary is particularly important both because it serves as an objective correlative of mystical experience (which is itself ineffable) and because it permits the individual employing it to reconcile the outstanding contradictions of the phenomenal universe with the intrinsic unity of the noumenal world. Chief among these symbols are the still point, the cone, and the dance.

Huxley often used images of stillness and peace, of quiet and tranquility, even in such early works as *Antic Hay,* to objectify his experience of that mysterious "blessedness lying at the heart of things." Yet perhaps his most remarkable use of these metaphors comes in the concluding passages of

Eyeless in Gaza, in which Anthony Beavis (a cerebrotonic ectomorph who represents Huxley's *Doppelgänger*) recounts his first full-blown mystical experience. The language is already familiar. Beavis describes his descent into "a dark peace" (Saint John of the Cross's "Dark Night of the Soul"), his descent into "an absolute stillness" after his passage from "one argument to another, step by step, towards a consummation where there is no more discourse, only experience, only unmediated knowledge, as of a colour, a perfume, a musical sound." In the absolute stillness of the Dark Night, Beavis achieves liberation from "pride and hatred and anger, peace from cravings and aversions, peace from all the separating frenzies" of the ego. He gains "peace in this profound subaqueous night, peace in this silence, this still emptiness *where there is no more time,* where there are no more images, no more words." And yet, there are certain images—nondiscursive ones—which evidently are actually apprehended during mystical experience. Beavis gives the following description:

> Peace beyond peace. . . . Peace at the tip, as it were of a narrowing cone of concentration and elimination, a cone with its base in the distractions of the heaving surface of life and its point in the underlying darkness. And in the darkness the tip of one cone meets the tip of another; and from a single, focal point, peace expands and expands towards a base immeasurably distant and so wide that its circle is the ground and source of all life, all being.[105]

This description of mystical awareness provides us with a model of Reality, a description of the reconciliation of time and eternity, and indirectly with another example of how spatialization permits a time-symbol to be turned into an image of eternity. The temporal world, represented by the first cone ("with its base in the distraction of the heaving surface of life"), culminates in a point, an apex which marks the end of time and the beginning of eternal peace (symbolized by the tip of the opposite, or second, cone). Together, the points of both cones blend into a single point of stillness, into what Huxley elsewhere calls the "glassy centre" of "the sphere's surface," or cycle of time.[106] This point serves as the center of the timeless and limitless circle that represents the totality of being.

The intricate image corresponds to (although it is not exactly identical with) Yeats's famous description of time and eternity in *A Vision.* The Irish poet imagined time as a series of interrelated gyres, cycles, or cones. Each gyre is composed of two opposing cones ("the base of each cone has as its center the apex of the other cone"). And since gyres have varying magnitudes, "The *smaller* gyres or cycles are seen as phases of a *larger* gyre or wheel representing twenty-eight incarnations, the peak of which is a phase producing temporary 'Unity of Being'; and twelve such wheels form a single *great cone.*" Every gyre in the great cone revolves "toward a final 'Unity of Being,' which is achieved upon reaching a 'Thirteenth Cone' or 'phaseless sphere,' signifying one's complete delivery from 'the twelve cycles of time and space.' "[107] Thus, we again have the image of two opposing cones: on a microcosmic level, in the smaller gyres themselves; on a macrocosmic plane, in the opposing yet reconcilable symbols of the great cone, or gyre, and the thirteenth cone, or phaseless sphere. Aside from its complexity, this image and Huxley's are virtually the same. Time and eternity are reconciled at a point—the apex of opposing cones—and Reality is depicted as a sphere or circle.

Twenty years before Huxley used the image of the two cones in *Eyeless in Gaza,* he applied another (although similar) analogy to the time-eternity relationship. In his first book of poetry, *The Burning Wheel* (1916), Huxley contrasted the wheel of time or "speed" with "the motionless centre" of eternity:

Wearied of its own turning,
Distressed with its own busy restlessness,
Yearning to draw the circumferent pain—
The rim that is dizzy with speed—
To the motionless centre, there to rest,
The wheel must strain through agony
On agony contracting, returning
Into the core of steel. . . .
. . . the wheel that yearns—
Sick with its speed—for the terrible stillness
Of the adamant core. . . .[108]

The family resemblance between this metaphor and Eliot's description of the "still point" and "the turning world"; Auden's conception of "the centre / Time turns on when completely reconciled," "that holy centre where / All time's occasions are refreshed"; Hesse's "Magic Theater" or moment of intuition (in which the "cycle of change," "the dividing line that seems to lie between this world and eternity" is revealed as "an illusion"); Charles Williams's image of "the separate center of the created dance"; Yeats's (and Huxley's own) cones and gyres; and Berdyaev's "point" of existential time should be obvious.[109] Each of these men is using a similar image to express his conception and experience of timeless reality. Each is employing a spatialized conception of time (frequently, although not exclusively, symbolized by the circle). This conception can also be transformed, through mystical experience and, of course, through the intrinsic tendency of spatialized time-concepts to deprive the temporal process of its dynamic content, into images of eternity.

Yeats and Huxley, for example, use the cycle to portray the time-process, but they also use it to describe Reality. The cycle itself orders time and virtually freezes the temporal process—or at least slows it sufficiently for the circular flux of events to be transfigured into an image of timelessness (or in Eliot's case into a "pattern / Of timeless moments"). Huxley, Yeats, and Eliot refer to time as a circle, wheel, or cone and infer a timeless center, or still point, from its circumference—a point of eternal peace, which (in the case of Yeats and Huxley) is also conceived as the center of another circle, the timeless and spaceless circle of Reality. Even Berdyaev, the linear apocalyptist, conceives of Reality as a circle: "Eternity is not a cessation of movement and of creative life; it is creative life of a different order, it is movement which is not spatial and temporal but inward, symbolized not by a straight line but by a circle, i.e., it is an inner mystery play, a mystery play of the spirit which embraces the whole tragedy of cosmic life."[110] Temporal movement—the linear time of history as well as the cyclical time of the cosmos—is transfigured (to borrow Eliot's phrase) into the unmoving movement of the circle of eternity. And once more we see man adopting space as an ally in his perennial war against time.

Another image of transcendent Reality favored by Huxley and other contemporary writers is that of the dance. References to it can be found in Huxley's early works (for example, in *Eyeless in Gaza,* where Helen's "dancing" is described as "a timeless present of consummate happiness").[111] But the image receives its fullest expression in Huxley's last novel, *Island.* Perhaps Huxley discovered the iconographical and religious significance of the Indian diety Shiva-Nataraja from Ananda Coomaraswamy's notable essay on *The Dance of Shiva.*[112] In any event, he used the image of Shiva-Nataraja, the Lord of the Dance, to describe the reconciliation of time and eternity in *Island,* one of his most memorable novels. The full meaning of Shiva's Dance can be grasped only by an individual who has succeeded in modifying his consciousness. This, of course, can be accomplished by the gift of mystical experience; but it can also be achieved with the assistance of what Huxley refers to in *Island* as "*moksha*-medicine"—i.e., hallucinogenic drugs such as mescaline or lysergic acid diethylamide (LSD).

Under the influence of hallucinogens it is possible to see Shiva-Nataraja "dancing through time and out of time, dancing everlasting and in the eternal now. Dancing and dancing in all the worlds at once." Shiva dances in the material world of time and space; indeed his dance can be viewed as "the dance of endless becoming and passing away." And in this respect, Nataraja's dance is a form of "cosmic play. Playing for the sake of playing, like a child. But this child is the Order of Things. His toys are galaxies, his playground is infinite space and between finger and finger every interval is a thousand million light-years." As he is portrayed in art, Nataraja is a man-made image, "a little contraption of copper only four feet high. But Shiva-Nataraja fills the universe, *is* the universe." Yet he is more than the universe, more than the spinner of the cosmic illusion or maya: he is eternity itself. "Eternity in love with time. The One joined in marriage to the many"—a concept symbolized by Shiva's union with the Goddess— "the relative made absolute by its union with the One. Nirvana identified with samsara, the manifestation in time and flesh and feeling of the Buddha Nature." The union of Shiva and his Shakti symbolizes the reconciliation of opposites—the transformation of time into eternity, the metamorphosis of matter into spirit. Time is lost within Shiva's embrace—it is contained, assimilated, and transfigured: "the relative" is "made absolute by its union with the One." Shiva's dance is also a symbol of transformation—"the symbol of release, of *moksha,* of liberation." For, "Nataraja dances in all the worlds at once—in the world of physics and chemistry, in the world of ordinary, all-too-human experience, in the world finally of Suchness, of Mind, of the Clear Light."[113] The dance, then, is a symbol for the flux of events as well as for what Berdyaev calls the "inner mystery play" of eternity. The image reveals the great primordial fact that samsara and nirvana are one and the same—that Reality is an eternal dance, a process of timeless, unmoving movement.

Huxley's identification of samsara and nirvana reveals the thoroughgoing reductionist logic of his monism. If numerical distinctions are illusory, then everything is really one and the same. T. S. Eliot's radio commentary, broadcast on the B.B.C., on Charles Williams provides an apt description of Huxley's position: Williams was "a man who was always able to live in the material and the spiritual worlds at once, a man to whom the two worlds were equally real because they are one world."[114] And Huxley's monism was just as consistent as it was thoroughgoing: he remained a convinced advocate of what Professor Zaehner terms "monistic mysticism" from the publication of *Eyeless in Gaza* onward. Yet this point is often missed by Huxley's critics and by scholars. One of them, for example, asserts that Aldous Huxley has "reverted more obviously to the Platonic and mystical tradition which views the temporal world as but an imperfect copy of eternity beyond nature."[115]

That Huxley has reverted to the "mystical tradition" is beyond question, but that he is (by implication) a Platonist is thoroughly untenable. Plato was an ontological dualist who recognized a radical and unbridgeable gulf separating the world of becoming from the world of Forms. He did not, however, believe that the phenomenal world was an illusion or that time and eternity were actually the same.[116] If "Platonic and mystical tradition" is meant to designate the philosophy of Neo-Platonism—notably that of Ammonius Saccas, Plotinus, Proclus, and Porphyry—then, and only then, does the author have a case because, of course, Plotinus was a monist.

This point is important because it is impossible to understand Huxley's reconciliation of time and eternity without realizing that he is a monist. It is impossible, in other words, to understand his concept of the dance—and those of Eliot, Williams, Yeats, and Hesse as well. Eliot's concept of the dance, for example, is virtually identical with Huxley's. "Except for the point," he tells us in "Burnt Norton," "the still point, / There would be no dance, and *there is only the dance.*"[117]

Helen Gardner has suggested that the source for Eliot's image of the dance is to be found in *The Greater Trumps* of Charles Williams.[118] Her hypothesis appears to be correct. Indeed, Williams uses a phrase which is almost identical with Eliot's description of the dance in "Burnt Norton": "Imagine, then," Williams writes, "that everything which exists takes part in the movement of a great dance—everything, the electrons, all growing and decaying things, all that seems alive and all that doesn't seem alive," for, "*there is nothing at all anywhere but the dance.* Imagine it—imagine it, see it all at once and in one!" The phrasing is quite close to Eliot's; the idea is identical with that expressed in "Burnt Norton." For like Eliot's dance, Williams's is not only synonymous with the measure and "meaning of all process," it is not simply "The Dance in the World," but the dance out of the world, the dance of timeless Reality.[119]

These opposites, however, are not ontological antinomies. There is no unbridgeable dualism separating phenomena and noumena, for the two worlds are really One. In fact (to paraphrase W. H. Auden), we actually live in eternity[120]—we already participate in the timeless and eternal dance—but we fail to realize that we do because our perceptual capacities have been distorted by Original Sin. Yet if we modify the conditions of our consciousness (by following either the way of affirmations or the way of refusals), we will see that time and eternity are One, that Reality is indivisible. This is a notion that Williams suggests with his image of the Fool of the Tarot pack in *The Greater Trumps:* The Fool (who is equivalent to the still point in "Burnt Norton") is "all-reconciling and perfect."[121] His dance (which, like Shiva's, can be seen only by the initiated) reconciles time and eternity.

In philosophical terms, the dance is comparable to Bradley's Absolute, for it assimilates Appearance and Reality; in poetic terms, it is synonymous with Eliot's notion of the dance (which also reconciles the still point and the turning world and transmutes time into a "pattern / Of timeless moments"). It is also analogous to Yeats's "magical dance" (which stimulates the Great Memory and allows the individual to participate in the rhythm of the "wheel of Eternity"); to Hermann Hesse's description of Steppenwolf's time-transcending dance (in which Steppenwolf not only "lost the sense of time" but achieved an awareness of the oneness of Reality); and to Carl Jung's description of the parallel between the mandala dance of India and the dances performed by various mental patients.[122]

The diffusion of dance imagery (as well as the broadcast use of the images of the point, cone, cycle, temenos, or rose garden) in the works of contemporary European intellectuals attests to the universality, the international scope, of Western man's attempt to "re-create" eternity in the twentieth century. This is not an isolated phenomenon. Indeed, it is part of a larger effort of Western man to discover, or return to, faith—whether it be the faith of one of the organized churches or what Franklin Baumer has called "layman's religion"—an effort aptly described by the title of one of Carl Jung's most popular essays, *Modern Man in Search of a Soul*.[123]

Huxley hoped that the Perennial Philosophy would serve as a universal religion for mankind. Whether or not his hope was in vain, it can be said that East and West have met in the effort to re-create eternity for modern man. All of the intellectuals mentioned above seem to be speaking the same language—the forgotten language of religious symbolism. As Erich Fromm has pointed out,

> Symbolic language . . . is the one universal language the human race has ever developed, the same for all cultures and throughout history. It is a language with its own grammar and syntax, as it were, a language one must understand if one is to understand the meaning of myths, fairy tales and dreams.

It is "the one foreign language each of us must learn." For,

> Its understanding brings us in touch with one of the most significant sources of wisdom, that of myth, and brings us in touch with the deeper layers of our own personalities. In fact, it helps us to understand a level of experience that is specifically human because it is common to all humanity, in content as well as in style.[124]

Huxley would modify Fromm's statement only by insisting that mysticism transcends myth.[125] But like other exponents of the Perennial Philosophy, as well as contemporary Christians, Huxley's message was based on a level of experience that "is common to all humanity." And undoubtedly he would have agreed that the current effort of intellectuals to re-create eternity represents an attempt to relearn the forgotten language of religious experience—an attempt which is not confined to national boundaries or to specific cultural traditions. Still, he would have insisted that although both Christian and Eastern writers were striving toward the same revelation, the only genuinely emancipated religion remained the Perennial Philosophy. And, he would have concluded, when Christian writers use the symbolic language of the authentic mystic, they are actually using the metaphors and images of the *philosophia perennis,* not of Christianity. For Huxley, a successful re-creation of eternity begins and ends in the journey to the East.

Drugs and the Mind: Mescaline

Until the spring of 1953 Huxley evidently felt that he had not realized the full meaning of the Perennial Philosophy in his own life. For although he had accepted the tenets of the *philosophia perennis* on an intellectual level—even though he had attempted to re-create eternity for himself and others—he had apparently not had what he considered a genuine mystical experience. However rewarding his Pythagorean experiments with music had been, they remained ersatz intimations of Reality, not full-blown mystical experiences of the divine Ground. Huxley had accepted the verbal message of the Perennial Philosophy, but (even though the experience of timelessness described in *Eyeless in Gaza* seems to be an exception) he apparently had not been able to reach the ineffable experience concealed behind the words of the Perennial Philosophers—that is, until the spring of 1953.

It was on "one bright May morning" in that year that Aldous Huxley "swallowed four-tenths of a gramme of mescalin dissolved in half a glass of water and sat down to wait for the results." What were they? The first was an extraordinary heightening of visual experience. Huxley seems to have been overwhelmed with this aspect of his mescaline experiment. For as long as he could remember, he had "always been a poor visualizer." Mescaline, however, allowed him to escape the linguistic strait jacket of his cerebrotonic intellect. Yet, what meaning did Huxley attribute to this enormous enhancement of his visionary powers? "Words like 'Grace' and 'Transfiguration'" immediately came to his mind. "The Beatific Vision, *Sat Chit Ananda,* Being-Awareness-Bliss—for the first time I understood, not on the verbal level, not by inchoate hints or at a distance, but precisely and completely what those prodigious syllables referred to." He was aware of "a transience that was yet eternal life, a perpetual perishing that was at the same time pure Being"—something he could only explain as the "divine source of all existence."[126] In other words, for the first time, Huxley was directly aware of what he later referred to as the Dance of Shiva-Nataraja.

He also felt, moreover, that he had at last experienced the Beatific Vision, that he had transcended the category of time in an eternal now—in a direct apprehension of Reality. The investigator assisting at the experiment asked Huxley if his perception of time had been modified by the drug. He replied that he was indifferent to time (and space). "I could, of course, have looked at my watch; but my watch, I knew, was in another universe. My actual experience had been, was still, of an indefinite duration or alternatively of a perpetual present made up of one continually changing apocalypse." This language appears very close to Bergson's; and in fact, Huxley cites with approval a statement of C. D. Broad's which suggests that "we should do well to consider much more seriously than we have hitherto been inclined to do the type of theory which Bergson put forward in connection with memory and sense perception." Huxley agrees with Bergson (and Professor Broad) that "the function of the brain and nervous system is to protect us from being overwhelmed and confused by . . . useless and irrelevant knowledge," so that we may perform the practical necessities of everyday life. According to this theory, the eliminative function of the brain not only prevents us from remembering everything that has happened to us; it also bars us from "perceiving everything that is happening everywhere in the universe." "To make biological survival possible, Mind at Large has to be funnelled through the reducing valve of the brain and nervous system." Thus, "Every individual is at once the beneficiary and the victim of the linguistic tradition into which he or she has been born."[127] Language allows man to create culture and survive, but it excludes—or at least reduces—his awareness of reality. Time itself seems to be nothing more than a product of symbol-formation, and as such, it reduces or irrevocably precludes one's ability to perceive eternity.

Bergson's conception of reality as a perpetually developing present, containing its own past, is not synonymous with the absolutely timeless Reality of the Perennial Philosophy. And yet, it is obvious from even a cursory reading of *The Doors of Perception* that Huxley definitely believed that mescaline had momentarily delivered him from "the world of selves, of time, of moral judgments and utilitarian considerations."[128] How can this apparent contradiction be reconciled? On the one hand, Huxley seems to accept Bergson's *durée réelle* as being final (i.e., equivalent to Reality). On the other hand, he insists that mescaline enabled him to escape time. Or perhaps there is no contradiction: perhaps Huxley believes that real duration is actually synonymous with eternity.

Huxley began to solve this problem in the later passages of *The Doors of Perception*. Initially, it should be remembered, Huxley had equated his mescaline experience with the Beatific Vision. Somewhat later in the same

essay, however, he modified this position. "I am not so foolish," he confesses, "as to equate what happens under the influence of mescalin or of any
other drug . . . with the realization of the end and ultimate purpose of
human life: Enlightenment, the Beatific Vision. All I am suggesting is
that the mescalin experience is what Catholic theologians call 'a gratuitous
grace.' "[129] Thus Huxley's mescaline experience belongs to the realm of
"visionary experience" (which "is not the same as mystical experience")
that is discoverable at the antipodes of the mind, beyond the collective subconscious and on the threshold of eternity. Unlike mystical experience,
"visionary experience is still within . . . the realm of opposites."[130] And yet the
gratuitous grace induced by mescaline undoubtedly results in a momentary
transcendence of time. But what kind of time? Huxley seems to say
chronological time. Does this imply that an experience of real duration is
equivalent to a gratuitous grace—a form of grace that can only be achieved
by gaining access to the world of Visionary Experience at the antipodes of
the mind? It does, but Huxley is not specific.

Indeed, on this point he evidently remained quite confused—confused,
that is to say, until he wrote *Island*. For in his last novel Huxley seems to
have returned to his earlier assumption that mescaline does (or at least can)
create the Beatific Vision. "In theological terms," we are told, "the *moksha*-
medicine" (mescaline or LSD) "prepares one for the reception of gratuitous
graces—premystical visions or the full-blown mystical experiences." The
conjunction "or" implies a reversal of Huxley's note of caution toward the
end of *The Doors of Perception*. This hypothesis is borne out in other
passages of *Island:* According to Dr. Robert (Huxley's principal mouthpiece), "Thanks to the *moksha*-medicine" individuals can have "an experience of the real thing." "*I* say that the *moksha*-medicine does something
to the silent areas of the brain which opens some kind of neurological sluice
and so allows a larger volume of Mind with a large 'M' to flow into your
mind with a small 'm'."[131] *Moksha*-medicine can create premystical visions,
but when it affects the silent areas of the mind, Dr. Robert says, they "don't
respond with visions or auditions, they don't respond with telepathy or
clairvoyance or any other kind of parapsychological performance. None
of that amusing premystical stuff. Their response is the full-blown mystical
experience. You know—One in all and All in one."[132]

Huxley's position now seems to have come full circle. From having
accepted the belief that mescaline produces the Beatific Vision and then
equated mescaline experience with gratuitous graces (as opposed to Enlightenment), he returned to the view "that the *moksha*-medicine can . . .
give you a succession of beatific glimpses, an hour or two, every now and
then, of enlightening and liberating grace."[133] Hence, Huxley believed that

he had, in fact, achieved mystical experience when he took mescaline on that fine May morning in 1953. And he corroborates this assumption himself in the conclusion to *Island* by reproducing (occasionally almost verbatim) his record of his first mescaline experience.

In the novel's last chapter, Will Farnaby, journalist, hired agent, cynic, and sceptic, has finally agreed to take the *moksha*-medicine. His experience is metamorphic. The first effect produced by the drug is the destruction of time; the second, the reconciliation of opposites:

> ONE, TWO, THREE, FOUR . . . THE CLOCK IN THE KITCHEN struck twelve. How irrelevantly, seeing that time had ceased to exist! The absurd, importunate bell had sounded at the heart of a timelessly present Event, of a Now that changed incessantly in a dimension, not of seconds and minutes, but of beauty, of significance, of intensity, of deepening mystery. . . . What he was seeing now was the paradox of opposites indissolubly wedded, of light shining out of darkness, of darkness at the very heart of light.[134]

This second result is extremely important, for it demonstrates that Huxley believed that he had not only transcended time, but that he had surmounted the opposites of the phenomenal world as well. In other words, he felt that he had transcended Visionary Experience (which is still within the realm of opposites)[135] and had actually experienced eternity directly. "There was a *tempo*" during his experience, "but no time. So what was there? Eternity."[136] Eternity and not real duration. Perhaps *durée réelle* can be experienced in the realm of Visionary Experience; perhaps a nonchronological experience of time is part of the premystical vision; but for the genuine mystic, *durée réelle* is, in Eliot's words, "simply not final." It is still part of the world of opposites; it may mark a step toward eternity, but it does not constitute the unmoving movement, the timeless tempo of eternity. Thus, in his last novel—in his summing up—Aldous Huxley believed that he had finally crossed the threshold of time and eternity, of Visionary Experience and Mystical Experience, of subconsciousness and superconsciousness. He had finally convinced himself that he had achieved the Beatific Vision.[137]

"Brave New World" or the "Island"?

Huxley's experiment with mescaline made him hopeful that more people could attain liberation, but he nevertheless feared that the political realities of the twentieth century would probably neutralize the potentially positive results of hallucinogenic or psychedelic drugs. In Huxley's opinion, the purpose of society is to produce saints—not directly, for environment cannot be an efficient cause of sainthood, but indirectly, by providing the greatest opportunity for individuals to seek their own salvation. He believed that the only social and political structure that permits the optimum conditions for potential liberation is a decentralized and self-sufficient community.

This community would be anarchic, not communal either in the sense of pure communism or in the manner of Eliot's *Idea of a Christian Society*. Rather, it would resemble the decentralized conception of society and government described by Paul Goodman in *People or Personnel* and by Henry Miller in *The Air-Conditioned Nightmare* and *Big Sur and the Oranges of Hieronymus Bosch*. Instead of concentrating power in the hands of a few rich industrialists and politicians, Huxley envisioned a society composed of self-regulated and autonomous units—small units, like Mr. Propter's "little farms" in *After Many a Summer Dies the Swan*. He felt that the decentralization of power could only be accomplished by compelling "a rational and planned decentralization of industry" and by restoring "the community sense in individuals." Like Miller and Goodman, Huxley admired the experiment being conducted at Black Mountain College in North Carolina and believed that "schools and colleges can be transformed into organic communities and used to offset, during a short period of the individual's career, the decay in family and village life." He thought country living was preferable: "life in the great city is atomistic."[138] But Huxley realized that it is unrealistic to think that "people will want to leave the cities and live . . . on little farms."[139]

Nevertheless, a community or neighborhood spirit must be generated in the city if the anomie of modern life is ever to be transcended. Huxley believed that the recent tendency of politicians to solve the two basic problems of power and force through massive centralization can only increase the alienation of modern man, for it destroys his identity and dignity by abolishing his self-reliance and assimilating him into a mechanistic and impersonal order. The specter of Ortega y Gasset's mass man—as well as White's *Organization Man* or Riesman's man of *The Lonely Crowd*—can only be haunted out of twentieth-century history if statesmen renounce their obsession with centralized authority.

Huxley would have us continue in the back-swamp Yankee tradition of New England—the tradition characterized by Emerson's "self-reliance" and Thoreau's *Walden*—for he believed that human liberty would be lost in a one-dimensional society. "Goodness politics"—i.e., "the art of organizing on a large scale without sacrificing the ethical values which emerge only among individuals and small groups"—cannot be practiced by monolithic states. It appears to be a fact of history, moreover, that "large-scale organizations are capable . . . of going down," or declining, with far more celerity than small-scale organizations. "The history of any nation follows an undulatory course," and it "invariably carries within itself the seeds of its own decadence." But small units, states in which power is allocated to small self-reliant communities, have a greater chance of enduring the oscillating pattern of history.[140]

Even decentralization, however, will not succeed in creating a peaceful and productive nation if it is not accompanied by an adoption of the method of the mystics. We must not delude ourselves like "Poor Bentham . . . with the notion that the greatest happiness of the greatest number could be achieved on the strictly human level—the level of time and evil, the level of the absence of God."[141] No, in order to create a viable community, Huxley argued, its members must adopt a theocentric religion, namely, the Perennial Philosophy.

But will there ever be such a community? What hope can we hold for such a project? Huxley tackled this problem for the last time in what is probably his final essay in Utopia-building, *Island*. In its early chapters, he describes an ideal community established on a commonly held faith in the *philosophia perennis,* a faith encouraged (with the assistance of the *moksha*-medicine) by direct mystical experience of the divine Ground. Yet the whole experiment—"the work of a hundred years"—was "destroyed in a single night" by political ambition and outside economic interests.[142] The message is inescapable: even if we were able to create an island of paradise in the wasteland of the twentieth century, it would be devoured by the unregenerate. When Huxley wrote *Brave New World,* he "was convinced that there was still plenty of time" before the "nightmare of total organization" actualized itself. "Twenty-seven years later," however, he felt "a good deal less optimistic." For, in fact, it appears that the brave new world "is now awaiting us, just around the next corner."[143] Thus, there is very little chance of our cultivating an island Utopia. Indeed, "if history is an expression of the divine will, it is so mainly in a negative sense. The crimes and insanities of large-scale human societies are related to God's will only insofar as they are acts of disobedience to that will."[144]

The disobedient and unregenerate nature of modern man probably ensures the failure of the island and the triumph of ape over essence, of the brave new world of Total Organization. Yet we must not give up the struggle; we must not give up the fight against our own selfishness, our own egotistical ambition and desires. We must continue to strive for redemption, for the timeless vision of the saints. We must continue to learn: *aun aprendo.*

CHAPTER 5

C. G. Jung and the Masks of God

> I am mortal for everyone, yet I am not touched
> by the cycle of aeons.
> —*Memories, Dreams, Reflections*

The House at Bollingen

In 1922, the year Aldous Huxley was composing *Antic Hay*—the same year in which T. S. Eliot published *The Waste Land* and Nicolas Berdyaev neared completion of *The Meaning of History*—Carl Gustav Jung purchased some property in Bollingen on the upper lake of Zurich. The purchase was to become significant, for in three intervals during the next twelve years Jung designed and had built there a house that represents one of his most remarkable protests against time. Casting its reflection onto the blue green waters of the lake, etched by sunlight and the shadow of the surrounding trees, Jung's stone house at Bollingen expresses the innermost convictions of a man who spent his life exploring the timeless dimensions of the psyche.

When he first planned the house at Bollingen, Jung envisaged a single tower that would serve as a retreat from the responsibilities of his analytical practice in Zurich. But as the years passed, he felt the urge to add a second tower, a courtyard, and a loggia. Jung's periodic desire to build was always impulsive: work on the "Tower" (Jung's name for the Bollingen residence in its entirety) proceeded spontaneously. Thus, the architectural pattern which eventually emerged (a building with four different parts designed in a style reminiscent of the sixteenth century) developed without conscious premeditation. Indeed, it was only after the house had been completed that Jung realized what he had been doing: unconsciously creating a concrete symbol of psychic wholeness—a testament of the imperishable and transcendental elements in human nature.

To Jung, the four sections of the Tower represented a quarternity, a mandala, an image of the individuated personality. Quarternity—whether depicted by the number 4, the square, or the cross (often in combination with a circle)—expresses completeness, integration, the reconciliation of psychic opposites. This condition of being is symbolized by the archetype of the Self, the God-image in man, which is "eternally present"[1] in the collective unconscious. The Self is at once the center and circumference of the psyche.[2] It participates in time insofar as it serves as a focus or point of reference by which an individual organizes the totality of his personal and nonpersonal psychological experience. In itself, however, the God-image is beyond time; it participates in the objective nontemporal and nonspatial depths of the collective unconscious. It cannot be known directly by the intellect; it can only be experienced, for it is a transcendental, as opposed to a rational, concept. Thus, when an individual achieves selfhood, he participates paradoxically in two worlds at once, one in time and one out of time. His experience in producing symbols of the Self (in dreams, visions, fantasies, or active imagination) is analogous to mystical experience. It is virtually ineffable and can only be expressed in "non-directed"[3] symbols such as mandala drawings or—as in the case of Jung's house at Bollingen—in an architectural "confession of faith in stone."[4]

Jung bought the site of his future retreat a decade after his 1912 break with Freud. For several years before he first met the Viennese psychoanalyst in 1907, Jung had publicly defended Freud's theories. The two men had already corresponded with each other (Jung sent Freud his *Studies in Word Association* in 1906) and had rapidly formed a close friendship. Jung came to view Freud as a wiser man—indeed, as a father figure—and Freud soon regarded Jung as his successor in the psychoanalytic movement: "If I am Moses, then you are Joshua and will take possession of the promised land of psychiatry, which I shall only be able to glimpse from afar."[5] This sympathetic relationship, however, did not last, and in 1909, during a seven-week trip to the United States, Jung's respect for Freud's authority was severely, if not irreparably, damaged. Both men had agreed at the outset of the voyage to analyze each other's dreams. On one occasion, however, Freud refused to supply Jung with all of the information about a particular dream. In astonishment, Jung asked for an explanation, to which Freud replied that he could not fill out the context of the dream because it would endanger his authority. "At that moment," Jung later confided, "he lost it altogether."[6]

Eventually Jung brought this betrayal of trust to Freud's attention during the climax of a stormy sixteen-month period from 1911 to early 1913, a period which marked the decline and ultimate collapse of their personal relationship. In an extraordinary exchange in which both men accused each other of behaving neurotically, Jung (whom Freud had reproached for acting "abnormally" while "shouting that he is normal")[7]

C. G. Jung

attacked his former mentor and collaborator in an outburst that is almost a parody of classical oedipal hostility:

Dear Professor Freud,

May I say a few words to you in earnest? I admit the ambivalence of my feelings towards you, but am inclined to take an honest and absolutely straightforward view of the situation. If you doubt my word, so much the worse for you. I would, however, point out that your technique of treating your pupils like patients is a *blunder*. In that way you produce either slavish sons or impudent puppies (Adler-Stekel and the whole insolent gang now throwing their weight about in Vienna). I am objective enough to see through your little trick. You go around sniffing out all the symptomatic actions in your vicinity, thus reducing everyone to the level of sons and daughters who blushingly admit the existence of their faults. Meanwhile you remain on top as the father, sitting pretty. For sheer obsequiousness nobody dares to pluck the prophet by the beard and inquire for once what you would say to a patient with a tendency to analyse the analyst instead of himself. . . . You see, my dear Professor, so long as you hand out this stuff I don't give a damn for my symptomatic actions; they shrink to nothing in comparison with the formidable beam in my brother Freud's eye. . . . If ever you should rid yourself entirely of your complexes and stop playing the father to your sons, . . . I will mend my ways and . . . uproot the vice of being in two minds about you. Do you *love neurotics* enough to be always at one with yourself?[8]

During their sojourn to the United States, however, this dramatic finale still lay three years away, and although at the time Jung did not forgive Freud's refusal of confidence (and his insistence on "placing personal authority above truth"),[9] the two men continued their mutual dream analyses.

Throughout this period Jung, who was thirty-four, was experiencing a series of extremely unusual dreams, so unusual, in fact, that Freud found them virtually impossible to interpret. One dream in particular was decisive, for it not only affected the relationship of the two men, but played a crucial role in the formation of Jung's own psychology and, ultimately, of his attitude toward time. Jung dreamed that he was in a two-story house. He found himself in the upper story, which was decorated in rococo style. He descended subsequently to the ground floor, which seemed to have been built during the fifteenth or sixteenth century and was outfitted with medieval furnishings. Following an urge to explore the entire house, Jung discovered

[163]

a door that led to a stone stairway which ended in a cellar. Examining the walls of the cellar, he determined that they dated from the Roman period. While he was searching about the room he noticed a ring connected to one of the stone slabs of the floor. He lifted it and descended the narrow steps it revealed, until he entered a cave covered with the debris of a primitive culture (bones, potsherds, dust). Then he noticed two human skulls that were partially disintegrated, and awoke. Freud interpreted the appearance of the two skulls as a death-wish, but Jung refused to accept this conclusion. He felt that the dream clearly contained impersonal contents, symbolical material of a collective nature. It was, in fact, this dream that led him "for the first time to the concept of the 'collective unconscious' and thus formed a kind of prelude to my book, [*The Psychology of the Unconscious*] *Wandlungen und Symbole der Libido*" (1916).[10]

In contrast to Freud, Jung interpreted the dream as a model of the psyche. In terminology he subsequently developed, he equated the second floor of the house with consciousness; the first floor, with the personal unconscious; the cellar, with the first levels of the collective unconscious; and the cave, with the most primitive antipodes of the collective unconscious—regions of the human psyche which border on "the life of the animal soul."[11]

Jung studied the implications of this dream for nearly three years before unveiling his reappraisal of Freud's theory of mind. Despite Freud's hope that Jung would eventually return to the fold, publication of *The Psychology of the Unconscious* (1916) actually marked Jung's formal departure from the psychoanalytic movement. At issue were three interrelated ideas: the concept of libido; the function of dreams; and the nature of the unconscious.

Jung repudiated Freud's theory of sexuality because he believed it was too restrictive. He regarded libido as a potentially liberating energy, as a process capable of transforming a person into a whole man, as a force, or tendency, with the inherent ability to attain nonsexual or spiritual goals. Similarly, Jung viewed dreams (whose symbols manipulate and transform psychic energy) as spontaneous and teleological products of the unconscious. In contrast to Freud, the Swiss psychologist believed that dreams must be taken for themselves, as they are, and not as masks, or disguises, for latent antisocial desires. A dream is a confession, or disclosure, of an individual's psychic state, but it is not always a product of dream-work or repression. Surely, there are many dreams which seem to exemplify repressive contents; and, as Jung would readily admit, repression exercises a limited influence on the psyche. But its function only applies to the personal sphere of the unconscious; it has absolutely no effect upon the collective or impersonal levels of the psyche. Thus, there are "small" as well as "big" dreams—

dreams that reflect the personal biography of the dreamer, and dreams that manifest the autonomous factors of the unconscious. It is on this point that the differences between the two psychologists become dramatic. For while Freud recognized the existence of archaic vestiges, memory traces, from previous generations in the psyches of his patients, he did not accept the theory of archetypes advocated by Jung.

In fact, the notion of an objective mind, or psyche, of the species, whose contents (i.e., the archetypes) live an autonomous and dynamic existence in the spaceless and timeless depths of the collective unconscious, is thoroughly foreign to Freud's thought. It is true, of course, that he believed that time and space are virtually destroyed in the unconscious, but he did not think that the structure of the human psyche contained an objective and entirely independent dimension of activity—an autonomous and impersonal sphere of process underlying the temporal and spatial boundaries of the personal psyche. Yet Freud's and Jung's divergence in viewpoint does not end here. Indeed, their differences are enlarged enormously if the implications that Jung gradually drew from his understanding of the unconscious are taken into account.

In 1909, two years after their first meeting, Freud became aware of Jung's keen interest in telepathic phenomena. Freud was extremely distressed by his heir-apparent's curiosity and did his best to discourage Jung's serious examination of the occult—but without success. After Jung's initial formulation of the theory of archetypes, he increasingly came to believe that the collective unconscious is intrinsically capable of perceiving telepathic events. The implications of this hypothesis, of course, are enormous. It suggests not only that the objective psyche is spaceless and timeless, but that it is capable of perceiving causeless and, hence, nontemporal and nonspatial events. The hypothesis also indicates the existence of a "wholly other" order of being. Jung continued studying (and experiencing) telepathic phenomena long after his break with Freud and in later years formulated the concept of "synchronicity" to explain the occurrence of telepathic, or acausal, yet meaningful, events. Along with his interpretations of myth and of the individuation process, synchronicity provided him with one of his three principal ways of overcoming time.

Jung believed that myths, like synchronistic coincidences, represent manifestations of timelessness in time. A myth is an embodiment, a concrete manifestation, of a timeless and constantly repeated motif of human experience. It is the symbolic product of an unconscious archetype, which, insofar as it is reexperienced, allows the perceiver to participate in a mode of experience that subsists beyond time. It is a nonrational and numinous universal which, when experienced as a meaningful and living reality, unites the individual with the timeless wisdom of the human species. Thus, "The religious myth is one of man's greatest and most significant achievements, giving him the security and inner strength not to be crushed by the monstrousness of the universe."[12] Yet, although a person may find an ancient myth meaningful, he must incorporate it within his own field of consciousness; he must, in other words, stamp the timeless themes of mythology with his own identity, create his own myth from the archetypal motifs common to all humanity.

When an individual succeeds in creating what Jung's collaborator, Karl Kerényi, called an "individual mythology," he is said to be individuated, or psychically whole. Individuation is virtually synonymous with that form of religious phenomenology known as mysticism, for it entails the notion of transferring the center of one's personality from the time-bound ego to the nontemporal Self. Yet, since the Self represents the totality of the psyche, it would be more accurate to say that the Self participates both in the timeless world of the unconscious and in the temporal world of consciousness. Nevertheless, an individual who has achieved psychic integration may be said to have transcended time because the archetype of the Self, when made conscious, unites and reconciles the three-dimensional universe of consciousness with the timeless and transpersonal realm of the unconscious. Thus, the Self is synonymous with the "still point" of the mystic. Just as "there is an old saying that 'God is a circle whose center is everywhere and the circumference nowhere,'" so it is a brute fact of empirical psychology that the Self is at once the center, or midpoint, and circumference of the psyche.[13]

The reconciling function of the Self is graphically portrayed by mandala symbols which can be found throughout the world at every cultural level—for example, on neolithic pottery, in the iconography of Tibetan Buddhism, in the spontaneous drawings of mental patients, and in the architectural design of Jung's house at Bollingen. The Tower itself actually represents the culmination of Jung's own individuation process which began immediately following his break with Freud, and continued into the early 1920s.

Soon after publication of *The Psychology of the Unconscious,* Jung was deluged by an extraordinary sequence of dreams and visions. At first he thought he was threatened with a psychosis. (He had had several terrifying visions which he later regarded as anticipations of World War I.) Eventually he decided to resign his position at the University of Zurich, where he had lectured since 1905. Jung momentarily tried to resist his encounter with the unconscious, but shortly before Christmas 1913 he finally decided to take "the decisive step." "It cost me a great deal," he later confided, "to undergo" the confrontation with the unconscious, "but I had been challenged by fate. Only by extreme effort was I finally able to escape from the labyrinth."[14] In retrospect, it is quite probable that had Jung himself not undergone the experience he eventually called individuation, analytical psychology would have remained stillborn in the pages of *The Psychology of the Unconscious.*

Jung's psychology derives from the ground of his own experience. Indeed in its initial formulation his psychology appears to be nothing less than an argument from limited experience, for Jung's analytical theories were originally developed as a personal psychotherapy. "All my works, all my creative activity, has come from those initial fantasies and dreams which began in 1912. . . . Everything that I accomplished in later life was already contained in them, although at first only in the form of emotions and images."[15] Before he could explain his inner images, Jung had to understand each one—separately—as it presented itself in his dreams and visions.

At the outset, Jung could see no relationship between his unconscious states and his conscious life, but as his self-induced therapy progressed, he gradually realized that the unconscious bore a compensatory relationship to consciousness and that it was possible to reconcile the opposite halves of the psyche. Jung achieved this insight (which enabled him slowly "to emerge from the darkness" "toward the end of the First World War") by drawing and understanding mandalas. He had painted his first mandala in 1916 but had failed to grasp its import. Then between 1918 and 1919, while he was medical administrator of the English prisoner-of-war camp at Château d'Oex, Jung "sketched every morning in a notebook a small circular drawing, a mandala, which seemed to correspond to my inner situation at the time. With the help of these drawings I could observe my psychic transformations from day to day."[16] The unpremeditated drawing of mandalas soon forced Jung "to abandon the idea of the superordinate position of the ego"; and he eventually "saw that everything, all the paths I had been following, all the steps I had taken, were leading back to a single point—namely, to the mid-point. It became increasingly plain to me that the mandala is the center. It is the exponent of all paths. It is the path to the center, to individuation." This discovery prefigured the culmination of Jung's decisive confrontation with the unconscious: he had begun

> to understand that the goal of psychic development is the self. There is no linear evolution; there is only a circumambulation of the self. Uniform development exists, at most, only at the beginning; later, everything points toward the center. This insight gave me stability, and gradually my inner peace returned. I knew that in finding the mandala as an expression of the self I had attained what was for me the ultimate. Perhaps someone else knows more, but not I.[17]

When Jung began building the Tower in 1923, he had attained his "ultimate"; he had successfully sailed through the cutwaters of the unconscious to become a "new" man. And in the next twelve years he carved his own myth—his mandala—in the form of the stone house at Bollingen.

One cannot help wondering what Jung's father, a Protestant minister, would have thought of his son's "individuation." When Carl Gustav Jung was born on 26 July 1875, his father was a pastor in Kesswil, Switzerland. As young Carl matured, he gradually became aware that his father was losing his faith. This tragedy nearly destroyed the senior Jung, and it made a lasting impression on his son. When he was fifteen, Carl prepared—under his father's supervision—for his confirmation in the Lutheran church. But even though he tried to immerse himself in the spirit of the ceremony, he found it both dull and meaningless. This dissatisfying experience gave Jung an insight into his father's agonizing predicament and precipitated his own religious crisis. On the one hand, he believed in God; on the other, he could not accept the God of his father. He thought that church organization and dogmatic theology vitiated the living experience of God, but he could not find a suitable alternative to institutional Christianity.

Jung grew increasingly sceptical of the existence of the deity of the churches, a view that may have been abetted by his scientific knowledge which was "thoroughly saturated with the scientific materialism of the time," yet he continued to believe in the arbitrary omnipotence of God.[18] His growing knowledge of science did not resolve the situation. Indeed, just as he missed the factor of empiricism in religion, so he missed that of meaning in science. And yet this was precisely the point—the point that his father, in particular, and organized Christianity, in general, had failed to grasp: religion must be a meaningful experience. It cannot be purely dogmatic or thoroughly intellectualized, for then it is simply a matter of hollow phrases and fossilized metaphors. Religion must be empirical and personal; it must involve a constant encounter between man and God—as Jung would later put it, between the conscious and the unconscious, the temporal and the eternal halves of the psyche. Religion, however, cannot merely be a matter of experience; it must also involve understanding. Like T. S. Eliot, Jung believed that reason and feeling must be unified: a dissociated sensibility can only lead to extreme intellectualism or to unfettered emotionalism. There must be a balance, an interaction between the extremities of the mind—an interpenetration of emotion and reason—a balance which Jung missed in organized Christianity but was soon to find in the writings of such mystics as Meister Eckhart. Jung's early preference for the mystics over the schoolmen continued for the rest of his life; he felt that they, like the alchemists (but unlike his pathetic father), really understood the phenomenology of religion.

When Jung graduated from the gymnasium, he enrolled in the University of Basel. He had found the gymnasium boring and enjoyed the new environment immensely. The university atmosphere inspired him (he later remembered with enthusiasm when Burckhardt and Bachofen walked in the streets of Basel) and provided him with abundant freedom to pursue his philosophical interests. To his budding interest in mysticism, he added a systematic investigation of the philosophies of Schopenhauer, Goethe, Nietzsche, Kant, Carus, and Von Hartmann. However, while still an undergraduate, Jung decided to study medicine, and upon completing his baccalaureate he entered the university's school of medicine. In 1898 (the year Berdyaev was exiled to Vologda) Jung had to choose a field of specialization. With the enthusiasm engendered from a reading of Krafft-Ebing, he informed a disappointed professor of internal medicine that he would become a psychiatrist.

Jung's psychiatric career, however, really did not begin until December 1900, when he joined the staff of the Burghölzli Clinic in Zurich. The years at the clinic marked his apprenticeship. There he had the invaluable opportunity of conducting a variety of experiments (some of which helped to provide him with the information necessary to produce the word-association test and the galvanometer) and of gaining experience in a new, and still disreputable, field of science. Yet Jung's subsequent friendship and break with Freud, his attempt to strike new paths in depth psychology, his personal encounter with the unconscious, and his reaction to the First World War soon dwarfed the early triumphs at Burghölzli. The war affected Jung profoundly; and indeed it is ironic that just as he was unraveling his own internal difficulties and discovering the skeleton key to the unconscious, the outside world—the external world of time, causality, space, and consciousness—should be doing its best to annihilate itself.

Before the war Jung had believed in the idea of Progress. He thought history (or, in any case, the history of the West) exemplified a linear pattern of development. Western man had made moral (as well, of course, as material) progress over the ages and appeared to be building an enlightened civilization based on order and freedom. But then unfortunately, tragically, the war struck and demonstrated the utter bankruptcy of the idea of progress. In a 1928 essay entitled "The Spiritual Problem of Modern Man," Jung spoke for many when he described the "shattering" effects of the war. "The revolution in our conscious outlook," he stated,

> brought about by the catastrophic results of the World War, shows itself in our inner life by the shattering of our faith in ourselves

and our own worth. We used to regard foreigners as political and moral reprobates, but the modern man is forced to recognize that he is politically and morally just like anyone else. Whereas formerly I believed it my bounden duty to call others to order, I must now admit that I need calling to order myself, and that I would do better to set my own house to rights first. I admit this the more readily because I realize only too well that my faith in the rational organization of the world—that old dream of the millennium when peace and harmony reign—has grown pale.[19]

Jung's loss of the dream of the millennium was as significant as were Berdyaev's repudiation of Marxism, Eliot's denial of Bergsonism, and Huxley's rejection of the idea of Progress. The loss marked Jung's renunciation of time-philosophy and his adoption of an extremely critical attitude toward the development of Western culture. Abandoning the idea of progress forced Jung to ask himself why the war had occurred. And in "Wotan," an essay published eight years later, he began to formulate a psychological theory of the historical process, a theory which he eventually spelled out fully in *Aion* (1951) and in *Flying Saucers: A Modern Myth of Things in the Sky* (1958).

The concept of historical time that gradually emerged from Jung's works enabled him to fill the void left by his rejection of the idea of Progress, for it provided him with a philosophy of history which gave time a meaning by imposing a purposive pattern on the temporal process. At least as early as 1928 (and quite possibly before), Jung discovered the psychological "law" which he believed would permit him to penetrate the apparent absurdity of historical time.

In an essay (republished in his popular book *Modern Man in Search of a Soul*), Jung suggested that history is governed by the same law that governs psychic processes. Following Heraclitus, Jung called this law *enantiodromia,* or the reversal of opposites.[20] The concept of *enantiodromia* is derived from observing the process known as psychological compensation. Just as the unconscious contradicts conscious attitudes that jeopardize psychic equilibrium, so one aeon, or historical period, contradicts another. According to Jung's full-blown theory, which he disclosed some twenty-three years after he had first used the law of compensation to interpret history, this dialectical process (which resembles Hegelian logic) is an immutable part of history: every culture necessarily entails the seeds of its own destruction. And yet on the basis of the law of compensation, civilization—or aeons themselves (i.e., Platonic months of over two thousand years)—need not disintegrate. For the very dialectic which gives history its dynamic meaning

C. G. Jung

—the process of *enantiodromia* itself—could be suspended if only an aeon could achieve integration.

This is the critical point: If it is possible for the individual to achieve psychic wholeness (symbolized by the mandala or archetype of the self), it is equally possible for a historical period to achieve integration. And if integration can be attained at this level, it is possible, though no more than possible, for mankind to achieve a final resolution of the contradictions of history—to create a new and final synthesis, an age of integration that will mark the end of historical time.

Jung emphasized this message with increasing intensity as he grew older. Yet he believed that the next aeon would be peaceful only if mankind created a new and viable myth. To do this, man would have to undergo individuation; he would have to experience a rebirth, or spiritual transformation. But Jung insisted that man could only accomplish this spiritual metamorphosis if he achieved union—integration—with the timeless dimensions of the collective psyche, if he succeeded in transferring the center of his personality from the time-bound ego to the transcendental and eternal self.

Although Jung was honored during his lifetime by many famous universities (in the United States, India, Europe, and Great Britain), his later work was often misunderstood or greeted with derision. When Jung stressed the necessity of individuation or the prospects for a new and regenerate period of history, he was frequently discounted, ignored, or heartily condemned as an anachronistic advocate of mysticism, romanticism, or atavism. And yet, these condemnations or misinterpretations merely confirmed Jung's view of contemporary man as a statistical cipher, a mechanical function whose instincts have atrophied. No wonder, Jung would argue, that modern man cannot understand me: he has lost contact with the roots of his being; he has disavowed the significance of creative fantasy; and because of this, he has jeopardized the future of his existence. This unconscious will not hesitate to compensate for the folly of consciousness. And—here is the danger—if the unconscious is neglected, if it is not recognized, accepted, and integrated with consciousness, it will erupt like a volcano, submerging in its wake the fragile accomplishments of civilization. Let it not be forgotten that war is a symptom of a maltreated unconscious—of a refusal to confront the impersonal, or external, side of our own nature and to incorporate it within the field of our everyday experience.

Jung continued to stress the importance of individuation and the possibility of transforming society through the transformation of the personality until his death, on 6 June 1961, at age eighty-six. Jung's legacy was enormous: voluminous published works (books, essays, and articles), a successful medical practice, the famous institute named after him in Zurich. But what underlies and unites all of these different facets of Jung's life—the accomplishment for which, in all probability, he will be chiefly remembered —is his understanding of the unconscious, his inspiration. It once prompted him to chisel the following inscription into a stone facing the lake in front of his house at Bollingen: "I am mortal for everyone, yet I am not touched by the cycle of aeons."[21]

Unconscious Platonism

The Structure of the Unconscious

E. R. Goodenough once observed that Jung probably saved himself from the chaotic depths of the psyche by "formulating the idea of the collective unconscious as a name and hence 'explanation' for these depths: for when a phenomenon gets a name it becomes less formidable on the same principle that a god with a name is less of a threat than a nameless god."[22] Jung would have agreed that his discovery of the collective unconscious had (like Nietzsche's intuition of eternal recurrence) redeemed his life. But he would have opposed Goodenough's suggestion that the collective unconscious was merely a "name," for Jung believed that the idea of an objective psyche necessarily entailed its own reality. In asserting the objective reality of a priori concepts, Jung realized that he was contradicting the triumphant epistemology of contemporary empiricism. "Once again," he lamented, "in the age-old controversy over universals, the nominalistic standpoint has triumphed over the realistic, and the Idea has evaporated into a mere *flatus vocis.*" Yet let it not be forgotten, he continued, that "every victory contains its own defeat." And, "In our own day signs foreshadowing a change of attitude are rapidly increasing."[23]

What are these signs? What indications are there of a counterrevolution in metaphysics? According to Jung there are two: the perduring popularity of Kant and the increasing acceptance of analytical psychology. It is true, of course, that Kant's doctrine of categories destroys traditional metaphysics, "but at the same time it paves the way for a *rebirth of the Platonic spirit.* If it be true that there can be no metaphysics transcending human reason," Jung wrote, "it is no less true that there can be no empirical knowledge that is not already caught and limited by the *a priori* structure of cognition."[24] The a priori structure to which Jung is alluding, however, is not the rational mind (with its categories and forms of intuition) described in the pages of *The Critique of Pure Reason.* On the contrary, it is a nonrational a priori structure, "namely the inborn, preconscious and unconscious . . . structure of the psyche." Jung usually refers to this "collective a priori beneath the personal psyche" as the collective unconscious, or the objective psyche.[25] He chose

> the term "collective" because this part of the unconscious is not individual but universal; in contrast to the personal psyche, it has contents and modes of behaviour that are more or less the same everywhere and in all individuals. It is, in other words, identical in all men and thus constitutes a common psychic substrate of a suprapersonal nature which is present in every one of us.[26]

Because it is universal and present in every individual, the collective unconscious is essentially timeless and spaceless. It comprises a form of being which is "wholly other," different from that of everyday experience. Yet not only is it "relatively trans-spatial and trans-temporal," but its contents—"its treasure-house of eternal images"—the archetypes, are also timeless and spaceless.[27] Yet one may ask: can an archetype be perceived in other than spatial terms? The answer is no. But, then, why is an archetype essentially nonspatial and nontemporal? Because, Jung would say (seemingly echoing Kant), there is a difference between the archetype in itself and the archetype as it appears to us. We always perceive the actualized or concretized archetype, never the archetype per se. And, unfortunately, we can only infer the existence of an unconditioned archetype (as Locke inferred the existence of his "Substance-I-know-not-what") from its manifestations. Although Jung does not draw this comparison, a psychological analogy to Heisenberg's law of indeterminancy seems to be operating: any attempt to perceive an archetype in its pure state merely distorts our visions of the original. Thus, the archetype (as opposed to the archetypal "idea") remains "a hypothetical and irrepresentable model,"[28] yet one without which it would be impossible to explain the appearance of archetypal symbols.

Jung originally seems to have derived the concept of the archetype from observing parallels between his own dreams and visions and the motifs of myths, legends, and fairy tales. Having failed initially to explain his dreams and visionary experiences by free association, he sought to amplify their meaning by subjecting them to different, but evidently related, contexts for interpretation. By using the comparative method, Jung found a correspondence between the symbolic content of his own dreams and the religious experience of other historical epochs and cultures. The innumerable analogies between his own symbolic experience and that of different civilizations —archaic as well as modern, Western as well as Eastern—led him to postulate the existence of an impersonal mind, underlying individual consciousness, whose contents are universally the same.

From "the repeated observation that, for instance, the myths and fairy-tales of world literature contain definite motifs which crop up everywhere" and from the recognition that "we meet these same motifs in the fantasies, dreams, deliria, and delusions of individuals living today,"[29] Jung inferred the existence of archetypes, primordial types or images, below the threshold of consciousness. An archetype is an immemorial pattern of human be-havior—psychological behavior—which appears to us as a symbolic portrait of the basic instincts (i.e., hunger, reproduction, the will to dominate, crea-tivity)[30] or conversely as a psychic process which has been transformed into a primordial image.[31] According to Jung, "The term 'image' is intended to express not only the form of the activity taking place, but the typical situation in which the activity is released." Thus, an archetype is at once a form, a pattern of functioning, and a motif in which unconscious processes are objectified. It is important to remember, however, that "whatever we say about the archetypes, they remain visualizations or concretizations which pertain to the field of consciousness."[32]

We cannot know the archetype in itself: the symbols, images, patterns, or ideas which we observe to be archetypal are not identical with the archetype per se. It transcends the devices of conscious elaboration and cannot be equated with its historical formula. The archetype per se is not a symbol: it is a form that produces symbols. In other words, "the archetype in itself is empty and purely formal, nothing but a *facultas praeformandi,* a possibility of representation" that produces a primordial image. In this sense, the archetype per se "might perhaps be compared to the axial system of a crystal, which, as it were, preforms the crystalline structure in the mother liquid, although it has no material existence of its own." For just "as the axial system determines only the stereometric structure but not the concrete form of the individual crystal,"[33] so the archetype per se supplies only the basic pattern of a primordial image, not its individual or concrete features. Thus the archetype in itself is at once a possibility for representation and the primordial mold in which an archetypal symbol is cast.

Although Jung refutes the doctrine of innate ideas, he insists that the mind is not a tabula rasa. In his view, the archetype per se is transmitted to the entire human species through heredity. If heredity were excluded it would be impossible to explain the fact that archetypes not only are dis-seminated by diffusion, but are equally capable of arising spontaneously. Thus, while inherited ideas are out of the question, Jung maintains that the notion of "inherited *possibilities* of ideas" is crucial and a necessary part of his concept of the archetypes.[34] To assume that the potentiality for producing archetypal symbols "is not inherited but comes into being in every child anew would be just as preposterous as the primitive belief that the sun which rises in the morning is a different sun from that which set the evening before."[35]

Jung did not claim to be the first to have formulated the theory of archetypes; indeed, as he readily admitted, "The honour belongs to Plato."[36] And while it is true that precedents for his psychological theories can be found in the works of Nietzsche, Bastian, Carus, Hubert and Mauss, Durkheim, and Lévy-Bruhl, as well as Hermann Usener, Jung himself seems to have considered his affinity with Plato—and the tradition of realism in general—to have been of cardinal importance. Like Plato, Jung believed that ideas—archetypal ideas—are intrinsically real, not (as the nominalist contends) merely names, fictions, or tautologies. Both Plato and Jung accepted the Idea as an eternal object of knowledge—a preexisting, or self-subsistent, form of being—which could only be known by anamnesis, or remembrance.[37] The similarity between these two men, however, does not end here: just as Plato believed in a timeless and spaceless world of Forms, so Jung maintained the existence of a trans-personal and trans-spatial world of archetypes.

For Jung, as for Plato, the archetypes are arranged hierarchically. In Plato's system the Forms are subordinated and unified by the Form of the Good, or the Form of Forms. In Jung's psychology the archetypes are subordinated and encompassed by the mandala, "the structure of which symbolizes the centre of order in the unconscious."[38] The analogy can be carried further: like Plato, Jung believed that particulars imitate or participate in universals. Jung observed that our individual lives are grounded in psychic processes which are common to the whole species; and quite often (although not always) our actions imitate or reflect the ancient paradigms of psychological behavior preserved in the timeless recesses of the unconscious.

At this point these important analogies between Jung's and Plato's thought begin to resolve themselves into contrasts. Plato regarded his archetypes as the ultimate forms of knowledge. His concept of the Idea entailed the notion of unsurpassable perfection and goodness, of a different form of being which, although vaguely reflected in the world of becoming, was virtually the antithesis of the phenomenal world. The Idea possessed the only claim to knowledge because it was synonymous with Truth. Jung, on the other hand, not only viewed the archetypal symbol as an imitation, or product, of the unconditioned archetypal form (a distinction which is absent in Plato), but as Jung said in his essay "The Soul and Death," he believed "that the psyche touches on a form of existence outside space and time."[39] In other words, while he regarded the collective unconscious as a timeless treasure house of eternal images, he also postulated the existence of an absolute (and not entirely psychic) form of being underlying the objective psyche. On the basis of his own experience and research, Jung

hazarded the postulate that the phenomenon of archetypal config-urations . . . may be founded upon a *psychoid* base, that is, upon an only partially psychic and possibly altogether different form of being. For lack of empirical data I have neither knowledge nor understanding of such forms of being, which are commonly called spiritual. . . . But insofar as the archetypes act upon me, they are real and actual to me, even though I do not know what their real nature is . . . all that is comprehended is in itself psychic, and to that extent we are hopelessly cooped up in an exclusively psychic world. *Nevertheless, we have good reason to suppose that behind this veil there exists the uncomprehended absolute object which affects and influences us.*[40]

Hypothetically, then, if an individual were to penetrate to "the un-comprehended absolute object," he would have to transcend not only the world of consciousness, but also the realms of actualized archetypes and of archetypes per se. In contrast, Plato would argue that an individual in search of Reality would have to reach the "absolute object" by the exercise of the rational faculty of the soul. Yet, Plato was forced to admit that the final comprehension of the world of Forms could be achieved only by mystical intuition—a form of preternatural experience which (in the West as well as the East) is often attributed to the agency of superconsciousness. According to Jung, however, superconsciousness, or the "higher conscious-ness," is nothing less than the unconscious.[41] Whether or not Jung's supposition is correct, it may be that his approach to reality is not as different from Plato's as it initially seems. Nevertheless, the theory of education described in the *Republic* and the *Symposium* differs considerably from Jung's "theory of knowledge" in that Plato stresses the gradual appropriation of reality through the emancipation of thought from myth—the liberation of consciousness from the control of the passionate and appetetic segments of the psyche. These differences notwithstanding, Jung's belief in the reality of archetypal ideas, his conception of the archetypal structure which produces the mandala symbol as a Form of Forms, and his insistence on the space-timelessness of the primordial images (as well as the "uncomprehended absolute object") make him a twentieth-century realist—that is, an "un-conscious" Platonist.

The Mandala

Although, as Professor Goodenough has pointed out, Jung's psychology represents a revival of Platonism, some critics have detected a Manichean

C. G. Jung

streak in his thought. This observation is not totally without foundation, for while Plato held that the Forms are absolutely good, Jung recognized a bipolarity of good and evil in the archetypes. And yet his psychology is not Manichean, nor (like Plato's) is it ultimately dualistic. Indeed, it is the very reverse of ontological dualism, for the major theme of his psychology—individuation, the transcendence of the time-bound ego and the attainment of the transcendental self—stresses the unity (and not the division) of the entire personality.

It is undeniable that Jung recognized the existence of dualistic tendencies within the psyche. In fact, he not only thought that there could be no reality without polarity, but that the cure of souls necessarily begins with the patient's acknowledgment of contradictory tensions within his own psyche. Yet the focus of Jung's psychology continually emphasizes the achievement of unity and harmony through the reconciliation and, hence, transcendence of the opposites immanent in the personality. He constantly stresses the necessity of transforming the antithetical relationship between the temporal and the eternal dimensions of the psyche—of transfiguring the time-oriented ego and the timeless unconscious into an all-inclusive and transcendental harmony: the self.

When a person decides to begin his odyssey into selfhood, he must start by admitting the existence within himself of characteristics popularly called "evil." The initial encounter with the dark side of one's personality may be shattering, but it is necessary before the collective contents of the unconscious can be integrated with consciousness. The destructive, evil, dark side of an individual's personality is depicted (in the personal unconscious) by the archetype of the shadow. The shadow can be both helpful and terrifying. In its positive aspect, the shadow inaugurates the process of individuation by "leading" the ego to its encounter with the collective unconscious. The first content of the collective unconscious to appear during psychic integration is usually the anima or animus. Since the psyche is inherently androgynous, a man possesses an anima; a woman, an animus—archetypal images which act as spokesmen for, or symbolic personifications of, the objective psyche. The anthropomorphic terminology is apposite, for not only do the archetypal images often project themselves in a human guise, but the personalization of the archetypes is essential to successful individuation.[42] If an individual fails to personify the collective material emerging from the unconscious, he runs the risk of being assimilated by the archetypes themselves—a catastrophe which can only lead to the destruction of the ego and ultimately to psychosis. If, on the other hand, a patient succeeds in personifying the archetypes, he can divest them of their mana, or potentially destructive power. Then, instead of facing the danger of being overwhelmed by the unconscious, he will be in a position to integrate the archetype with consciousness, thus preserving the existence of his ego.

After an individual succeeds in depriving the anima or the animus of its destructive power, he can establish contact with the next major figures in the hierarchy of the collective unconscious: namely, the archetype of the wise old man or the image of the great mother. The wise old man seems to be autochthonous to the male psyche, while the great mother (as well as the maiden) is evidently indigenous to the female unconscious. Together the syzygy anima-animus and the pair formed by the great mother and the wise old man constitute what Jung refers to as the marriage *quaternio,* a complex symbol of psychic harmony which represents the union of the four dimensions or principal opposites of the collective unconscious.[43]

While there are many variants and analogues of the basic archetypes, an individual begins to approach the goal of his psychic odyssey when he confronts either the image of the chthonic mother or the wise old man. These images contain the potentiality, or "secret," of integration: they establish the final differentiation of the unconscious opposites and prepare the way for the appearance of another symbol which transforms the division of the personality into unity. The final symbol to appear—the third term (which, in this sense, is analogous to Bradley's Absolute) to emerge from the polar opposites of the psyche—is the mandala, or symbol of the (transcendental) self.

"The Sanskrit word *mandala* means 'circle' in the ordinary sense of the word. In the sphere of religious practice and in psychology it denotes circular images, which are drawn, painted, modelled, or danced." Mandalas, Jung wrote, usually "appear in connection with chaotic psychic states of disorientation or panic. They then have the purpose of reducing the confusion to order, though this is never the conscious intention of the patient. At all events they express order, balance, and wholeness."[44] It is quite

> easy to see how the severe pattern imposed by a circular image of this kind compensates the disorder and confusion of the psychic state—namely, through the construction of a central point to which everything is related, or by a concentric arrangement of the disordered multiplicity and of contradictory and irreconcilable elements. This is evidently an *attempt at self-healing* on the part of Nature, which does not spring from conscious reflection but from an instinctive impulse.[45]

Obviously not every attempt to heal the psyche is successful, and occasionally some mandalas fail to perform their function. They may tempo-

C. G. Jung

rarily enable a patient to order his realities, yet ultimately fail to produce a new and permanent center of the personality.[46] When a mandala (or more likely, a series of mandalas) has succeeded in rechanneling, or reorienting, the flow of psychic energy toward the center of the entire psyche, individuation—"the process by which a person becomes a psychological 'in-dividual,' that is, a separate, indivisible unity or 'whole' "[47]—has reached its climax.

Thereafter, the mandala functions as both the center and the circumference of the transfigured psyche—as the self. For although its "centre is represented by an innermost point, it is surrounded by a periphery" (i.e., its circumference) "containing everything that belongs to the self—the paired opposites that make up the total personality." This totality (which represents a reconciliation of the temporal and eternal dimensions of the psyche) "comprises consciousness first of all, then the personal unconscious, and finally an indefinitely large segment of the collective unconscious whose archetypes are common to all mankind."[48]

Jung is saying that the upper half of the self—which faces the outer world, the world of time—is composed of the persona (the mask of conventional behavior assumed by consciousness when dealing with society), the ego (the focal point of the nonindividuated personality), and the superior function of consciousness (i.e., thinking, feeling, sensation, or intuition), as well as its attitudinal type (extraversion or introversion). The lower half of the self, on the other hand—which faces the inner world, or timeless recesses of the psyche—is composed of the personal unconscious (symbolized by the shadow), the archetypes of the collective unconscious (ranked according to their respective hierarchical status), and the inferior function of consciousness (thinking, feeling, sensation, or intuition), as well as the unconscious attitudinal type (extraversion or introversion).

Having arranged the contents of the psyche according to a circular order, the self serves both as the center and as the circumference of the personality. After the culmination of the individuation process, all contents of the personality (both conscious and unconscious) orient themselves by referring to the self. Hence, instead of attempting to develop in a linear fashion (which usually causes fragmentation or dissociation), the elements of the personality establish themselves on the rim of the psyche and circumambulate the self. Thus, the mandala (which appears to us as the actualized archetype of wholeness) "has the dignity of a 'reconciling symbol.' "[49] It forms a relationship between consciousness and unconsciousness, unites the various components of the psyche, and transfers the center of the personality from the time-bound ego to the transcendental self.

It is true that "the ego is the only content of the self that we do know";

[179]

yet, "the individuated ego senses itself as the object of an unknown and superordinate subject." It feels that it has been united and transformed, that it has become complete and whole by communing with and participating in a higher reality. Thus, while "the idea of a self is itself a transcendental postulate" which "does not allow of scientific proof," it is nevertheless "justifiable psychologically": it refers to and is grounded in an experience which, while intensely subjective, is discoverable in every age.[50]

In its function as the center of the transfigured personality, the self acts as a mediator between the temporal world of consciousness and the timeless world of unconsciousness. The mandala, in its capacity as a unifying symbol, achieves a reconciliation between "the still point" of the collective unconscious and "the turning world" of the ego. The self is, therefore, analogous to the "dance"[51] of Huxley, Eliot, Williams, and Yeats: it transforms the chaotic events in the life of the nonindividuated personality into a "pattern / Of timeless moments"; it incorporates the life of temporal man into the framework of the eternal in man, thereby rendering individual existence significant and meaningful. From the opposition of time and eternity, consciousness and unconsciousness, good and evil, the self emerges as the great reconciler. The mandala resolves the antitheses of the psyche and blends them into a transcendental harmony. Time and eternity, the ego and the objective psyche, join together to circumambulate the self: "God is a circle whose centre is everywhere and the circumference nowhere."

Before his individuation, Jung underwent a period of enormous inner turbulence. He was prey to "the uncanny grotesqueness of the irrational world of chance" and believed that "the storm pushing against me was time . . . [which] ceaselessly dogs our heels." Jung saw time "exert[ing] a mighty suction which greedily draws everything living into itself."[52] After his individuation, however, he felt that he had succeeded in creating a personal myth, an inward vision, that enabled him to defy the crushing forces of the universe. An individual mythology allows a person to express what he is under the aspect of eternity. It permits him to integrate himself with the cycle of the aeons and the phylogenetic content of human experience—to identify himself with the eternal core of meaning concealed in the heart of life.

According to Jung, life is "like a plant that lives on its rhizome. . . . The part that appears above ground lasts only a single summer. Then it withers away—an ephemeral apparition." And yet, while the flower may perish, the rhizome of the plant remains. Analogously, although an individuated person's "conventional" achievements (for example, professional success) may vanish, his authentic life's work—his personal myth—will withstand the flux of time. In Jung's case, his own myth made him aware of something constant and stable, underlying the vicissitudes of phenomenal experience. "When we think of the unending growth and decay of life and civilizations, we cannot escape the impression of absolute nullity. Yet I have never lost a sense of something that lives and endures underneath the eternal flux. What we see is the blossom, which passes. The rhizome remains."[53]

At first glance, Jung's view of myth seems to stress Bergsonian duration as a means of escaping the serial order of time. Once, for example, during a visit to North Africa, Jung observed that it would not be long before the "pocket watch, the symbol of the European's accelerated tempo," destroyed the static existence of the Arab states. Industrialization, he said, would eventually come to North Africa, and with it "the god of time" (and his "synonym, progress"), who would "inevitably chop into the bits and pieces of days, hours, minutes, and seconds that duration which is still the closest thing to eternity."[54] This statement is not atypical. Certainly Jung emphasized duration; but it is equally true that his concept of duration entailed the notion of timelessness in time. He disliked the chronological order of time as much as Bergson did, but he nevertheless posited a reality behind time, spatialized time as well as real duration. A personal myth, for instance, which is ultimately dredged up from what Thomas Mann called the "time-coulisse" of the past—i.e., the unconditioned archetypes of the collective unconscious—subsists above the temporal process, above change or creative evolution. Jung confirms this himself when he describes his own individuation—those precious moments during his life when "the imperishable world irrupted into this transitory one."[55]

Jung actually had two experiences of individuation: the first, during the decade from 1912 to 1923; the second, in 1944 while recuperating from an illness. The first period culminated with the construction of his Bollingen residence (on the walls of which he painted "all those things which have carried me out of time into seclusion, out of the present into timelessness") and with the composition of his *Red Book* (in which he painted a mandala representing "a window opening on to eternity").[56]

Jung's second all-important encounter with the unconscious (which he thought represented the effects of a completed individuation) has been vividly recorded in his autobiography. While convalescing from a broken foot and a heart attack, Jung experienced a series of amazing visions—visions that contain all of the essential ingredients of mystical phenomenology. Throughout the course of these supranormal experiences, Jung came to disbelieve in the reality of the "three-dimensional world." He repeatedly felt that the phenomenal space-time universe had been artificially constructed (perhaps, one is tempted to speculate, for perpetuating the illusion of multiplicity). During this period Jung would usually spend the day uncomfortably, fall asleep in the evening, and awake around midnight for about an hour "in an utterly transformed state." It was, he said, "as if I were in an ecstasy. I felt as though I were floating in space, as though I were safe in the womb of the universe—in a tremendous void, but filled with the highest possible feeling of happiness. 'This is eternal bliss,' I thought. 'This cannot be described; it is far too wonderful.' "[57] Jung had, he said, never "imagined that any such experience was possible." But

> it was not a product of imagination. The visions and experiences were utterly real; there was nothing subjective about them; they all had a quality of absolute objectivity.
>
> We shy away from the word "eternal," but I can describe the experience only as the ecstasy of a non-temporal state in which present, past, and future are one. Everything that happens in time had been brought together into a concrete whole. Nothing was distributed over time, nothing could be measured by temporal concepts.[58]

Jung's experience of eternity liberated him from time—from the past-present-future structure of linear time and from the constantly developing present of *durée réelle*: "Everything that happens in time had been brought together into a concrete whole." The qualitative flow of creative evolution, as well as the quantitative development of temporal succession, had been eliminated from his consciousness. He felt as though he were "interwoven into an indescribable" and timeless "whole" which he could observe "with complete objectivity."[59] His consciousness was not destroyed; nor did he feel that he was about to be absorbed into a nondifferentiated Absolute.

Jung's mysticism, then, cannot be equated with Huxley's Perennial Philosophy. Rather, it is quite similar to the "personal" monism of Eliot and Williams. Although R. C. Zaehner would probably disagree (he uses Jungian psychology to explain nonpersonal monistic and nature mysticism in order to preserve the purity of the Christian concept of mystical communion), Jung's mysticism emphasizes two factors which are also found in the works of Eliot and Williams: namely, the transcendence of dualism and the preservation of the personality during "the ecstasy of a non-temporal state." Individuation, in Jung's view, is not limited to the concept of a trans-temporal union with nature; nor is it synonymous with the monistic notion of union through elimination of the personality. On the contrary, its motive concept is much closer to the theist's (or personal monist's) definition of mysticism as a nontemporal yet conscious communion with God. The individuated personality communes with the "absolute object" through the mediation of the symbol of the self (Christ or some other mandala symbol) and thus establishes a personal relationship with eternity. Whether the "absolute object" is ultimately "personal" or "impersonal" we cannot say, but its existence is undeniable: we can experience it through the aegis of the archetypes (from which the individuated personality fashions its own "timeless" myth); and we can penetrate the time barrier when we achieve psychic wholeness.

In attempting to categorize Jung's mysticism, it is also extremely important to remember that he insisted on the absolute objectivity of his experiences. Although he would admit that his "ecstasy" was a "psychological" experience, he nevertheless believed that it was objectively real. At any rate, what is significant is that Jung's "ecstasy" meant as much to him as the "unattended moment" did to Eliot or the successful passage through the "way of affirmations" did to Williams.

Still, in one respect there does appear to be a difference between the preternatural experiences of Eliot and of Jung. Jung stressed the fact that our perceptions are "cooped up in an exclusively psychic world." This notion implies that when we transcend time, we are only communing with the collective unconscious. And although the collective unconscious is itself timeless and spaceless, it does not fit the standard descriptions of supernatural reality. Jung could reply that the term "collective unconscious" is simply a neologism for supernatural reality. But while he would, no doubt, argue that individuation is synonymous with what is usually called mystical experience, he would insist that the psychological conditions of mysticism in no way repudiate its validity. On the contrary, the fact that traditional wisdom recognizes the objective validity of mystical experience suggests not only that it is absolutely real for those people who experience it, but that mystical experience is probably grounded in an absolute reality underlying the objective psyche.

Jung actually believed that there was an "uncomprehended absolute object" beneath the structure of the unconscious. And although he thought that it was twice removed from that "absolute object," Jung felt that when an individual visually experienced his own psychic integration (in the form of dreams, visions, fantasies, or active imagination) by seeing his self emerge as the pattern of the mandala, he had indeed transcended time. This view is similar to Berdyaev's conception of superconscious images as well as to Huxley's conception of visionary experience. But Jung may have gone farther in those 1944 visions. He seems to imply that he had crossed the barrier separating the phenomenal world from the timeless world of visionary, or archetypal, experience and had actually established contact with the "uncomprehended absolute object which affects and influences us."[60]

"Aion" and Synchronicity

Whether or not Jung thought that he had penetrated to the absolute, he did believe that he had transcended time and that by integrating himself with the "treasure house of eternal images" in the collective unconscious, he had achieved a transcendental identity. His ego might still be "mortal for everyone," but the authentic center of his personality—his self—could not be "touched by the cycle of aeons." By attaining individuation, Jung also became aware of his relationship to the timeless, or immutable, psychological law which supplies the basic pattern of history.

From his clinical observations, Jung had evidently learned that the unconscious compensates for the deficiencies of consciousness. If, for instance, an individual identifies himself with his persona and ignores the demands of the inner world, his unconscious will react by projecting images which contradict his conscious situation. The projected images, or archetypes, will attempt to restore psychic equilibrium by reversing the deleterious trend of consciousness. They will assert a significance, or condition of being, which represents the exact opposite of the conscious attitude. Thus, if an individual were a thoroughgoing rationalist who refused to ascribe an importance to his feelings, his unconscious would inevitably manifest itself in emotional terms which would seek a compromise with the exaggerated intellectualism of consciousness. If, however, the attempt to regain a balance between consciousness and unconsciousness were a failure—if the hyper-intellectual failed to acknowledge the significance of his emotions—a neurosis, or perhaps even a psychosis, would inexorably follow.

According to Jung, this pattern of polar complementarity is universal. It was operative in the past; it is functioning at present; and it will govern psychological development in the future. It functions in the individual as well as in the species. Hence, "the collective psyche shows the same patterns of change as the psyche of the individual," and the individual can be used as a model for historical explanation.[61]

Jung argued that if a historian wishes to understand the past or anticipate the future he must penetrate the surface of history, "for the true historical event lies deeply buried, experienced by all and observed by none. It is the most private and most subjective of psychic experiences. Wars, dynasties, social upheavals, conquests, and religions are but the superficial symptoms of a secret psychic attitude unknown even to the individual himself, and transmitted by no historian."[62] Yet, the meaning of history need not be esoteric; it is quite possible to discover and interpret the subterranean processes that control historical time as long as we remember the law of psychological opposites. For just as the psyche of the individual operates according to the law of complementary opposites, so the inner processes of history follow the inexorable law of *enantiodromia*.

As early as 1928 Jung used this term, which he derived from the "cosmic fragments" of Heraclitus of Ephesus, to interpret the historical process. In his popular essay "The Spiritual Problem of Modern Man," for example, he suggested that "an intimation of the terrible law that governs blind contingency, which Heraclitus called the rule of *enantiodromia* (a running toward the opposite), now steals upon modern man through the by-ways of his mind."[63] This statement (which precedes the fully developed version of his theory of history by some twenty-three years) indicates that a decade after he had undergone his first individuation experience—the experience which actually marked the beginning of his career as an "analytical psychologist"—Jung had started constructing his philosophy of history. Yet although he had already begun by 1928 to use the concept of *enantiodromia* to explain the dialectic of history, Jung does not appear to have associated the rule of *enantiodromia* with the notion of successive aeon-cycles (each periodized by the appearance of a different symbol of the self) until the late '40s.

Now while the date of Jung's full-blown theory may be in question, it is also uncertain whether he actually acquired the concept of the reversal of opposites from Heraclitus or whether he simply found his notion of complementarity confirmed by the sixth- (and fifth-) century B.C. philosopher. At any rate, it is not an exaggeration to say that Heraclitus stands in the same relation to Jung as Empedocles does to Freud. Jung readily admits that his reading of Heraclitus assisted and inspired him in formulating his theory of history. In Jung's view, the law of *enantiodromia* can be satisfactorily described by a mandala—in particular, the circular symbol of the Yang and the Yin found in classical Chinese philosophy:

> Of these it is said that always when one principle reaches the height of its power, the counter-principle is stirring within it like a germ. This is another, particularly graphic formulation of the psychological law of compensation by an inner opposite. Whenever a civilization reaches its highest point, sooner or later a period of decay sets in. But the apparently meaningless and hopeless collapse into a disorder without aim or purpose, which fills the onlooker with disgust and despair, nevertheless contains within its darkness the germ of a new light.[64]

The processes of history, then, follow a circular course. There are periods of growth and decay, ebullience and disintegration. At the conclusion of a historical cycle, when hope has been dissolved by despair, the possibility of regeneration emerges from the darkness, for, as Berdyaev puts it, "stars shine through the night and dawn is coming."⁶⁵

This portrait of historical process could just as well have been drawn from observing the correspondence between human life, on the one hand, and nature, or the waxing and waning of the moon or sun, on the other, as it could have been from studying the behavior of mental patients. Yet Jung's theory of history—especially as it is developed in his later works, for instance, *Aion* (1951), *Answer to Job* (1952), and *Flying Saucers: A Modern Myth of Things Seen in the Skies* (1958)—represents an unusual formulation of the cyclical theory. Starting from analytical psychology, Jung interprets the meaning of history as a cyclical, or spiral, succession of self-images.

Approximately every two thousand years, Jung believes, the collective unconscious creates a new representation, or archetypal image, of the self. This periodic recasting of the principal archetype, which is accompanied by important changes in the structure of society, represents the commencement of a new aeon in the history of mankind. According to Jung the supercession of aeons is controlled by a psychological law—the dialectical law of *enantiodromia*—which imparts meaning to history and evidently preestablishes (without directly causing) the pattern of external historical events such as war and revolution or the rise and fall of civilizations. The core of meaning underlying the historical process is, therefore, psychological, or spiritual: it contains the code for the continuous reformulation and representation of the meaning of life to individuals. Since the archetype of wholeness is intrinsically immutable, and since every age demands a remolding of the meaning of the principal archetype, a re-creation of eternity, the self must appear to each successive epoch in a different actualized archetype, or symbol. The various historical embodiments of the self reflect the particular needs of an age and, consequently, should be used to distinguish historical periods.

Unabashedly borrowing from astrology, Jung maintained that each aeon was actually equivalent to a "Platonic month," or 2,150 years. Our own age, he wrote, "the Christian aeon of the Fishes," is "now running to its end."⁶⁶ It began with the appearance of Jesus of Nazareth (who, although he was human, was identified by his contemporaries as the Messiah) and coincided with the commencement of the astrological month of the Fishes. This complex parallelism in time was not fortuitous. Jesus (upon whom the archetypal notion of the Messiah was projected) became not only the harbinger of a new age, but the historical figure around whom the God-image (i.e., the mandala, or symbol of the self) crystallized into a new image of wholeness—an image destined to symbolize the highest spiritual aspirations of the West for over two millennia. Now, however, our aeon is swiftly

C. G. Jung

drawing to a close. This view is not based on dogma, for there are many current indications, of a psychological nature, that foreshadow the conclusion of our epoch. "As we know from ancient Egyptian history," Jung wrote, peculiar psychological phenomena, such as a widespread belief in flying saucers or Unidentified Flying Objects,

> are manifestations of psychic changes which always appear at the end of one Platonic month and at the beginning of another. Apparently they are changes in the constellation of psychic dominants, of the archetypes, or "gods" as they used to be called, which bring about, or accompany, long-lasting transformations of the collective psyche. This transformation started in the historical era and left its traces first in the passing of the aeon of Taurus into that of Aries, and then of Aries into Pisces, whose beginning coincides with the rise of Christianity. We are now nearing that great change which may be expected when the spring-point enters Aquarius.[67]

The coming historical transformation may prove to be more important than previous aeon-changes, for it contains the possibilities of spiritual rebirth and world peace. Like Berdyaev, Jung believed that although the modern period had virtually run its course, the present contained the potentiality of a new and regenerate aeon. He felt, however, that mankind would probably have to suffer through a period of darkness (analogous to Berdyaev's New Middle Ages) before this hope could be realized. Nevertheless, like his Russian contemporary, Jung believed that the future would see the rebirth of man.

As he implied in his 1951 study of the phenomenology of the self, Jung seems to have possessed confidence in the future of humanity even though he detested the materialistic and rationalistic tendencies of contemporary society. He steadfastly believed in the law of compensation and the regular succession of aeons. According to his interpretation, every aeon consists of two periods (symbolized in our own ages by the two zodiacal Fishes, Christ and Anti-Christ, or the motif of the hostile brothers): a generative or creative phase, in which the foundations of a new culture are established; and a destructive phase, in which the unifying symbol of an age loses its validity, thus plunging civilization into chaos (mental, social, political, economic) before a new symbol appears to restore order.

This thematic exposition of historical process bears a striking resemblance to Saint-Simon's differentiation of "critical" and "natural" ages. This prophet of Paris contended that after a period of organic growth, centrifugal forces appear which disrupt the cohesion of society. The confusion, however, which inevitably follows the disintegration of an "organic" period, does not last indefinitely. And upon assimilation of the disruptive elements that were responsible for destroying the equilibrium of the previous organic age, another natural period eventually establishes itself, resolving former contradictions into a new synthesis.

As presented here, this conception of temporal process is both pessimistic and optimistic: pessimistic because it entails the notion of immanent decline; optimistic because it presupposes the recrudescence of organic periods. And yet, implicit within the historical theories of both Jung and Saint-Simon is the belief, the fervent hope, in the possibility of ending the oscillating pattern of history and establishing a permanent (but dynamic) culture, or civilization. For Saint-Simon, this New Jerusalem resolves itself into a scientific state, or technocracy; for Jung, it suggests an age of individuation.

The Age of Fishes, like all previous aeons, began to disintegrate as it reached its midpoint (A.D. 1075). For it was at this pivotal juncture that the *enantiodromia* of our aeon occurred, inaugurating the second phase of the Aion of Pisces. The creative, or generative, phase of our aeon, characterized by the stability of an organic ethos, gradually began to wane. At first the process of deterioration was barely perceptible. But during the twelfth and thirteenth centuries, the initial effects of the countervailing thrust of our aeon made themselves explicit in a syndrome of religious fanatacism. The primary sources of this "religious inflation"—millenarian sects such as "the Cathari, Patarenes, Concorricci, Waldenses, Poor Men of Lyons, Beghards, Brethren of the Free Spirit, 'Bread through God'"—had "their visible beginnings . . . in the early years of the eleventh century."[68] But their impact was only felt later, especially during the next two centuries, when Europe developed many of the characteristics of a mass psychosis.

The great hero of this time of troubles was Joachim of Flora, who "unwittingly ushered in a new 'status,' a religious attitude that was destined to bridge and compensate the frightful gulf that had opened out between Christ and Antichrist in the eleventh century."[69] As Europe reeled under the impact of the reversal of opposites, Joachim, unconsciously and single-handedly, attempted to compensate for the psychological cleavage, or dissociation, besetting Western man. But it was Jung's opinion, and Berdyaev's also, that Joachim was ahead of his time. Yet it is not Joachim's fault that contemporary Europeans did not heed his message. On the contrary, "The antichristian era is to blame that the spirit [projected by Joachim] became non-spiritual and that the vitalizing archetype [of the spirit] gradually degenerated into rationalism, intellectualism, and doctrinairism, all of which leads straight to the tragedy of modern times now hanging over our heads like a sword of Damocles."[70] Europe lost a momentous opportunity when it repudiated the Calabrian monk and the archetype of creative spirituality

C. G. Jung

which he exemplified. The failure to absorb the teachings—the pneuma—
of Joachim of Flora precluded the possibility of stemming (or perhaps even
transmuting) the dialectic of the Aion of Pisces.

After the outburst of millenarian frenzy during the Middle Ages, the
next important step in the *enantiodromia* of our aeon occurred during the
Reformation. The schism with Rome, the destruction of Christian unity
(in the West), and the segregation of Europe into two armed camps added
to the disorientation of Western history and, viewed from the present, prefigured the schism between the two contempory superpowers, the Soviet
Union and the United States. When the dust of the Reformation's religious
wars had settled, Europe eventually experienced a period of pseudo-Enlight-
enment—false enlightenment because the excessive rationalism of the eighteenth century (tantamount, in Jung's view, to what the Greeks called
hubris) led to "the rationalistic and political psychosis that is the affliction
of our day."[71]

Today, as the aeon of the two Fishes rapidly approaches its end, the
"loss of roots and lack of tradition neuroticize the masses and prepare them
for collective hysteria." The rationalistic materialism of our age turns
human beings into machines, and states "into lunatic asylums." Yet, we
must not despair, for there are indications that the new aeon will be far
better than the past. "Naturally," however, "the present tendency to destroy
all tradition or render it unconscious could interrupt the normal process of
development for several hundred years and substitute an interlude of bar-
barism." But, "If, as seems probable, the aeon of the fishes is ruled by the
archetypal motif of the hostile brothers, then the approach of the next
Platonic month, namely Aquarius, will constellate the problem of the union
of opposites."[72]

Jung's implications are clear. The next aeon will probably be an age
of synthesis—that is to say, an age of individuation. Following the law of
compensation, the next age will reverse the deleterious trends of the current
cycle and prepare the way for a reconciliation of opposites. A new unifying
symbol (or image of the self) will appear and enable not only the exceptional individuals, but—and this is the staggering implication—the majority
of people living during the next two thousand years to achieve psychic
integration.

If this event ever comes to pass (and Jung is inclined to think that it
will), history will come to an end—unless, of course, the law of *enantiodromia* inaugurates a new historical cycle. But—and this is the quintessential
question—why should it? For if the collective psyche of mankind is integrated, the functioning of the law of compensation would cease to exist or,
at least, would operate only as a harmonious condition of a balanced psycho-

logical state. It would never function as a disruptive agency because every time it manifested itself, its "intention" would be known and accepted.

Thus, the motion (i.e., the flow of psychic energy) of the collective psyche of mankind would be eternally circular—the different dimensions of the psyche would intersect harmoniously. There would always be a mutual reciprocity between consciousness and unconsciousness; and the soul of humanity would correspond, as Plato would put it, to the circular motion of the moving image of eternity. The entire psyche of mankind—what Teilhard de Chardin would call the "noosphere"—would "constitute in its totality a sort of timeless and eternal world-image," an image which in its perfection would approximate the "uncomprehended absolute object." For those who live in the aeon of Aquarius, the past and future will cease to exist. And just as the collective unconscious possesses an absolute knowledge and subsists "in a timeless present,"[73] so the inhabitants of the new world will live in a nontemporal present—in what Norman O. Brown would call the way out of the struggle between Life and Death, *eros* and *thanatos*.

The conflict between unconsciousness and consciousness, between the ego and the self, as well as the conflict between the primary mental characteristics of man and woman, *logos* and *eros* (which, in a macrocosmic context, signify the eternal struggle between destruction and creation), will come to an end. The collective mind of humanity will have then reached a condition of being analogous to Father Teilhard's "point Omega" or Yeats's "phaseless sphere." Mankind will order its collective sensibility under the aspect of eternity and objectify itself in the form of a concrete image of eternity—a mandala—which will be the symbol of the new age.

This sketch of the implications of Jung's theory of history is admittedly conjectural. Unfortunately, he was as succinct in his descriptions of the future aeon as Marx was in his allusions to conditions in the classless society. Thus, it is impossible to say definitely whether Jung envisaged the Platonic month of Aquarius as the culminating point of history. For while his occasional references to the next aeon presuppose the probability of a reconciliation of the opposites in the collective psyche of mankind, his discussion of the causation of historical events does not preclude an eternal alteration between "critical" and "organic" stages.

The difficulty of ascertaining the exact intention of Jung's theory of history is compounded even further by the opaqueness of his later thought. Indeed, to borrow Winston Churchill's famous phrase, it often seems "a riddle wrapped in a mystery inside an enigma." The vagueness which surrounds Jung's later thought is limited not only to his notion of the Aion of Aquarius—the approaching, but evidently hypothetical, age of integration. It also obfuscates his conception of the relationship between the

C. G. Jung

cycles of historical time, on the one hand, and the archetypes of the collective unconscious and eternal reality (the "absolute uncomprehended object"), on the other.

This relationship warrants further analysis, for it not only sheds greater light on Jung's conception of historical "causation," or *enantiodromia,* but demonstrates the deeper implications of his theory of history as well as the manner in which he ultimately overcame the apparent meaninglessness of historical time. By first examining his conception of phylogenesis and ontogenesis in relation to the rule of *enantiodromia* and, second, by analyzing his conception of the causal role of the archetypes in effecting historical situations, it will be possible to dispel some of the ambiguities surrounding Jung's view of the relationship between (historical) time and timeless reality, or the absolute.

According to Jung, phylogenesis is recapitulated in ontogenesis—that is, the individual repeats the psychological history of the species in his own life-cycle. Just as the embryo passes through previous phases of biological evolution, so the human psyche retraces in its development the earlier psychological history of mankind. Jung supports this hypothesis, first, by observing the parallel between the mythopoeic mentality of the child and the world-view of primitive societies and, second, by pointing out that in its absence, it would be impossible to maintain the existence (which he assures us has been established by clinical observation) of archetypal images. Thus the pattern of childhood behavior and the process of archetypal configuration are necessarily linked together: both are intrinsic facts of human experience; and both are transmitted by heredity.

But what bearing does this have on Jung's theory of history? First of all, the phylogenetic foundation of ontogenesis presupposes the existence of a law governing the mental evolution of mankind. Just as there are biological laws that control the physical development of each human being, so there are laws that impose a pattern upon the growth of the individual psyche; just as there is a genetic code that determines heredity, so there is a psychological code that decides the general outline of a person's mental history. When this aspect of our psychological evolution is examined in connection with the fact of the periodic supercession of self-images, it is apparent not only that there is a universal code governing the inheritance of archetypal "possibilities" (in the individual as well as in the species), but also that there is a law that controls the changes in the representation of actualized archetypes themselves. These two interrelated codes, or laws (which are really two aspects of the same process), determine the psychological inheritance of people living today, as well as the archetypal configurations present in the collective mind of future ages.

[191]

The original formulation of both codes (i.e., the laws governing phylogenesis and ontogenesis as well as the rule of *enantiodromia,* which controls the succession of the aeons) derives from the "uncomprehended absolute object" which, although hidden behind the mask of the archetypes, "affects and influences" the course of history. Speaking as a loyal Jungian, Erich Neumann once said that the archetypes, "being essential components and organs of the psyche from the beginning, mold the course of human history."[74] While he would have concurred with his brilliant colleague, Jung might have added that the archetypes in themselves spring from a psychoid base (that is, from a form of being which is "commonly called spiritual"), which is itself the ultimate molder of history.[75] Taking account of Jung's later thought (especially as it is represented in his autobiography), it is impossible to doubt that he believed in an absolute which controlled human destiny through the archetypes of the collective unconscious. In *Answer to Job,* Jung imagined "God as an eternally flowing current of vital energy that endlessly changes shape."[76]

From the standpoint of analytical psychology, it is obvious that Jung understood the archetypes (in themselves and as they appear to us) to be the shapes, or forms, assumed by the eternally flowing current of spiritual energy. Thus, the archetypes are what Joseph Campbell has called them, *The Masks of God,* intermediaries between the divine and the human. They represent timeless reality to us and in us; they control the rites of passage through which every individual must pass; and they govern the cycles of the aeons. They are our end (in the sense that they contain the potentiality of individuation) and our beginning (in the sense that they supply us with the inherited wisdom of past generations).

As indicated earlier, terms such as "control" and "determine" present a problem in interpreting Jung's theory of history. He frequently uses these verbs to describe the functioning of the unconscious and the pattern of historical cycles. For instance, he often talks of "destiny" and "fate" affecting the life of the individual, and it is not impossible to find him describing contemporary changes in the psychic dominants, or archetypes, as the result of changes in the position of the symbols of the zodiac. But although he employed this terminology, Jung ultimately founded his conception of historical time upon an acausal theory of events.

The first experiences that eventually led Jung to formulate his concept of acausal occurrences date from his association with Freud. These experiences were of a telepathic nature and, in Jung's opinion, offered evidence which suggested that the psyche possessed depths that transcended time and space. Freud did his best to dissuade Jung, his intended scion, from pursuing his avid interest in telepathy. Freud not only wrote Jung cautioning letters but composed several essays repudiating the claims of parapsychology.[77] But Jung was not to be influenced, and from the mid 1920s on, he set himself the task of formulating an explanation for telepathic events.

Two external sources played significant roles in shaping Jung's concept of acausality. The first was the *I Ching,* or *Book of Changes* to which he had been introduced by Richard Wilhelm, the noted sinologist with whom he had collaborated in producing a commentary on the Taoist text *The Secret of the Golden Flower* (1929). The second was the research of J. B. Rhine. The Duke University psychologist's experiments with extrasensory perception and psychokinesis confirmed Jung's own suspicions about the psyche: namely, that the unconscious possesses an intrinsic ability to break through the space-time barrier of consciousness.[78] Jung thought that Rhine's experiments and his own experience demonstrated that "the psyche's attachment to the brain, i.e., its space-time limitation, is no longer as self evident and incontrovertible as we have hitherto been led to believe." In other words, the existence of ESP implies not only that the objective psyche operates according to its own nondirected "logic" (what Ernst Cassirer would call the "law of metamorphosis"), but that it actually transcends time and space and represents a substantially different form of being from that associated with consciousness.

Jung initially described the conclusions he drew from the ESP experiment with caution, yet the caution was intended to encourage belief:

> The fact that we are totally unable to imagine a form of existence without space and time by no means proves that such an existence is in itself impossible. And therefore, just as we cannot draw, from an appearance of space-timelessness, any absolute conclusion about a space-timeless form of existence, so we are not entitled to conclude from the apparent space-time quality of our perception that there is no form of existence without space and time. It is not only permissible to doubt the absolute validity of space-time perception; it is, in view of the available facts, even imperative to do so. The hpyothetical possibility that the psyche touches on a form of existence outside space and time presents a scientific question mark that merits serious consideration for a long time to come.[79]

In later years, this "hypothetical possibility" became a fundamental certainty of Jung's world-view. It is probably true that he was even convinced of the space-timelessness of the psyche. during his association with Freud. But, undoubtedly because his pronouncements were often greeted with scepticism, he remained reluctant to express his belief in the existence of "occult" phenomena. This is not to say that he refrained from developing the implications of telepathy. On the contrary, his own encounters with supra-normal phenomena—as well as his keen interest in Rhine's research—kindled, rather than diminished, his enthusiasm. And over the succeeding years, Jung not only continued to collect parapsychological data, but persisted in his search for a model that could be used to explain the nature of telepathic events.

He was aided in this search by his discovery of the *I Ching,* or *Book of Changes.* From his acceptance of the existence of ESP, Jung had concluded that the objective psyche is timeless and spaceless. Now, from his interpretation of the *Book of Changes,* Jung decided that telepathic events represent significant (as opposed to chance) occurrences in time. He was particularly struck by the method which the authors of the ancient Chinese text had developed for establishing an apparently meaningful correspondence between a given mental state and the configuration of an external object or objects (e.g., coins or yarrow stalks). Upon analysis of various telepathic events, Jung discovered that the parallelism in time of meaning and external situation, which he had previously encountered in the *I Ching,* also adhered between different samples of parapsychological occurrences. The outstanding feature of both the events produced by the "mantic" method of the *I Ching* and the events collected from Jung's research was that while they appeared to be meaningful, they could not be related causally. Two events (or sets of events) which existed simultaneously were found to coincide as a consequence of their equivalence in meaning although they stood in an acausal relationship to each other.

Jung sought to explore the full implications of this puzzling phenomenon in two of his later and (from our standpoint) most significant essays: "Synchronicity: An Acausal Connecting Principle" (1952) and "On Synchronicity" (1951). From his observations and empirical research (especially his astrological experiment),[80] Jung formulated his concept of "synchronicity" to designate "the parallelism of time and meaning between psychic and psychophysical events, which scientific knowledge so far has been unable to reduce to a common principle." Actually, "the term [synchronicity] explains nothing, it simply formulates the occurrence of meaningful coincidences which, in themselves" cannot be explained by temporal, spatial, or causal categories.[81] Synchronistic events are not synchronous—that is, they are not simply simultaneous occurrences. They possess a common meaning, which is perceived as a consequence of their parallelism in time. So far, synchronistic events appear to fall under three rubrics:

1. The coincidence of a psychic state in the observer with a simultaneous, objective, external event that corresponds to the psychic state or content . . . where there is no evidence of a causal

connection between the psychic state and the external event, and where, considering the psychic relativity of space and time, such a connection is not even conceivable.

2. The coincidence of a psychic state with a corresponding (more or less simultaneous) external event taking place outside the observer's field of perception, i.e., at a distance, and only verifiable afterward. . . .

3. The coincidence of a psychic state with a corresponding, not yet existent future event that is distant in time and can likewise only be verified afterward.[82]

From each of these categories Jung adduced examples which repeatedly demonstrate the impossibility either of dismissing synchronistic events as chance occurrences or of reducing them to causal explanations. Again and again, the coincidence in time of a "psychic state" (i.e., an archetype) and an objective situation is found to be meaningful—not fortuitous—and acausal. Jung continually maintains that since his own experience and observation (as well as the results of Rhine's experiments) have conclusively "shown that under certain conditions space and time can be reduced almost to zero, causality disappears along with them, because causality is bound up with the existence of space and time and physical changes, and consists essentially in the succession of cause and effect." Thus, for this reason, "synchronistic phenomena cannot in principle be associated with any conception of causality."[83]

The constant discovery of significant conjunctions between archetypes and external occurrences ultimately compelled Jung to attribute to the unconscious an immediate perception, or absolute foreknowledge, of events. In turn, this timeless knowledge of future events convinced Jung that the human psyche actually does touch on a form of existence outside time and space. Jung concluded that whereas extrasensory perception proves the space-timelessness of the objective psyche, synchronicity establishes the psyche's ability to perceive manifestations of a realm of being beyond space, time, and causality. This other, or trans-temporal, form of being (upon which the antipodes of the collective unconscious are rooted) itself possesses a foreknowledge of events (which, Jung implies, it transmits to the unconscious), as well as an ability to effect the temporal world (a feat it evidently accomplishes through the archetypes). Synchronistic events are, thus, projections of this eternal order of being, manifestations of eternity in time. They are causeless events which must be regarded "as *creative acts*"—i.e., "as the continuous creation of a pattern that exists from all eternity, repeats itself sporadically, and is not derivable from any known antecedents."[84] The existence of synchronistic, or parapsychological, coincidences, in other words, forces us to "face the fact that our world, with its time, space, and causality, relates to another order of things lying behind or beneath it, in which neither 'here and there' nor 'earlier and later' are of importance."[85]

We are compelled to recognize that there is an "uncomprehended absolute object" which, operating through the archetypes of the collective unconscious, "affects and influences us." And yet, this causeless order, or "pattern / Of timeless moments," affects and influences us in a noncausal manner: it makes us aware of eternity by manifesting itself in series of acausal events. This is true even when it preestablishes the harmonious succession of aeons. For, to return to the problem of the causation of historical cycles, aeons neither are caused nor are themselves causes. The appearance of a new self-image (for example, the anthropos, or the two fishes) does not cause the appearance of a world historical figure such as Jesus (Christ the Redeemer). It simply coincides in a meaningful, yet acausal, relationship to a specific historical situation, condition, or object (in the case of our own aeon, Jesus of Nazareth). The point that Jung wishes to make is that while an aeon does not cause things to happen, it contains within it a pattern of preestablished possibilities—a pattern which is itself preestablished by the "uncomprehended absolute object."

Everything that occurs, then, necessarily develops according to the paradigm—or, to use an Aristotelian metaphor, specific form—of possible development contained within the preestablished structure of each aeon. Aeons are, thus, synchronistic events on a cosmic scale. They do not cause things, but events coincide significantly within them. Of course, space, time, and causality function during an aeon; they are ontological conditions of the physical world. But alongside time, space, and causality stands synchronicity. Together these four dimensions compose a quaternity symbol, or mandala, signifying the immanence of eternity in time and the possibility of transforming time into eternity, which transmits (yet not causally) a transcendental scheme upon history.[86]

In his description of synchronicity, Jung is proposing a reformulation of the old "concept of correspondence, sympathy, and harmony"—of "Leibnitz' idea of pre-established harmony" which he believed was "based not on philosophical assumptions but on empirical experience and experimentation."[87] In other words, Jung thought that he had proved the existence of eternity—which he had experienced directly during his 1944 visions—on the basis of the scientific method. Eternity is, thus, not only the final cause of an individual's life, it is the final cause of science.

EPILOGUE

The men I selected for study were all born in the nineteenth century, in what William Inge, dean of St. Paul's, called "the most wonderful century in human history, . . . the age of hope" (1922).[1] Yet while they were still young or had just reached middle age, the Great War abruptly ended the Pax Victoriana and ushered in an age of disappointment, shattering "the mould in which the Victorian age cast its hope": the idea of Progress. To Dean Inge, as well as to my antitemporalist quartet, the conclusion was inescapable: "We have no [secular] millennium to look forward to." "Our apocalyptic dream is vanishing into thin air."[2] The loss or abridgement of the idea of Progress, both during and after the war, was an especially harsh blow, for that notion had provided a measure of cohesiveness, giving the nineteenth century the semblance of what Saint-Simon called an "organic age."

According to Saint-Simon and his followers, climates of opinion fall into one of two categories: the "organic" (or "natural") and the "critical." Following this view, the high Middle Ages was an organic age because it presupposed a common faith and dogma. In contrast the Scientific Revolution was a critical age because it questioned earlier metaphysical assumptions and, in the end, subverted both the conception of the closed organic universe and the principles of hierarchy and plenitude. Yet the intellectual confusion left in the wake of the collapse of the Middle Ages was not permanent. For just as Aquinas had achieved a synthesis of faith and reason in the thirteen century, so Newton, in his turn, created a new "organic" world view at the end of the seventeenth century. The mechanistic analogies drawn from the Newtonian synthesis proved remarkably disruptive, however, when employed by political thinkers of the eighteenth and nineteenth centuries.

At first, Newton's "world machine" gave the appearance of harmonious perfection ("From harmony, from heavenly harmony / This universal frame began"), but when the "covering metaphors" of mechanistic materialism (to which Newton gave final cosmological formulation) were incorporated into political and social theories that were used to advance (or retard) social change, the result was anything but harmonious. And when the idea of

Epilogue

ceaseless change, or becoming, was extracted from the common assumptions of mechanistic materialism in the late eighteenth and nineteenth centuries, the "organic" unity that Newton's synthesis had provided the Enlightenment erupted into a multitude of often conflicting "isms": e.g., utilitarianism, romanticism, socialism, nationalism, positivism, idealism, Darwinism, and vitalism.

This development disquieted some intellectuals who, like Matthew Arnold, noting the apparent anarchy in late nineteenth-century thought, lamented the loss of "certitude" that inevitably accompanied the "long withdrawing roar" of "The Sea of Faith":

And we are here as on a darkling plain,
Swept with confused alarms of struggle and flight,
Where ignorant armies clash by night.
[*Dover Beach*, 1867]

Although Arnold was not lamenting the disintegration of the unity that the Newtonian synthesis had imposed upon all branches of thought during the Enlightenment, his threnody for faith captures the bewilderment of a growing number of intellectuals who confronted the "multitudinousness" of late nineteenth-century thought. And yet there is a sense in which the nineteenth century can claim to be an organic, rather than a critical, age. For while important (and often combative) differences separate the various ideologies, there is undeniably a central theme underlying these conflicting strands of nineteenth-century thought. And that theme, of course, is the idea of Progress, "the mould in which the Victorian age cast its hope." It provided a focus, a center, around which most—I do not say all—nineteenth-century "post-theologies," or substitute religions, could arrange themselves in a coherent fashion. Indeed, Progress became (to borrow F. M. Cornford's phrase) part of the "unwritten philosophy" of the century. It was an unconsciously held presupposition which one absorbed from the cultural atmosphere.

With the advent of the Great War, however, matters changed quickly, and that semblance of order vanished with the political collapse of Europe. For those thinking men and women who had been nurtured on the sceptical tradition or who had lost their religious faith there seemed to be nothing left. The assumptions of optimistic secularism—the belief in man's innate goodness and rationality, as well as the doctrine of the inexorable moral and physical improvement of the human condition—appeared to be entirely thrown over by the most horrific war in Europe's history. In Yeats's words, "Things fall apart; the centre cannot hold." For many intellectuals the Age of Hope was irretrievably smashed. Like Donne's world three hundred years before, it was

> . . . all in peeces, all cohaerence gone;
> All just supply, and all Relation
> [*The First Anniversay,* 1611]

It is against this desolate background that Berdyaev, Eliot, Huxley, and Jung began their quest for transcendental meaning, their valiant attempt to create a new "organic" age. The challenge they faced in the most "critical" age in the history of the West was enormous, and it is remarkable that they were able to persevere to the end. In an ironic age of cynical disbelief and longing, it is amazing that they did not succumb to "despairing secularism," that they did not acquiesce in the face of overwhelming odds and abandon their search for absolute values and timeless meaning. They are also remarkable in that they did not immerse themselves in postwar decadence. Although aware, for instance, of the Dada movement, the dandies, and the Expressionists, they were not swayed from their own spiritual voyages until they had discovered a new center of their own being, firmly established on the foundations of a painfully gained religious truth. They were never members of a "lost generation." They rejected nihilism and secularism and repudiated Nietzsche's maxim that "God is dead." And from their explorations of myth and symbol, from their conversions to a religious perspective, they found their commitment to humanity.

Their conversions inevitably led them out of solipsism and despair toward a social concern, toward an affirmation of the value of humanity and a determination to rebuild Europe on spiritual foundations. In their quest for a spiritual explanation of life, the quartet discovered that the ugliness of modern civilization (symbolized, in particular, by the factory and the industrial metropolis—i.e., by the death of Nature) had cut them off from Being, the permanent and unshakable foundations of timeless Reality. They realized that rationalistic modes of thought had distorted their conception of truth, that the progress of science and technology had uprooted them from the ground of Being. Although Heidegger's interpretation of Being may be different from theirs, they would have agreed that the modern world has experienced a forgetfulness of Being *(Seinsvergessenheit)* and that the future of humanity—as well as the possibility of creating a new "organic" age—depends upon our relearning the "forgotten language" of Being, God, or the timeless Ground. Without contact with eternity we are destined to destroy ourselves.

While unsuccessful in reintegrating the drifting culture of the West, Berdyaev, Eliot, Huxley, and Jung were able to revolt against secularism and to transcend the hollow doctrines of linear time which they inherited as part of the "unwritten philosophy" of the nineteenth century. They were successful against formidable odds. But does their achievement mark the culmination of the twentieth-century revolt against time, or will it continue to flourish?

Until new symbolic forms are created (or until man learns to objectify all his concepts of time in nonpictorial symbols), I am convinced that the vast majority of human beings will continue to express their notion of psychological, or subjective, time in spatial patterns. Perhaps if our language did not contain words expressing the notion of time (e.g., mutability, succession, change, motion, becoming), we would not try to compensate for the irreversible fact of death (the end of one's life*time*) by attempting to order, control, and eliminate the temporal process with nondiscursive or mythological symbols. The epistemological function of time-symbols obviously fulfills a crucial and enduring psychological need: it enables human beings to order their temporal realities, to impose (and, therefore, to discover) a significant or meaningful pattern (gestalt) upon historical time, and—in many cases— to destroy the harbinger of death: the process of temporal decay itself.

Yet given the enduring use of spatial symbols to conquer time, will the twentieth-century revolt against time—and not simply the mutability tradition (for, after all, men can lament the fact of temporal decay without seeking to destroy time)—will this revolt continue to be an important current of twentieth-century thought? The Swedish historian of ancient Greek religions Martin P. Nilsson has interpreted religion as mankind's refusal to accept the meaninglessness of events. And surely men will continue to protest against the absurdity of temporal corruption through their institutionalized religions, private mythologies, or heroic defiance. But will a significant number of twentieth-century intellectuals continue to identify their attack on time with an attack on Western civilization? Will they follow the lead of Berdyaev, Eliot, Huxley, and Jung; of Wyndham Lewis, C. S. Lewis, James Joyce, Charles Williams, W. B. Yeats, W. H. Auden, E. M. Cioran, the later writings of Edmund Husserl,[3] and (insofar as they attack chronological time as a symptom of the modern malady) Virginia Woolf, Marcel Proust, Lawrence Durrell, Hermann Broch, D. H. Lawrence, and Martin Heidegger? Will intellectuals still be attracted by the diagnoses and proffered spiritual nostrums of Simone Weil, Ananda Coomaraswamy, Romain Rolland, May Sinclair, René Guénon, Dorothy Sayers, and Hermann Hesse? Or, like Teilhard de Chardin, Karl Barth, Léon Bloy, Karl Heim, and many Continental theologians, will they continue to insist that man's destiny cannot be anchored to temporal civilization—to the nightmarish dimension of modern history—or to the historical process itself? Will intellectuals con-

Epilogue

tinue to repudiate time-philosophy, especially what Dean Inge called the "superstitious belief in the automatic progress of humanity," and demand a massive spiritual reorienation of Western culture?

The answer may not be as obvious as it seems. But until Western intellectuals lose their sense of anomie and alienation and once again find meaningful roots in their culture, it appears that this century will see more "men and women against time." Indeed, the enduring interest in Eastern and Western mysticism (either traditional or innovative—for instance, Norman O. Brown's body-mysticism or Theodore Roszak's neoshamanism), the widespread use of drugs which distort or eliminate time-consciousness, and the lasting popularity of the occult indicate quite clearly that many people in the West (and not simply the intellectuals) are interested in finding a release from the pressures of time and the burden of history. Critics may lament this rise in irrationalism and deplore the archaic content of modern thought as an alarming and extremely dangerous element in contemporary culture. But until domestic and international tensions can be resolved—until, some would argue, the decline of the West can be reversed—men and women who feel especially powerless to end the conflicts of history are going to revolt against time.

If one assumes, as I do, that man is "a symbolizing, conceptualizing, meaning-seeking animal which . . . cannot live in a world it cannot understand,"[4] then it is logical to assume that people who are no longer willing to accept "the triumph of becoming" "with all its implications"—relativism (if not nihilism), the erosion of being, and the eclipse of eternity—are going to continue to explore ways of recapturing a view of life under the aspect of eternity *(sub specie aeternitatis)*. If the shape of Western civilization changes dramatically, if there is a widespread rediscovery of Eternity and Being and a concomitant cessation of the dehumanizing trends of Western society, then—and perhaps only then—will the revolt against time lose its intensity and purpose. Perhaps Berdyaev was right: we are living in the dark shadow of a catastrophic New Middle Age; but "stars shine through the night and dawn is coming."

NOTES

The Twentieth-Century Revolt against Time

1. Sir Walter Raleigh (?), "Even Such Is Time," in Norman Ault, *Elizabethan Lyrics* (New York: Capricorn Books, 1960), p. 489.
2. J. T. Fraser (ed., *The Voices of Time* [New York: George Braziller, 1966]) recently stressed this point in a letter to the author (17 March 1980): "The kind of revolt against the becoming aspect of time, which you so clearly identify in literature, has its twin revolt in contemporary science, especially in physics. The whole of Relativity Theory may be described as a spatialization and hence, the negation of creative time."
3. See J. A. Gunn, *The Problem of Time* (London: George Allen and Unwin, 1929), p. 173; and Hans Meyerhoff, *Time in Literature* (Berkeley: University of California Press, 1955), pp. 1–26.
4. Cf. H. G. Alexander, *Time as Dimension and History* (Albuquerque: University of New Mexico Press, 1945), p. 13.
5. Milič Čapek, *The Philosophical Impact of Contemporary Physics* (New York: D. Van Nostrand, 1961), p. 162.
6. Henri Bergson appears to have been the first to criticize "the fallacy of spatialization" in his *Essai sur les données de la conscience*. The essay (which was formulated and written between 1883 and 1887) was originally published in 1889; an English edition (*Time and Free Will*) appeared in 1910. Other works worth consulting on the problem of "spatialization" are: Ernst Cassirer, *The Philosophy of Symbolic Forms* and *Essay on Man;* Susanne Langer, *Philosophy in a New Key;* John Gunnell, *Political Philosophy and Time;* C. G. Jung's essays on mandala symbolism in *The Archetypes and the Collective Unconscious;* Carl Hentze, *Mythes et symboles lunaires;* Alfonso Ortiz, *The Tewa World;* Mircea Eliade, *Cosmos and History;* F. M. Cornford, *From Religion to Philosophy;* Heinrich Zimmer, *Myths and Symbols in Indian Art; Man and Time,* ed. J. Campbell; Erwin Panofsky, *Studies in Iconology;* Ananda Coomaraswamy, *The Dance of Shiva;* and M. H. Nicolson, *Breaking of the Circle.*
7. T. S. Eliot, *The Complete Poems and Plays, 1909–1950* (New York: Harcourt, Brace, 1952), pp. 124, 96.
8. For Berdyaev "cosmic time" represents the cyclical time of the physical uni-

verse; "historical time," on the other hand, is synonymous with the divine-
human drama which—as a finite series of unique events—unfolds as a linear
(and dialectical) progression. Finally, "existential time" designates the nontemporal time or period of world history (viz., the Age of the Spirit, which
is symbolized by a point) that precedes the final destruction of the time-
process.

9. Eliot, *Complete Poems and Plays,* p. 144.
10. Aldous Huxley, *Island* (New York: Bantam, 1965), pp. 170–73.
11. Williams James, *The Varieties of Religious Experience* (New York: Mentor,
1961), pp. 292–93.
12. *Ibid.,* p. 293.
13. Eliot, *Complete Poems and Plays,* p. 119.
14. Aldous Huxley, *The Perennial Philosophy* (New York: Harper, 1944), p.
165; *Collected Essays* (New York: Bantam, 1960), p. 233.
15. Nicolas Berdyaev, *The Beginning and the End,* trans. R. M. French (London: Geoffrey Bles, 1952), p. 177.
16. C. G. Jung, *Memories, Dreams, Reflections,* trans. Richard and Clara Winston (New York: Pantheon, 1963), pp. 295–96.
17. R. C. Zaehner, *Mysticism: Sacred and Profane* (New York: Oxford University Press, 1961), p. 30.
18. According to Professor Rhine, the existence of extrasensory modes of perception—which, he assures us, has been established by reliable experimentation—such as clairvoyance, precognition, telepathy, and intuition proves
unequivocally that part of man's nature is nonphysical. Man's ability to
anticipate or predict events, to perceive distant states of affairs spontaneously,
and to know the thoughts of others intuitively means that the human mind
transcends "the organic functions of the material brain." Rhine goes farther,
however, and posits not only the existence of a "psychical oversoul" but the
probability of immortality. The discovery that ESP can "function without
limitation from time and space" is "taken to mean that the mind is capable
of action independent to some degree of the space-time system of nature.
Now"—and this is Rhine's conclusion—since "all that immortality means is
freedom from the effects of space and time," it follows "as a logical deriva-
tion from the ESP research" that "there is at least some sort of technical
survival" after death (J. B. Rhine, *The Reach of the Mind* [New York:
William Sloane, 1962], pp. 206, 211, 213).
19. Jung, *Memories, Dreams, Reflections,* p. 296.
20. Owen Chadwick, *The Secularization of the European Mind in the Nineteenth Century* (Cambridge: Cambridge University Press, 1975), pp. 17–18.
21. *Ibid.,* p. 11.
22. Examples of this attitude can be found in nineteenth-century thought (for

instance, in the work of Schopenhauer). But the few nineteenth-century intellectuals who may qualify as "rebels against time" (in the sense that the term is used above) are not representative of any major pattern of nineteenth-century opinion. Indeed, they (as opposed to Berdyaev, Eliot, Huxley, and Jung, as well as the many other twentieth-century intellectuals who share their hostility to time) often appear to be isolated from the main currents of contemporary thought. Furthermore, it should be noted that even the ("non-Heglian") Idealists, who flourished in the 1890s and early years of the twentieth century, did not aim their attack on time against nineteenth-(or twentieth-) century culture. Nor, for that matter, did the Theosophists or, apparently, the members of the Society for Psychical Research. For while they may have been interested in mysticism, in communing with supernatural powers, they did not interpret their desire to transcend time as a repudiation of the presuppositions of the "bourgeois century." On the contrary, as Carlton Hayes has pointed out, the program of the Theosophical Society represented but one of "many different ways of being enlightened and progressive" (*A Generation of Materialism,* p. 332).

23. Franklin Baumer, *Modern European Thought: Continuity and Change in Ideas, 1600–1950* (New York: Macmillan, 1977), p. 20.

24. Maurice Nicoll, *Living Time,* cited in J. B. Priestly, *Man and Time* (New York: Dell, 1968), p. 309. Nicoll also equates *"Now"* with "the sense of higher space."

25. Franklin Baumer, "Twentieth-Century Version of the Apocalypse," *Cahiers d' histoire mondiale (Journal of World History)* 1, no. 3 (January 1954): 623–40; see also Franklin Baumer, *Religion and the Rise of Scepticism* (New York: Harcourt, Brace, and World, 1960), pp. 12, 261.

26. Hayden White, "The Burden of History," *Tropics of Discourse* (Baltimore: Johns Hopkins University Press, 1978), pp. 27–50. History was also attacked (although sometimes indirectly) for preserving decadent traditions: see Filippo Marinetti, *Futuristic Manifesto* (1909), and Tristan Tzara, *Dada Manifesto* (1918). André Breton also attacked history, especially when it was defined as (scientific) progress, for he believed that the doctrine of progress presupposed the suppression of dream and fantasy (*What Is Surrealism?* [1936]).

27. Carlton J. H. Hayes, *A Generation of Materialism* (New York: Harper Torchbook, 1963), p. 328.

28. W. W. Wagar, *Good Tidings: The Belief in Progress from Darwin to Marcuse* (Bloomington: Indiana University Press, 1972), pp. 23–28.

29. "Positivism" refers to what H. Stuart Hughes would call the philosophical side of materialism—that is, a form of thinking characterized by the use of analogies drawn from both Newtonian mechanics and Darwinian biology.

One of the earliest discussions of the revolt against positivism is found in Alfred Fouillée, *Le Mouvement idéaliste et la réaction contre la science positive* (Paris: Germer Bailliere, 1896). For further discussion of the revolt, see Baumer, *Modern European Thought,* pp. 371–78; Wagar, *Good Tidings,* p. 27; and H. Stuart Hughes, *Consciousness and Society* (New York: Vintage, 1958), pp. 59, 47.

30. Hughes, *Consciousness and Society,* pp. 59, 47.
31. F. M. Cornford, "The Poems of George Meredith," *Supplement to the Working Men's College* (a lecture delivered 21 March 1903), pp. 10, 118.
32. Hayes, *Generation of Materialism,* p. 332.
33. For a discussion of the growing uncertainty about the condition of Western civilization in late nineteenth-century thought see Franklin Baumer, *Main Currents of Western Thought* (New York: Knopf, 1970), pp. 451–59, *Modern European Thought,* pp. 389–400; Richard Altick, *Victorian People and Ideas* (New York: W. W. Norton, 1973), pp. 107–13. I should note here my agreement with Warren Wagar that Europeans continued to believe in the vitality of their civilization until the First World War (Wagar, *Good Tidings,* pp. 22–28).

NICOLAS BERDYAEV

1. Nicolas Berdyaev, *The Beginning and the End,* trans. R. M. French (London: Geoffrey Bles, 1952), p. v.
2. *Ibid.,* p. 209.
3. Nicolas Berdyaev, *Dream and Reality,* trans. K. Lampert (London: Geoffrey Bles, 1950), pp. x, 296.
4. Nicolas Berdyaev, *Slavery and Freedom,* trans. R. M. French (London: Geoffrey Bles, 1944), p. 258; Nicolas Berdyaev, *The Destiny of Man,* trans. Natalie Duddington (London: Geoffrey Bles, 1959), p. 295.
5. *Beginning and the End,* p. 229; *Dream and Reality,* p. 294.
6. *Slavery and Freedom,* p. 257.
7. *Dream and Reality,* p. 294; *Slavery and Freedom,* p. 267.
8. *Dream and Reality,* p. 291.
9. *Ibid.,* p. 2.
10. *Ibid.,* pp. 86–87.
11. *Ibid.,* pp. 78, 80, 79.
12. *Ibid.,* pp. 79, 80.
13. *Ibid.,* pp. 115, 116.
14. *Ibid.,* pp. 115, 118.
15. It is true that Berdyaev read Hegel before Marx, but even though Berdyaev's "three-ages" scheme of history (analogous to the unconscious, con-

scious, and self-conscious stages of the Absolute in Hegel's dialectic) may have been influenced by the German philosopher, it appears that Marx's philosophy of history captured Berdyaev's imagination before Hegel's did. In any event, it was not until Berdyaev had had his initial "encounter with Marxism" that he began to shift his philosophical allegiance to Hegel and German idealism.

16. *Dream and Reality,* p. 123.
17. Nicolas Berdyaev, *The Russian Idea,* trans. R. M. French (Boston: Beacon Press, 1962), p. 250.
18. *Dream and Reality,* pp. 91–92.
19. *Ibid.,* pp. 91–92, 122.
20. *Ibid.,* pp. 124–25, 126.
21. *Ibid.,* p. 125.
22. *Ibid.,* p. 133.
23. *Ibid.,* p. 134.
24. *Ibid.,* pp. 127–28.
25. Donald Lowrie, *Rebellious Prophet* (New York: Harper, 1960) p. 81.
26. Will Herberg, *Four Existentialist Theologians* (New York: Anchor, 1958), p. 100.
27. *Dream and Reality,* p. 141.
28. Lowrie, *Rebellious Prophet,* p. 82.
29. *Ibid.,* p. 84.
30. *Dream and Reality,* p. 153.
31. *Ibid.,* p. 176.
32. *Ibid.,* p. 175.
33. *Ibid.,* p. 174.
34. *Ibid.,* p. 226.
35. *Ibid.,* p. 225.
36. *Ibid.,* p. 250.
37. For an account of the debates at Meudon and Clamart (the homes of Maritain and Berdyaev, respectively) see Julie Kernan, *Our Friend, Jacques Maritain: A Personal Memoir* (Garden City, N.Y.: Doubleday, 1975), pp. 67, 82.
38. *Dream and Reality,* p. 268.
39. Nicolas Berdyaev, *Truth and Revelation,* trans. R. M. French (London: Geoffrey Bles, 1953), p. 90.
40. *Ibid.,* pp. 274, 275; see also Kernan, *Our Friend, Jacques Maritain,* p. 78.
41. *Dream and Reality,* p. 325.
42. *Ibid.,* p. x.
43. Nicolas Berdyaev, *The Fate of Man in the Modern World,* trans. Donald A. Lowrie (Ann Arbor: University of Michigan Press, 1961), p. 34.

44. *Beginning and the End,* p. 241.
45. *Ibid.,* pp. 244, 245, 247; *Dream and Reality,* p. 296.
46. Nicolas Berdyaev, *The Divine and the Human,* trans. R. M. French (London: Geoffrey Bles, 1949), p. 112.
47. *Fate of Man in the Modern World,* p. 28; *Beginning and the End,* p. 172.
48. *Dream and Reality,* p. 45.
49. Herberg, *Four Existentialist Theologians,* p. 7.
50. *Dream and Reality,* p. 286.
51. Herberg, *Four Existentialist Theologians,* pp. 6–7.
52. *Beginning and the End,* p. 97; *Dream and Reality,* p. 113.
53. *Beginning and the End,* p. 40.
54. Berdyaev considered other "religious existentialists," especially the neo-Thomists, guilty of "ontologism," While he consistently maintained that "ontology should be replaced by pneumatology" (*Beginning and the End,* p. 96), they stressed the *kataphatic* doctrine which defines God in terms of pure being, or act—a concept Berdyaev believed was "merely a product of hypostatized existence" (p. 97) and was opposed to the proper *apophatic* description of God as *supra*-being.
55. *Destiny of Man,* pp. 290, 291.
56. *Ibid.,* p. 290.
57. *Dream and Reality,* p. 210.
58. Nicolas Berdyaev, *The Meaning of the Creative Act,* trans. Donald Lowrie (New York: Collier, 1962), pp. 12, 11.
59. *Dream and Reality,* p. 209.
60. Evidently Berdyaev had not read Freud or Jung when he wrote *The Meaning of the Creative Act,* but he became acquainted with their works during the interwar years. And when he returned to the problem of creativity in *Dream and Reality* and *The Beginning and the End,* he was definitely aware of their respective concepts of mind.
61. *Beginning and the End,* p. 176.
62. *Ibid.,* pp. 209–10.
63. *Ibid.,* p. 177.
64. *Ibid.,* p. 210.
65. *Dream and Reality,* p. 83.
66. Nicolas Berdyaev, *The Meaning of History,* trans. George Reavy (Cleveland: Living Age Books, 1962), p. 58.
67. *Divine and the Human,* p. 200.
68. *Beginning and the End,* p. 185.
69. *Ibid.,* p. 174.
70. *Ibid.,* p. 185.
71. *Meaning of the Creative Act,* p. 97.

72. *Beginning and the End*, pp. 177, 187.
73. *Slavery and Freedom*, p. 261.
74. *Meaning of the Creative Act*, p. 97; *Divine and the Human*, p. 198.
75. *Dream and Reality*, p. 216.
76. *Ibid.*
77. *Divine and the Human*, p. 191.
78. *Ibid.*, p. 190.
79. *Slavery and Freedom*, pp. 60, 69.
80. *Ibid.*, pp. 210, 218.
81. *Meaning of History*, p. 172.
82. *Ibid.*, p. 165.
83. *Dream and Reality*, p. 294.
84. *Meaning of History*, p. 173.
85. *Dream and Reality*, p. 211.
86. *Ibid.*, p. 220.
87. *Beginning and the End*, p. 181.
88. *Meaning of the Creative Act*, p. 298.
89. *Dream and Reality*, p. 63.
90. *Ibid.*, pp. 112, 158.
91. *Ibid.*, p. 137.
92. *Slavery and Freedom*, p. 267.
93. *Beginning and the End*, pp. 198, 209, 200, 213, 208.
94. *Ibid.*, p. 208.
95. *Meaning of History*, p. 31.
96. *Dream and Reality*, p. 181.
97. *Meaning of History*, pp. 55, 62.
98. *Beginning and the End*, p. 239.
99. *Destiny of Man*, p. 285.
100. Eliade, *Cosmos and History*, pp. 58, 76–77.
101. *Beginning and the End*, p. 199, 198.
102. *Ibid.*, p. 200.
103. *Ibid.*, p. vi.
104. *Destiny of Man*, p. 290.
105. *Dream and Reality*, p. 294.
106. *Fate of Man in the Modern World*, p. 8.
107. *Dream and Reality*, p. 296.
108. *Ibid.*, p. 295.
109. *Meaning of History*, p. 11.
110. Walter Horton, *Contemporary Continental Theology* (New York: Harper, 1938), p. 140.

111. Rudolf Bultmann, *History and Eschatology* (Edinburgh: Edinburgh University Press, 1957), pp. 152–53.
112. Erich Frank, cited in *ibid.*, p. 153.
113. *Beginning and the End*, p. 183.
114. Baumer, "Twentieth-Century Version of the Apocalypse," pp. 623–40.
115. *Dream and Reality*, pp. 290, 295; *Meaning of History*, p. 18.
116. *Meaning of History*, p. 11.
117. *Dream and Reality*, p. 290.
118. Baumer, *Religion and the Rise of Scepticism*, p. 12.
119. *Meaning of History*, p. 180.
120. *Ibid.*, p. 188.
121. Nicolas Berdyaev, *The End of Our Time*, trans. Donald Atwater (London: Sheed and Ward, 1934), p. 69.
122. *Ibid.*
123. *Meaning of the Creative Act*, p. 86.
124. *Ibid.*, p. 87.
125. *Dream and Reality*, p. 22.
126. *Ibid.*, p. 29.
127. *Ibid.*, p. 294; *Slavery and Freedom*, p. 258.
128. *Dream and Reality*, pp. 298, 294, 296.
129. *Ibid.*, pp. 28, 42, 29, 30.
130. *Ibid.*, pp. 45–46.
131. *Beginning and the End*, p. 211.
132. *Ibid.*, p. 209.
133. *Divine and the Human*, p. 186.
134. *Ibid.*, pp. 186, 193.
135. *Beginning and the End*, pp. 232–33.
136. Karl Löwith, *Meaning in History* (Chicago: University of Chicago Press, 1958), p. 148. It is interesting to note that, like Berdyaev, Spengler was strongly influenced by Joachim; for Joachim's (and Nietzsche's) influence on Spengler, see H. Stuart Hughes, *Oswald Spengler* (New York: Scribner's, 1962), p. 51.
137. *Divine and the Human*, p. 199.
138. *Meaning of the Creative Act*, p. 215; *Meaning of History*, pp. 114, 115.
139. *Meaning of the Creative Act*, p. 215.
140. *Beginning and the End*, p. 206.
141. *Ibid.*, p. 253.
142. *Ibid.*, p. 207.
143. *Divine and the Human*, p. 199.
144. *Ibid.*; *Slavery and Freedom*, p. 72; *Beginning and the End*, p. 207; *Divine and the Human*, p. 197.

145. *Divine and the Human,* p. 197.
146. *Ibid.*
147. *Dream and Reality,* p. 295.
148. *Beginning and the End,* pp. 213, 254.

T. S. ELIOT

1. T. S. Eliot, *The Sacred Wood* (London: Methuen, 1920), p. 53.
2. T. S. Eliot, *Selected Essays* (New York: Harcourt, Brace, 1932), pp. 202, 356–57, 400; T. S. Eliot, *Essays Ancient and Modern* (New York: Harcourt, Brace, 1932), p. 117.
3. Allesandro Pellegrini, "A London Conversation with T. S. Eliot," trans. Joseph Frank, *Sewanee Review* 57 (1949): 291; *Selected Essays,* p. 332.
4. T. S. Eliot, "Commentary," *The Criterion* 12 (October 1932): 78–79; *Selected Essays,* p. 332.
5. But Berdyaev was a romantic only in the sense that he strove "relentlessly toward the transcendent in an intense endeavor to cross the boundary and surpass the limits of this world" (*Dream and Reality,* p. 29).
6. T. S. Eliot, *The Complete Poems and Plays, 1909–1950* (New York: Harcourt, Brace, 1952), p. 128.
7. T. S. Eliot, lecture given in acceptance of the Hanseatic Goethe Prize, quoted in F. O. Matthiessen, *The Achievement of T. S. Eliot* (New York: Oxford University Press, 1959), p. 200.
8. Berdyaev, *Dream and Reality,* p. 83.
9. *Complete Poems and Plays,* p. 136.
10. Although Eliot believed that "natural" man could not progress in time, he nevertheless regarded the Age of Dante as superior to contemporary civilization. And he also felt—as he implies in *The Idea of a Christian Society*—that it might be possible to regain the universal Christian ethos of Dante's age. In other words, he thought that there was a possibility of overcoming the "metaphysical tragedy" of twentieth-century history by resuscitating Christian culture. Yet Eliot would still have insisted that a revitalized Christian society would not be representative of temporal progress, for fallen man cannot progress in time. Moral progress, as the saint knows, is made outside of time.
11. T. S. Eliot, *American Literature and the American Language* (St. Louis: Washington University Studies, 1953), pp. 4–5 Appen.
12. Cleanth Brooks, *The Hidden God* (New Haven: Yale University Press, 1963), p. 71.
13. *Complete Poems and Plays,* p. 199.

14. Herbert Howarth, *Notes on Some Figures behind T S. Eliot* (Boston: Houghton Mifflin, 1964), pp. 5–6.
15. See, for example, "Commentary," pp. 78–79; *Complete Poems and Plays,* p. 199.
16. *Complete Poems and Plays,* p. 136.
17. T. S. Eliot, "Talk on Dante," *Adelphi* (October 1951), p. 107.
18. T. S. Eliot, *A Sermon Preached in Magdalene College Chapel* (Cambridge: Cambridge University Press, 1948?), p. 5.
19. Quoted in Matthiessen, *The Achievement of T. S. Eliot,* p. 183.
20. F. H. Bradley, *Appearance and Reality* (Oxford: Oxford University Press, 1930), p. 207.
21. T. S. Eliot, *After Strange Gods* (New York: Harcourt, Brace, 1934), p. 43.
22. T. S. Eliot, *Knowledge and Experience in the Philosophy of F. H. Bradley* (London: Faber and Faber, 1964), pp. 9–10.
23. *Ibid.*
24. *Selected Essays,* pp. 6, 4.
25. *Ibid.,* p. 11.
26. *Ibid.,* p. 4.
27. A. Seth Pringle-Pattison, *The Idea of God* (Oxford: Oxford University Press, 1917), p. 363.
28. *Selected Essays,* p. 5.
29. Wyndham Lewis, *Time and Western Man* (New York: Harcourt, Brace, 1928), p. xv.
30. T. S. Eliot, "Introduction" to Simone Weil, *The Need for Roots,* trans. Arthur Wills (New York: G. P. Putnam's Sons, 1952), p. vi.
31. Wyndham Lewis, "Early London Environment," in *T. S. Eliot: A Collection of Critical Essays,* ed. Hugh Kenner (Englewood Cliffs, N.J.: Prentice Hall, 1962), p. 33.
32. T. S. Eliot, cited in Valerie Eliot, *The Waste Land: A Facsimile and Transcript of the Original Drafts* (New York: Harcourt Brace Jovanovich, 1971), pp. xxi–xxii.
33. Valerie Eliot, *ibid.*
34. *Ibid.,* p. xxv.
35. T. S. Eliot, in N. A. Scott, *Rehearsals of Discomposure* (London: J. Lehman, 1952), p. 201.
36. *Essays Ancient and Modern,* p. 158.
37. T. S. Eliot, "Charles Williams," *The Listener,* 9 January 1947.
38. T. S. Eliot, "On Conversion," *The Listener,* 16 March 1932.
39. T. S. Eliot, *For Lancelot Andrewes* (London: Faber and Gwyer, 1928), p. ix.
40. T. S. Eliot, in John Baillie, *The Idea of Revelation in Recent Thought* (New York: Columbia University Press, 1956), p. 15.

41. *Essays Ancient and Modern,* p. 162.
42. "Talk on Dante," pp. 106–14.
43. T. S. Eliot, "*Ulysses:* Order and Myth," *Dial* 75 (Nov. 1923): 481.
44. *Complete Poems and Plays,* p. 42.
45. *Ibid.,* p. 43.
46. *Selected Essays,* p. 332.
47. Cleanth Brooks, "*The Waste Land:* An Analysis," in *T. S. Eliot: A Study of His Writings by Several Hands,* ed. B. Rajan (London: D. Dobson, 1948), p. 32; Staffan Bergsten, *Time and Eternity: A Study in the Structure and Symbolism of T. S. Eliot's Four Quartets* (Stockholm: Svenska bokfor laget, 1960), p. 26.
48. *Selected Essays,* p. 314.
49. *Ibid.,* p. 235.
50. T. S. Eliot, *On Poetry and Poets* (New York: Farrar, Straus and Cudhay, 1957), p. 10.
51. Eliade, *Cosmos and History,* p. 153.
52. *Ibid.,* pp. 3–6; Mircea Eliade, *Myths, Dreams and Mysteries,* trans. Philip Mairet (London: Harvill, 1960), pp. 39–72.
53. (New York: Anchor, 1957), chap. 9. According to medieval tradition, Christ entrusted Joseph of Arimathea with the Grail He used to celebrate the first Eucharist at the Last Supper. After the Crucifixion and the disbandment of the Disciples, Joseph and his followers left the Holy Land, taking the sacred Grail with them. Once, during their wanderings, they faced a food shortage, and Joseph appealed for divine guidance; whereupon an angel instructed him to ask his brother, Brons, to fish in a nearby stream. Brons complied, subsequently catching a large fish, which enabled his friends to escape starvation and earned him the sobriquet "Rich Fisher" or "Fisher King." Eventually Joseph and his followers arrived in Great Britain, where they established a community which was later known as the realm of the Fisher King. When Joseph died, Brons succeeded him as guardian of the Grail. But his succession was not auspicious, for he eventually fell mysteriously ill, and his kingdom—formerly a demesne of luxuriant meadows, bountiful game, large quantities of legumes, and plentiful water—was laid waste. After this tragic occurrence, Brons and his subjects learned that they would have to await the arrival of a hero, a knight (in the literature, Gawain, Perceval, or Galahad) before the wasteland could be restored. In most versions of the legend, the knight completes what Joseph Campbell, in his book *The Hero with a Thousand Faces,* calls the monomythic cycle of the hero: he usually effects at least a partial restoration of the stricken land (and the sick king) by asking appropriate questions about the Grail and the Lance (i.e., the spear, customarily associated with the Cup, which pierced

Christ's side at the Crucifixion), and/or by killing a foe of the Fisher King's.

54. Weston, *From Ritual to Romance,* pp. 203, 174.

55. *Selected Essays,* p. 125. For a study that regards Frazer's influence upon Eliot as being more crucial than Weston's, see John B. Vickery, *The Literary Impact of the Golden Bough* (Princeton: Princeton University Press, 1973): "Indeed, in a very real sense, it may have been Sir James Frazer who, ironically enough, brought Eliot to the Anglican Communion and an acceptance of orthodox Christianity. For though it did not create it, *The Golden Bough* did accentuate the pattern of death and resurrection with which Eliot was overwhelmingly concerned" (p. 243).

56. *Complete Poems and Plays,* p. 38.

57. Here, as elsewhere, Eliot departs from the traditional Tarot pack "to suit my own convenience" (*ibid.,* p. 51).

58. *Ibid.,* pp. 38, 43.

59. *Ibid.,* pp. 47, 49, 50, 49.

60. Eliade, *Cosmos and History,* p. 85.

61. Mircea Eliade, *Patterns in Comparative Religion,* trans. Rosemary Sheed (New York: Sheed and Ward, 1958), p. 396.

62. *Ibid.,* pp. 402, 407.

63. *Ibid.,* p. 407.

64. "*Ulysses:* Order and Myth," p. 481.

65. *Complete Poems and Plays,* p. 58.

66. *Essays Ancient and Modern,* pp. 158, 160.

67. *Ibid.,* pp. 160, 167.

68. *Complete Poems and Plays,* pp. 126, 61, 65.

69. *Ibid.,* p. 127.

70. *Ibid.,* pp. 120–21.

71. Dante Alighieri, *Purgatorio,* canto xxvi, ll. 145–48, trans. T. S. Eliot, "Dante," *Selected Essays,* p. 217.

72. *Complete Poems and Plays,* p. 63.

73. *Ibid.*

74. Two short stories, *The Dead,* by James Joyce, and *The Shadow in the Rose Garden,* by D. H. Lawrence (both of which Eliot criticized in *After Strange Gods*), as well as *Le Roman de la Rose,* and Dante's descriptions of the "Rose of Paradise" and of the garden in the *Paradiso* probably exercised some influence on Eliot's development of the image.

75. Louis L. Martz, "The Wheel and the Point: Aspects of Imagery and Theme in Eliot's Later Poetry," in *T. S. Eliot: A Selected Critique,* ed. Leonard Ungar (New York: Holt, Rinehart and Winston, 1948), pp. 447–50.

76. *Complete Poems and Plays,* p. 234.

77. *Ibid.,* p. 49.

78. *Ibid.*, pp. 234–35.

79. *Ibid.*, p. 252.

80. *Ibid.*, pp. 276–77.

81. *Ibid.*, pp. 274, 277.

82. Brooks, *The Hidden God*, p. 71.

83. F. R. Leavis, "T. S. Eliot's Later Poetry," in *T. S. Eliot: A Collection of Critical Essays,* ed. Hugh Kenner (Englewood Cliffs, N.J.: Prentice-Hall, 1962), p. 119.

84. Eliade, *Patterns in Comparative Religion,* pp. 372, 378, 408.

85. Brooks, *The Hidden God,* p. 73.

86. W. H. Auden, *The Collected Poetry of W. H. Auden* (New York: Random House, 1945), pp. 355, 202, 206.

87. *Ibid.*, p. 251.

88. *Ibid.*, p. 129.

89. *Complete Poems and Plays,* p. 129.

90. Auden, *Collected Poetry,* p. 11.

91. *Ibid.*, p. 291.

92. *Ibid.*, pp. 395, 402.

93. *Ibid.*, p. 14.

94. *Ibid.*, pp. 278, 291.

95. *Ibid.*, p. 431.

96. *Ibid.*, pp. 396–97.

97. W. B. Yeats, *Collected Plays* (London: Macmillan, 1935), p. 378.

98. *Ibid.*, p. 152.

99. W. B. Yeats, *The Cutting of an Agate* (New York: Macmillan, 1912), p. 131.

100. *Lawrence Durrell and Henry Miller: A Private Correspondence,* ed. George Wickes (New York: Dutton, 1963), p. 19.

101. *Ibid.*, p. 23.

102. Lawrence Durrell, *The Dark Labyrinth* (New York: Cardinal Books, 1963), p. 232.

103. Charles Williams, *Arthurian Torso, Containing the Posthumous Fragment of The Figure of Arthur by Charles Williams and a Commentary on the Arthurian Poems of Charles Williams by C. S. Lewis* (London: Oxford University Press, 1948), p. 65. For an analysis of Williams's use of the Arthurian legend, see Charles Moorman, *Arthurian Triptych: Mythic Materials in Charles Williams, C. S. Lewis and T. S. Eliot* (Berkeley: University of California Press, 1960), pp. 38–102.

104. John Heath-Stubbs, *Charles Williams* (London: Longmans, Green, 1955), p. 15.

105. Charles Williams, *The Descent of the Dove* (London: Faber and Faber, 1939), p. 18.

106. Heath-Stubbs, *Charles Williams,* p. 18.

107. "Dedication," Dorothy L. Sayers, in her translation of Dante's *Inferno* (London: Penguin, 1949); T. S. Eliot, "The Significance of Charles Williams," *The Listener,* 19 December 1946, pp. 894–95.

108. C. S. Lewis, *Miracles* (New York: Macmillan, 1974), p. 139 n. 1. Tolkien (who was a close friend of both Lewis's and Williams's) believed that the mythic force of a successful fairy tale permits the individual enchanted by the "arrested strangeness" of its story to surmount the barrier of time: "Such stories have . . . a mythical or total (unanalysable) effect . . . they open a door on Other Time, and if we pass through, though only for a moment, we stand outside our own time, outside Time itself, maybe" (*Tree and Leaf* [New York: Ballantine Books, 1966], p. 32).

109. T. S. Eliot, *Quatre Quatuors,* trans. P. Leyris, notes by J. Hayward (Paris: Editions du seuil, 1950), p. 131.

110. *Complete Poems and Plays,* p. 118.

111. Berdyaev, *Dreams and Reality,* p. 176; Helen Gardner, *The Art of T. S. Eliot* (New York: E. P. Dutton, 1959), p. 163.

112. T. S. Eliot, *Elizabethan Essays* (London: Faber and Faber, 1934), p. 194.

113. *Complete Poems and Plays,* p. 118.

114. *Ibid.,* pp. 129, 136.

115. Kristian Smidt, *Poetry and Belief in the Work of T. S. Eliot* (London: Routledge & Kegan Paul, 1961), pp. 174–75 (emphasis added).

116. *Complete Poems and Plays,* p. 136.

117. *Ibid.,* p. 199.

118. Huxley, *Perennial Philosophy,* p. 68.

119. *Complete Poems and Plays,* p. 136.

120. *Ibid.,* pp. 139, 142, 126.

121. *Times Literary Supplement,* 7 November 1929, pp. 35–37; *Essays Ancient and Modern,* p. 167.

122. "The Significance of Charles Williams," *The Listener,* 19 December 1946), pp. 894–95.

123. *Complete Poems and Plays,* p. 136.

124. *Ibid.,* p. 119.

125. *Selected Essays,* p. 233; *Complete Poems and Plays,* p. 118.

126. *Selected Essays,* p. 234.

127. *Complete Poems and Plays,* pp. 130–31.

128. *Ibid.,* p. 131.

129. *Ibid.,* pp. 123–24.

130. *Ibid.,* 184.

131. *Ibid.,* p. 192.
132. Sir Philip Sidney, *Arcadia.*
133. *Complete Poems and Plays,* p. 184.
134. *Ibid.,* p. 130.
135. *Ibid.,* p. 117.
136. *Ibid.,* p. 184.
137. Auden, *Collected Poetry,* p. 409.
138. "Commentary," p. 77.
139. Eliot's use of the cycle in *Four Quartets* enabled him to control the temporal process after all. Although he may not have been able to extract himself permanently from the cycle of temporal corruption, he was able to "turn" sufficiently "the wheel on which he turns" to transmute time into eternity—that is, to escape the time-process by realizing (through the crystallization of mystical experience) that time and eternity, appearance and reality, ultimately blend into the all-inclusive harmony of a nontemporal "dance."
140. *Complete Poems and Plays,* p. 86.
141. *Ibid.,* p. 96.
142. *Ibid.,* p. 119.
143. Huxley, *Perennial Philosophy,* p. 35; *Complete Poems and Plays,* p. 122.
144. Bradley, *Appearance and Reality,* p. 210.
145. Seth Pringle-Pattison, *The Idea of God,* pp. 363–64.
146. *Complete Poems and Plays,* pp. 128, 142, 144.
147. *Ibid.,* pp. 119, 65, 127.
148. *Ibid.,* pp. 144, 119, 121, 133.
149. Berdyaev, *Beginning and the End,* pp. 209–10.
150. *Complete Poems and Plays,* pp. 119–20.
151. *Ibid.,* pp. 136, 142.
152. *Essays Ancient and Modern,* p. 148.
153. *After Strange Gods,* p. 12.
154. *Selected Essays,* p. 247.
155. *Essays Ancient and Modern,* pp. 113, 127; "Commentary," p. 77.
156. *Essays Ancient and Modern,* p. 138; "The Idea of a Christian Society," in *The Idea of a Christian Society* and *Notes towards the Definition of Culture* (New York: Harvest, 1940), pp. 14, 15, 19.
157. Pellegrini, "A London Conversation with T. S. Eliot," p. 291; *Selected Essays,* p. 332.
158. *Essays Ancient and Modern,* p. 123.
159. "Commentary," pp. 78–79.

ALDOUS HUXLEY

1. Aldous Huxley, *Time Must Have a Stop* (New York: Harper, 1944), p. 296.
2. Aldous Huxley, *Collected Essays* (New York: Bantam, 1960), pp. 233, 276. For a discussion of the Perennial Philosophy, see pp. 131–39.
3. *Ibid.,* p. 286. Like Eliot, Huxley considered "saint" and "mystic" to be synonymous. But unlike Eliot, Huxley also used the term "theocentrism" as a synonym for both "saint" and "mystic." But it is important to remember that when Huxley uses the term "mystic," he is referring to the nonpersonal variety of monistic mysticism endorsed by the Perennial Philosophy.
4. Aldous Huxley, *Eyeless in Gaza* (New York: Harper, 1936), p. 177.
5. Aldous Huxley, *Brave New World Revisited* (New York: Bantam, 1960), pp. 26–27.
6. Aldous Huxley, *Proper Studies* (London: Chatto and Windus, 1933), p. 210.
7. *Collected Essays,* p. 278.
8. *Ibid.,* p. 362.
9. *Ibid.,* p. 281.
10. *Proper Studies,* p. 208.
11. Eliot, *Complete Poems and Plays,* p. 96.
12. *Collected Essays,* p. 214; Eliot, *Complete Poems and Plays,* p. 234; Berdyaev, *Fate of Man in the Modern World,* p. 8.
13. It is true that material culture, or civilization, is not an "external" event in the same sense as are the processes of the natural world; it is a symptom or objectification of man's internal struggle for salvation. But as a symptom it exists in the "outside" and is subject to the conditions of the natural world. This is analogous to Croce's and Collingwood's concept of "self-expression." Art is not synonymous with its material manifestation or embodiment, but with the act of expression inside the mind of the artist. History is equivalent neither to nature nor to the material objectification of thought in the space-time world, but to thought itself. "All history is the history of thought" as Collingwood says; as Berdyaev, Eliot, or Huxley might phrase it: human history is the history of salvation. Eliot summarizes this notion in the final movement of "Little Gidding": "A people without history / Is not redeemed from time, for history is a pattern / Of timeless moments" (*Complete Poems and Plays,* p. 144). In this sense, then, "history" is a process which, while it runs parallel with and affects the development of civilization, remains above time. The history of salvation concerns man in time, and man's success in achieving salvation is measured by his ability to create a temporal society which enables the greatest number of people to transcend time.
14. Aldous Huxley, *The Perennial Philosophy* (New York: Harper, 1944), p. 95.
15. *Ibid.,* p. 77; *Proper Studies,* p. 207.

16. Aldous Huxley, in Alexander Henderson, *Aldous Huxley* (London: Chatto and Windus, 1935), p. 14; cf. George Woodcock, *Dawn and the Darkest Hour: A Study of Aldous Huxley* (New York: Viking Press, 1972), p. 44.
17. Aldous Huxley, obituary, *New York Times,* 24 November 1963, p. 22.
18. Huxley, "The Burning Wheel," cited in Sybille Bedford, *Aldous Huxley: A Biography* (New York: Alfred Knopf, 1974), p. 67.
19. Huxley, London interview with John Chandos, cited in *ibid.,* p. 57.
20. Huxley lost the manuscript to his first novel and did not try to rewrite it.
21. See Nand Kumar Pandey, "The Influence of Hindu and Buddhist Thought on Aldous Huxley" (Ph. D. diss., Department of English, Stanford University, 1963); Charles Rolo, ed., *The World of Aldous Huxley* (New York: Harper & Row, 1947).
22. Aldous Huxley, *Brave New World* (New York: Modern Library, 1946), p. 3.
23. *Brave New World Revisited,* p. 30.
24. *Ibid.*
25. Aldous Huxley, *Those Barren Leaves* (New York: Avon, 1925), p. 41.
26. Zaehner, *Mysticism: Sacred and Profane,* p. 16.
27. Aldous Huxley, *Crome Yellow* (London: Chatto and Windus, 1949), pp. 37–38.
28. *Eyeless in Gaza,* p. 85.
29. *Crome Yellow,* pp. 273–74.
30. *Ibid.,* p. 274.
31. Lewis Gannett, "Introduction," in Aldous Huxley, *Antic Hay* (New York: Modern Library, 1923), p. viii. It should be noted that while Huxley may have been exploring mysticism at an early period, his public thought of him as an arch-critic of religion of any sort. The most dramatic example of this reputation appeared during the thirties when the *Sunday Express* "carried a two-page attack on him under the headline, Aldous Huxley—THE MAN WHO HATES GOD" (Bedford, *Aldous Huxley,* p. 302). On his ambivalent attitude toward mysticism, see also Ronald W. Clark, *The Huxleys* (London: Heinemann, 1968), p. 168.
32. Aldous Huxley, *After Many a Summer Dies the Swan* (New York: Avon, 1939), p. 87.
33. *Antic Hay,* pp. 201, 202.
34. *Ibid.,* p. 213.
35. *Those Barren Leaves,* pp. 100, 369, 370, 376.
36. *Ibid.,* p. 372.
37. *Ibid.,* pp. 377–78.
38. Seán O'Faoláin, *The Vanishing Hero* (New York: Grosset and Dunlap, 1956), p. 19.

39. Aldous Huxley, *Jesting Pilate* (London: Chatto and Windus, 1948), pp. 109–10.

40. *Ibid.*, pp. 110–11.

41. *Ibid.*, pp. 130, 214, 82–86.

42. *Collected Essays*, p. 128. See also Bedford, *Aldous Huxley*, p. 209.

43. Aldous Huxley, *Point Counter Point* (New York: Avon, 1928), p. 204.

44. *Ibid.*, p. 205.

45. It must be recognized, however, that five years later, when Huxley wrote *Brave New World*, he thought of himself as "an amused, Pyrrhonic aesthete."

46. Laura Archera Huxley, *This Timeless Moment: A Personal View of Aldous Huxley* (London: Chatto and Windus, 1969), p. 126.

47. Aldous Huxley, cited in his obituary, *New York Times* 24 November 1963; for an account of Huxley's last days, see Huxley, *This Timeless Moment*, p. 295.

48. *Perennial Philosophy*, p. vii.

49. S. Radhakrishnan, *Eastern Religions and Western Thought* (New York: Oxford University Press, 1959), p. 116.

50. *Time Must Have a Stop*, p. 293; *Eyeless in Gaza*, p. 442.

51. *Time Must Have a Stop*, p. 293.

52. *Perennial Philosophy*, pp. x–xi.

53. *Time Must Have a Stop*, p. 297.

54. *Collected Essays*, p. 233; *Time Must Have a Stop*, p. 290.

55. *Collected Essays*, pp. 233–34. Huxley's point is that although Niebuhr says the meaning of history lies outside history, history is nevertheless meaningful (for Niebuhr) because it leads man on to the Last Judgment and the End of time. Thus, Niebuhr contradicts himself, for historical time is redemptive after all.

56. Berdyaev, *Dream and Reality*, p. 83.

57. *Perennial Philosophy*, pp. 36, 48, 36.

58. *After Many a Summer Dies the Swan*, p. 92.

59. Aldous Huxley, *Ends and Means* (New York: Harper, 1937), pp. 277–80.

60. *Perennial Philosophy*, pp. 133–34.

61. *Ends and Means*, p. 4.

62. *Ibid.*

63. *After Many a Summer Dies the Swan*, p. 96.

64. Huxley was especially influenced by the nondualistic doctrine of Sankara (c. A.D. 700–800) and Patanjali (second century B.C.?), by the *Bhagavad Gita* (the sayings attributed to the Buddha), and by the *Tibetan Book of the Dead*. While he also appreciated such Western mystics as François de Sales, St. John of the Cross, and Jakob Boehme, Huxley seems to have admired

them mainly because they embraced the tenets of his Perennial Philosophy. That is, he admired their doctrines insofar as they contradicted the traditional teachings of the Western (Christian) churches. Although he may have changed his mind toward the end of his life, Huxley usually took issue with Christian theology. He admired the teachings of Jesus and several Western mystics (*Ends and Means,* p. 5), but not the teachings of organized Christianity. He probably would not have gone so far as to call his favorite Christian mystics non-Christian, but he did believe that the mystic tradition of Christianity was ultimately based upon and derived from the Upanishads. Thus, Huxley appears to have looked favorably upon Boehme, for instance, not only because he was a monist, but because his religious philosophy seemed to be closer to the nondualistic teachings of the East than to the personalist traditions of Christian theology. For a discussion of Huxley's view of the origin of the mystic tradition in the West, see Pandey, "The Influence of Hindu and Buddhist Thought on Aldous Huxley," p. 16.

65. *Time Must Have a Stop,* p. 281.
66. *Perennial Philosophy,* p. 19; *After Many a Summer Dies the Swan,* p. 90.
67. *Perennial Philosophy,* p. viii.
68. *Collected Essays,* pp. 234–35.
69. Berdyaev, *Dream and Reality,* p. 83.
70. *Time Must Have a Stop,* pp. 280–81.
71. *Ends and Means,* p. 21.
72. Heinrich Zimmer, *Philosophies of India,* ed. Joseph Campbell (Princeton: Princeton University Press, 1971), p. 14.
73. *Perennial Philosophy,* p. 151.
74. *After Many a Summer Dies the Swan,* p. 91.
75. *Perennial Philosophy,* pp. 149, 148, vii, 153.
76. *Ibid.,* p. 158. Yet he still seems to reserve the privilege of mystical experience to the cerebrotonic: "Finally, there is the way of knowledge, through the modification of consciousness, until it ceases to be ego-centered and becomes centred in and united with the divine Ground. This is the way to which the extreme cerebrotonic is naturally drawn" (pp. 152–53).
77. *Perennial Philosophy,* pp. 149, 166–67, 115, 264; Aldous Huxley, *"The Doors of Perception" and "Heaven and Hell"* (New York: Harper, 1963), *Heaven and Hell,* p. 145.
78. *Crome Yellow,* p. 58.
79. *Perennial Philosophy,* p. 115; *Heaven and Hell,* pp. 84, 85, 96.
80. *Doors of Perception,* p. 73.
81. *Perennial Philosophy,* p. 192.
82. *Antic Hay,* p. 216.
83. *Collected Essays,* p. 244; *Jesting Pilate,* p. 6.

84. *Antic Hay,* pp. 213, 211; *Music at Night,* p. 35; Aldous Huxley, *The Genius and the Goddess* (New York: Bantam, 1956), p. 102.
85. *Time Must Have a Stop,* p. 296; *Antic Hay,* p. 210; *After Many a Summer Dies the Swan,* pp. 86, 88; *Eyeless in Gaza,* p. 22.
86. *After Many a Summer Dies the Swan,* pp. 90, 87.
87. *Time Must Have a Stop,* p. 282; *Genius and the Goddess,* p. 4.
88. *Time Must Have a Stop,* pp. 298, 296.
89. *Collected Essays,* p. 244 (emphasis mine).
90. *Ibid.,* pp. 230, 221, 223, 215, 222.
91. *Ibid.,* p. 214.
92. *Ibid.,* pp. 243–44 (emphasis mine).
93. Eliot, *Complete Poems and Plays,* p. 121.
94. T. S. Eliot, from a 1933 lecture given in New Haven, cited in Howarth, *Notes on Some Figures behind T. S. Eliot,* p. 278; *Point Counter Point,* p. 438 (cf. *Eyeless in Gaza,* p. 172).
95. Aldous Huxley, *On the Margin* (New York: George H. Doran, 1923), p. 45.
96. Aldous Huxley, *Music at Night and Other Essays* (London: Penguin, 1950), pp. 35–36, 40.
97. *Collected Essays,* p. 230.
98. *Ibid.,* p. 223.
99. Huxley, *Perennial Philosophy,* pp. 182, 228; *Eyeless in Gaza,* p. 468.
100. *Perennial Philosophy,* p. 182.
101. *Ibid.,* pp. 229, 183, 229.
102. *Proper Studies,* p. 208; *After Many a Summer Dies the Swan,* p. 221.
103. *Perennial Philosophy,* p. 53.
104. *Ibid.,* pp. 62, 299.
105. *Eyeless in Gaza,* pp. 471–72.
106. *Time Must Have a Stop,* p. 290.
107. W. B. Yeats, cited in Cornwell, *The Still Point,* pp. 112, 110.
108. Huxley, "The Burning Wheel," in *The Collected Poems of Aldous Huxley* (London: Chatto and Windus, 1970), p. 3.
109. Auden, *Collected Poetry,* pp. 361, 121; Hermann Hesse, *Siddharta,* trans. Hilda Rosner (New York: New Directions, 1957), pp. 146, 145; Charles Williams, *The Greater Trumps* (New York: Noonday Press, 1950), p. 177. Evelyn Waugh also uses a similar image in his first novel, *Decline and Fall* (Boston: Little, Brown, 1928), when he compares life to "the big wheel at Luna Park": "the nearer you can get to the hub of the wheel the slower it is moving. . . . There's generally some one in the centre who stands up and sometimes does a sort of dance. . . . Of course at the very centre there's a point completely at rest, if one could only find it" (pp. 282–83).
110. Berdyaev, *Destiny of Man,* pp. 288–89.

111. *Eyeless in Gaza,* p. 184.
112. Ananda Coomaraswamy, *The Dance of Shiva* (New York: Noonday Press, 1957), pp. 66–78.
113. Aldous Huxley, *Island* (New York: Bantam, 1963), pp. 170–71, 172–73.
114. Eliot, "The Significance of Charles Williams," *The Listener* (19 December 1946).
115. Baumer, *Religion and the Rise of Scepticism,* p. 263.
116. Cf. Huxley's comment in *Doors of Perception:* " 'Is-ness.' The Being of Platonic philosophy—except that Plato seems to have made the enormous, the grotesque mistake of separating Being from becoming and identifying it with the mathematical abstraction of the Idea" (p. 17).
117. Eliot, *Complete Poems and Plays,* p. 119 (emphasis mine).
118. Gardner, *The Art of T. S. Eliot,* p. 161 n. 1. It cannot be denied, however, that Eliot could have derived his image of the dance from Dante or the Elizabethans—Sir John Davies's *Orchestra* (1596) could be a likely source.
119. Williams, *Greater Trumps,* pp. 106–07 (emphasis mine), 20, 102.
120. Auden, *Collected Poetry,* p. 278; cf., however, Auden's attack on philosophical monism in "For the Time Being," p. 453.
121. Williams, *Greater Trumps,* p. 266.
122. W. B. Yeats, "Rosa Alchemica," *Early Poems and Stories* (New York: Macmillan, 1925), p. 489; Herman Hesse, *Steppenwolf,* trans. Basil Creighton (New York: Ungar, 1957), p. 240; C. G. Jung, *Psyche and Symbol,* ed. Violet de Laszlo (New York: Anchor, 1958), p. 320.
123. Baumer, *Religion and the Rise of Scepticism,* chap. 5.
124. Eric Fromm, *The Forgotten Language* (New York: Grove Press, 1957), pp. 7, 10.
125. Myth is apparently a product of visionary experience: see *Heaven and Hell,* p. 99.
126. *Doors of Perception,* pp. 12, 15, 18.
127. *Ibid.,* pp. 21, 22, 23.
128. *Ibid.,* p. 36.
129. *Ibid.,* p. 73.
130. *Heaven and Hell,* p. 138.
131. *Island,* pp. 189, 163, 141.
132. *Ibid.,* p. 140.
133. *Ibid.,* p. 173.
134. *Ibid.,* pp. 271, 288.
135. *Heaven and Hell,* p. 139.
136. *Island,* p. 275.
137. Yet he would have insisted that he had not achieved final liberation; and there is evidence that he may have believed in reincarnation (*Island,* pp.

193–94). We can catch beatific glimpses of the divine Ground, but this does not mean that we are united with it forever. After all, we must die, and Huxley believes that there is a posthumous state and progress of the spirit (cf. *Heaven and Hell*, p. 140). If we have, however, cooperated with the grace bestowed by mescaline, the possibility of retaining the Beatific Vision after death may be quite good. But it must be clear that by Beatific Vision, Huxley and the Christian theologian do not mean the same thing: Huxley's interpretation of final Enlightenment entails the notion of the destruction of the personality.

138. *After Many a Summer Dies the Swan*, p. 123; *Ends and Means*, pp. 90, 91.
139. *After Many a Summer Dies the Swan*, p. 123.
140. *Collected Essays*, pp. 280, 277.
141. *After Many a Summer Dies the Swan*, p. 118.
142. *Island*, p. 294.
143. *Brave New World Revisited*, pp. 1–2. It is worth noting that Huxley drew attention to this possibility at the outset of *Brave New World* by citing a passage from Nicolas Berdyaev.
144. *Collected Essays*, p. 275.

C. G. JUNG

1. C. G. Jung, *Aion: Researches into the Phenomenology of the Self*, trans. R. F. C. Hull (New York: Pantheon, 1959), p. 182.
2. C. G. Jung, *Psychology and Alchemy*, trans. R. F. C. Hull (New York: Pantheon, 1953), p. 41.
3. C. G. Jung, *Symbols of Transformation*, trans. R. F. C. Hull (New York: Pantheon, 1952), p. 28. This work was originally published in 1912 and translated in 1916 as *Psychology of the Unconscious;* it marked Jung's public break with Freud.
4. C. G. Jung, *Memories, Dreams, Reflections*, trans. Richard and Clara Winston (New York: Pantheon, 1963), p. 223.
5. Sigmund Freud to C. G. Jung (17 January 1909), *The Freud/Jung Letters*, ed. William McGuire, trans. Ralph Manheim and R. F. C. Hull (Princeton: Princeton University Press, 1974), pp. 196–97.
6. *Memories, Dreams, Reflections*, p. 158.
7. Freud to Jung (3 January 1913), p. 539.
8. Jung to Freud (18 December 1912), pp. 534–35.
9. *Memories, Dreams, Reflections*, p. 158.
10. *Ibid.*
11. *Ibid.*, p. 160.
12. *Symbols of Transformation*, p. 231.

13. C. G. Jung, *Civilization in Transition*, trans. R. F. C. Hull (New York: Pantheon, 1964), p. 327.
14. *Memories, Dreams, Reflections*, p. 178.
15. *Ibid.*, p. 192.
16. *Ibid.*, p. 195.
17. *Ibid.*, pp. 196–97.
18. *Ibid.*, p. 74.
19. *Civilization in Transition*, p. 81.
20. *Ibid.*, p. 82.
21. *Memories, Dreams, Reflections*, p. 227.
22. Erwin R. Goodenough, *Jewish Symbols in the Greco-Roman Period*, 12 vols. (New York: Pantheon, 1954), 4: 110.
23. C. G. Jung, *The Archetypes and the Collective Unconscious*, trans. R. F. C. Hull (Princeton: Princeton University Press, 1971), p. 76.
24. *Ibid.* (emphasis mine).
25. *Ibid.; Memories, Dreams, Reflections*, p. 161.
26. *Archetypes and the Collective Unconscious*, p. 4.
27. C. G. Jung, *The Structure and Dynamics of the Psyche*, trans. R. F. C. Hull (New York: Pantheon, 1960), p. 413; *Archetypes and the Collective Unconscious*, p. 7.
28. *Archetypes and the Collective Unconscious*, p. 5.
29. *Memories, Dreams, Reflections*, p. 392.
30. Jung regards the creative "instinct" as similar to, but not identical with, an instinct; see *Structure and Dynamics of the Psyche*, p. 118; M. Esther Harding, *Psychic Energy* (New York: Pantheon, 1963), p. 21.
31. Jolande Jacobi, *The Psychology of C. G. Jung* (New Haven: Yale University Press, 1962), p. 44.
32. *Structure and Dynamics of the Psyche*, p. 214.
33. *Archetypes and the Collective Unconscious*, pp. 79–80.
34. *Ibid.*, pp. 79, 66.
35. *Ibid.*, p. 78.
36. *Ibid.*, p. 79.
37. *Aion*, pp. 40, 180.
38. *Archetypes and the Collective Unconscious*, p. 337.
39. *Structure and the Dynamics of the Psyche*, p. 414.
40. *Memories, Dreams, Reflections*, pp. 351–52 (emphasis added). Although this citation is drawn from Jung's latest work—his posthumously published autobiography—there is evidence that proves not only that Jung believed in the timelessness of the objective psyche as early as 1927, but that by 1933, if not before, he had also posited the existence of a spiritual reality beyond time. See Jung's essays "Analytical Psychology and 'Weltanschauung' "—

first given as a lecture in 1927; "The Stages of Life"—first published in 1930; "The Real and Surreal" (1933) and "The Soul and Death" (1934) in *Structure and Dynamics of the Psyche,* pp. 358–415.

41. *Archetypes and the Collective Unconscious,* pp. 282–83.
42. C. G. Jung, *Two Essays on Analytical Psychology,* trans. R. F. C. Hull (New York: Pantheon, 1953), p. 226. The anima-animus (the feminine nature of man's psyche and the masculine nature of woman's psyche) is often the personification, or mouthpiece, of the collective unconscious, whereas the wise old man, or magician (who evidently appears only in man's psyche), represents wisdom and often reveals the secret of individuation. The hero and his odyssey symbolize the quest for self-realization; the great mother (sometimes in connection with the maiden) performs the same function in the female psyche as the magician does in the male.
43. *Aion,* p. 22; cf. C. G. Jung, *Mysterium Coniunctionis,* trans. R. F. C. Hull (New York: Pantheon, 1963), pp. 388, 425; see p. 430 for other examples of marriage *quaternios.*
44. *Archetypes and the Collective Unconscious,* pp. 387, 360–61.
45. *Ibid.,* p. 388.
46. Because mandalas occasionally fail to produce a new center of the personality, Jungians such as M. Esther Harding have differentiated between a self-producing mandala and the "Circle of the Psyche" (see *Psychic Energy,* pp. 303–59 and Plate XIV).
47. *Archetypes and the Collective Unconscious,* p. 275.
48. *Ibid.,* p. 357.
49. C. G. Jung, *Psychology and Religion* (New Haven: Yale University Press, 1960), p. 96.
50. *Two Essays on Analytical Psychology,* p. 238.
51. For a reference to the mandala as a dance and a discussion of mandala symbolism in general, see C. G. Jung, "Commentary," *The Secret of the Golden Flower,* in *Psyche and Symbol,* ed. Violet de Laszlo (New York: Anchor, 1958), pp. 319–20.
52. *Memories, Dreams, Reflections,* pp. 72, 88.
53. *Ibid.,* p. 4.
54. *Ibid.,* p. 240.
55. *Ibid.,* p. 4.
56. *Ibid.,* p. 224; it is worth noting that when Jung first published this mandala, he did not acknowledge its authorship (see *Archetypes and the Collective Unconscious,* pp. 364–65, Fig. 6). It was only known (to the uninitiated) who painted the mandala after the posthumous publication of Jung's autobiography—it is not reproduced in the Swiss edition (see *Memories, Dreams, Reflections,* Plate XI).

57. *Memories, Dreams, Reflections*, p. 293.
58. *Ibid.*, pp. 295–96.
59. *Ibid.*, p. 296.
60. *Ibid.*, p. 352.
61. *Civilization in Transition*, p. 80.
62. *Ibid.*, pp. 148–49.
63. *Ibid.*, p. 82.
64. *Ibid.*, p. 142.
65. Berdyaev, *Fate of Man in the Modern World*, p. 7.
66. *Aion*, p. 62.
67. *Civilization in Transition*, p. 311.
68. *Aion*, pp. 83–84.
69. *Ibid.*, p. 86.
70. *Ibid.*
71. *Ibid.*, p. 84.
72. *Ibid.*, pp. 181, 87.
73. *Structure and Dynamics of the Psyche*, p. 376.
74. Erich Neumann, *The Origins and History of Consciousness*, trans. R. F. C. Hull (New York: Pantheon, 1954), p. xxi. Jung maintained that whether the "psychic structure and its elements, the archetypes, ever 'originated' at all is a metaphysical question and therefore unanswerable" (*Archetypes and the Collective Unconscious*, p. 101).
75. *Memories, Dreams, Reflections*, p. 351.
76. C. G. Jung, *Psychology and Religion: West and East*, trans. R. F. C. Hull (New York: Pantheon, 1958), p. 361.
77. Cf. Sigmund Freud, *Studies in Parapsychology*, introduction by Philip Rieff (New York: Collier, 1963). Freud, however, eventually changed his mind and as of 1924 (if not 1922) was prepared "to lend the support of psychoanalysis to the matter of telepathy" (Arthur Koestler, *The Roots of Coincidence: An Excursion into Parapsychology* [New York: Vintage Books, 1973], p. 101).
78. Cf. J. B. Rhine's discussion of "ESP and its independence of space-time conditions" in *The Reach of the Mind*, p. 120 and chap. 5 ("Across the Barrier of Time").
79. *Structure and Dynamics of the Psyche*, p. 414.
80. *Ibid.*, pp. 459–84.
81. *Ibid.*, p. 531.
82. *Ibid.*, p. 526. An example of the first category of synchronistic events can be gathered from the following incident drawn from Jung's analytic practice. Jung had been trying unsuccessfully to treat a young female patient. The young lady possessed a hyper-intellectualized view of reality and tenaciously

suppressed the emotional side of her personality. Jung wanted to penetrate this rational façade but knew he could only do so if during analysis something irrational or unexpected occurred. The unexpected happened one day just as the patient was telling Jung of a dream she had had the previous night in which she had been given a golden scarab, a costly piece of jewelry. While the patient was still recalling her impressive dream, Jung heard a gentle tapping on the window pane. He

> turned round and saw that it was a fairly large flying insect that was knocking against the window-pane from outside in the obvious effort to get into the dark room. This seemed to me very strange. I opened the window immediately and caught the insect in the air as it flew in. It was a scarabaed beetle, or common rose-chafer . . . whose gold-green colour most nearly resembles that of a golden scarab. I handed the beetle to my patient with the words, "Here is your scarab." This experience punctured the desired hole in her rationalism. . . . The treatment could now be continued with satisfactory results.

The synchronistic connection, then, is obviously between the dream-scarab and the unexpected (yet, in Jung's view, nonfortuitous) appearance of the rose-chafer. They both coincided simultaneously in a meaningful (yet acausal) relationship. An example of the second category of synchronistic events can be found in "Swedenborg's well-attested vision of the great fire in Stockholm." For although he was miles away and could not possibly see the capital at the moment of the disaster, the Swedish theologian had a vision of the fire at approximately the same time it was devastating Stockholm. And, finally, an example of the third category of significant yet acausal events is discovered in "the recent report by Air Marshal Sir Victor Goddard about the dream of an unknown officer, which predicted the subsequent accident to Goddard's plane" (*ibid.*, pp. 525–26).

83. *Ibid.*, pp. 445–46.
84. *Ibid.*, p. 518.
85. *Memories, Dreams, Reflections*, p. 305.
86. The mandala arrangement of space, time, causality, and synchronicity (which composes a quaternity, or harmonious unity) indicates that Jung's metaphysics is ultimately nondualistic. His solution of the time-eternity problem seems, at least in one respect, to be analogous to Bradley's. Just as Bradley resolved the antithesis between time and timelessness by introducing a third term, the Absolute, which united and transmuted both forms of being into an all-inclusive harmony, so Jung seems to have resolved the antithesis between time, space, and causality, on the one hand, and synchro-

nicity, on the other, by subsuming temporal and eternal modes of being under the rubric of a "psychoid" absolute. His implied (I use the word "implied" advisedly because Jung does not discuss the problem at length) resolution of the dualism between the temporal and the eternal is derived from his concept of individuation. Arguing by analogy, Jung implies that just as the self transmutes the conscious and unconscious into a new unity, so the absolute object unites and transfigures time into "a pattern / Of timeless moments."

87. *Structure and Dynamics of the Psyche,* p. 531. Jung collaborated with the physicist Wolfgang Pauli (author of the "Exclusion Principle" and discoverer, in theory, of the neutrino) in attempting to elucidate the principle of synchronicity. Both men evidently hoped to devise a view of the universe that would unite the fields of science and psychology. Although critics have frequently dismissed the results of the effort, at least one has recognized the importance of their collaboration: "It was for the first time in the history of modern thought that the hypothesis of a-causal factors working in the universe was given the joint stamp of respectability by a psychologist and a physicist of international renown" (Koestler, *Roots of Coincidence,* p. 101).

EPILOGUE

1. William Inge, *Outspoken Essays* (London: Longmans, Green, 1925), pp. 185, 186.
2. *Ibid.,* pp. 179, 183, 180.
3. In his later investigations Husserl aroused controversy and dismay in phenomenological circles by proclaiming the existence of a Transcendental Ego, which he concluded would continue to exist even if our time-framed world were destroyed; for his treatment of the problem of time, see *The Phenomenology of Internal Time-Consciousness,* ed. Martin Heidegger (Bloomington: Indiana University Press, 1964).
4. Clifford Geertz, cited in Ortiz, *The Tewa World,* p. 27.

BIBLIOGRAPHY

THE TWENTIETH-CENTURY REVOLT AGAINST TIME

Alexander, H. G. *Time as Dimension and History*. Albuquerque: University of New Mexico Press, 1945.

Altick, Richard D. *Victorian People and Ideas*. New York: W. W. Norton, 1973.

Baumer, Franklin Le Van. *Main Currents of Western Thought*. New York: Knopf, 1970.

———. *Modern European Thought: Continuity and Change in Ideas, 1600–1950*. New York: Macmillan, 1977.

———. *Religion and the Rise of Scepticism*. New York: Harcourt, Brace, and World, 1960.

———. "Twentieth-Century Version of the Apocalypse." *Cahiers d'histoire mondiale (Journal of World History)* 1, no. 3 (January 1954): 623–40.

Bergson, Henri. *Time and Free Will*. Translated by F. L. Pogson. New York: Harper, 1960.

Breton, André. *What Is Surrealism?* Translated by David Gascoyne. London: Faber and Faber, 1936.

Broch, Hermann. *The Sleepwalkers*. Translated by Willa and Edwin Muir. New York: Grosset and Dunlap, 1964.

Buckley, Jerome H. *The Triumph of Time*. Cambridge, Mass.: Harvard University Press, Belknap Press, 1966.

Čapek, Milič. *The Philosophical Impact of Contemporary Physics*. New York: D. Van Nostrand, 1961.

Cassirer, Ernst. *Essay on Man*. New Haven: Yale University Press, 1966.

———. *The Philosophy of Symbolic Forms*. Translated by Ralph Manheim. New Haven: Yale University Press, 1955.

Chadwick, Owen. *The Secularization of the European Mind in the Nineteenth Century*. Cambridge: Cambridge University Press, 1975.

Cornwell, Ethel. *The "Still Point."* New Brunswick, N.J.: Rutgers University Press, 1962.

Dentan, Robert C., ed. *The Idea of History in the Ancient Near East*. New Haven: Yale University Press, 1955.

Bibliography

Eddington, Arthur. *Mathematical Theory of Relativity.* Cambridge: Cambridge University Press, 1927.

Eliade, Mircea. *Cosmos and History: The Myth of the Eternal Return.* Translated by W. R. Trask. New York: Harper, 1959.

———. *Myths, Dreams and Mysteries.* Translated by Philip Mairet. London: Harvill, 1960.

Fraser, J. T. *Of Time, Passion, and Knowledge: Reflections on the Strategy of Existence.* New York: Braziller, 1975.

———. *Time as Conflict: A Scientific and Humanistic Study.* Basel and Boston: Birkhauser, 1978.

———, ed. *The Voices of Time.* New York: Braziller, 1966.

Fussell, Paul. *The Great War and Modern Memory.* New York and London: Oxford University Press, 1975.

Gilb, Corinne Lathrop. "Time and Change in Twentieth Century Thought." *Cahiers d'histoire mondiale (Journal of World History)* 9, no. 4m (1966): 867–83.

Goblet D'Alviella, Eugene F. *The Migration of Symbols.* New York: University Books, 1956.

Gunn, J. A. *The Problem of Time.* London: George Allen and Unwin, 1929.

Hayes, Carlton J. H. *A Generation of Materialism.* New York: Harper Torchbook, 1963.

Heller, Erich. *Disinherited Mind.* New York: Farrar, Straus and Giroux, 1957.

Hentze, Carl. *Mythes et symboles lunaires.* Antwerp: De Sikkel, 1932.

Holborn, Hajo. *The Political Collapse of Europe.* New York: Knopf, 1958.

Hughes, H. Stuart. *Consciousness and Society.* New York: Vintage, 1958.

Hughes, Richard. *The Fox in the Attic.* New York: Signet, 1963.

Inge, William Ralph. *Outspoken Essays.* London: Longmans, Green, 1925.

James, William. *The Varieties of Religious Experience.* New York: Mentor, 1961.

Jones, Peter. *Philosophy and the Novel.* Oxford: Oxford University Press, 1975.

Joyce, James. *Ulysses.* New York: Modern Library, 1946.

Kazantzakis, Nikos. *The Rock Garden.* New York: Simon and Schuster, 1963.

Lawrence, D. H. *The Rainbow.* New York: Viking Press, 1943.

Malraux, André. *Le Musée imaginaire.* Paris: Gallimard, 1965.

———. *Les voix du silence.* Paris: Gallimard, 1953.

Mann, Thomas. *Essays of Three Decades.* Translated by H. T. Lowe-Porter. New York: Knopf, 1947.

Marinetti, Filippo. "The Foundation of Futurism." Translated by Eugen Weber. In *Paths to the Present,* edited by Eugen Weber. New York: Meyerhoff, 1960.

Mendilow, A. A. *Time and the Novel.* London: Peter Nevill, 1952.

Bibliography

Meyerhoff, Hans. *Time in Literature*. Berkeley: University of California Press, 1955.

Mosse, George L. *The Culture of Western Europe: The Nineteenth and Twentieth Centuries*. Chicago: Rand McNally, 1961.

Ortiz, Alfonso. *The Tewa World: Space, Time, Being and Becoming in a Pueblo Society*. Chicago: University of Chicago Press, 1974.

Panofsky, Erwin. *Studies in Iconology*. New York: Harper, 1962.

Pouillon, Jean. *Temps et roman*. Paris: Gallimard, 1946.

Poulet, Georges. *The Interior Distance*. Translated by Elliott Coleman. New York: Harper, 1961.

—————. *Studies in Human Time*. Translated by Elliott Coleman. New York: Harper, 1959.

Priestly, J. B. *Man and Time*. New York: Dell, 1968.

Proust, Marcel. *A la recherche du temps perdu*. Paris: Gallimard, 1954.

Schneider, Daniel. *Symbolism: The Manichean Vision*. Lincoln: University of Nebraska Press, 1975.

Simon, Pierre-Henri. *Esprit et l'histoire*. Paris: Cohn, 1954.

Simpson, William. *The Buddhist Praying-Wheel*. New York: Macmillan, 1896.

Tobin, Patricia D. *Time and the Novel: The Genealogical Imperative*. Princeton: Princeton University Press, 1978.

Toulmin, Stephen, and June Goodfield. *The Discovery of Time*. New York: Harper, 1965.

Tzara, Tristan. *Dada III*. Translated by Eugen Weber. In *Paths to the Present*, edited by Eugen Weber. New York: Meyerhoff, 1960.

Wagar, Warren W. *Good Tidings: The Belief in Progress from Darwin to Marcuse*. Bloomington: Indiana University Press, 1972.

Wells, H. G. *The Time Machine*. New York: Bantam, 1968.

White, Hayden. *Tropics of Discourse*. Baltimore: Johns Hopkins University Press, 1978.

Wood, Douglas K. "Even Such Is Time: A Survey of Twentieth-Century Approaches to the Problem of Time." *Revision Journal* 1, no. 1 (Winter 1978).

Woolf, Virginia. *The Waves*. New York: Harcourt, Brace and World, 1931.

Yeats, William Butler. *Ideas of Good and Evil*. New York: Macmillan, 1912.

NICOLAS BERDYAEV

Primary Sources

Berdyaev, Nicolas. *The Beginning and the End*. Translated by R. M. French. London: Geoffrey Bles, 1952.

[233]

Bibliography

——. *The Destiny of Man*. Translated by Natalie Duddington. London: Geoffrey Bles, 1959.

——. *The Divine and the Human*. Translated by R. M. French. London: Geoffrey Bles, 1949.

——. *Dostoevsky*. Translated by Donald Atwater. New York: Meridian, 1957.

——. *Dream and Reality*. Translated by K. Lampert. London: Geoffrey Bles, 1950.

——. *The End of Our Time*. Translated by Donald Atwater. London: Sheed and Ward, 1934.

——. *The Fate of Man in the Modern World*. Translated by Donald A. Lowrie. Ann Arbor: University of Michigan Press, 1961.

——. "L'idée religieuse russe." *Cahiers de la nouvelle journée* 8 (1924).

——. *The Meaning of History*. Translated by George Reavy. Cleveland: Living Age Books, 1962.

——. *The Meaning of the Creative Act*. Translated by Donald Lowrie. New York: Collier, 1962.

——. *The Origin of Russian Communism*. Translated by R. M. French. London: Geoffrey Bles, 1955.

——. *The Russian Idea*. Translated by R. M. French. Boston: Beacon Press, 1962.

——. *Slavery and Freedom*. Translated by R. M. French. London: Geoffrey Bles, 1944.

——. *Solitude and Society*. Translated by R. M. French. London: Geoffrey Bles, 1934.

——. *Spirit and Reality*. Translated by R. M. French. London: Geoffrey Bles, 1937.

——. *Truth and Revelation*. Translated by R. M. French. London: Geoffrey Bles, 1953.

Secondary Sources

Allen, E. L. *Freedom in God: A Guide to the Thought of Nicholas Berdyaev*. New York: The Philosophical Library, 1951.

Barrett, William. *Irrational Man*. New York: Anchor, 1962.

Brown, Norman O. *Life against Death: The Psychoanalytical Meaning of History*. New York: Vintage, 1959.

Bultmann, Rudolf. *History and Eschatology*. Edinburgh: Edinburgh University Press, 1957.

Clarke, Oliver Fielding. *Introduction to Berdyaev*. London: Geoffrey Bles, 1957.

Herberg, Will. *Four Existentialist Theologians*. New York: Anchor, 1958.

Bibliography

Horton, Walter. *Contemporary Continental Theology*. New York: Harper, 1938.
Hughes, H. Stuart. *Oswald Spengler*. New York: Scribner's, 1962.
Kernan, Julie. *Our Friend, Jacques Maritain: A Personal Memoir*. New York: Doubleday, 1975.
Löwith, Karl. *Meaning in History*. Chicago: University of Chicago Press, 1958.
Lowrie, Donald. *Rebellious Prophet*. New York: Harper, 1960.
Nucho, Fuad. *Berdyaev's Philosophy*. London: Victor Gollancz, 1967.
Shklar, Judith N. *After Utopia: The Decline of Political Faith*. Princeton: Princeton University Press, 1957.
Spinka, Matthew. *Christian Thought from Erasmus to Berdyaev*. Englewood Cliffs, N.J.: Prentice-Hall, 1962.
Teilhard de Chardin, Pierre. *The Phenomenon of Man*. New York: Harper, 1959.
Tucker, Robert. *Philosophy and Myth in Karl Marx*. Cambridge: Cambridge University Press, 1965.

T. S. ELIOT

Primary Sources
Allen, Warner. *The Timeless Moment*. London: Faber and Faber, 1946.
Auden, W. H. *The Collected Poetry of W. H. Auden*. New York: Random House, 1945.
Durrell, Lawrence. *The Alexandria Quartet*. London: Faber and Faber, 1962.
――――. *The Dark Labyrinth*. New York: Cardinal Books, 1963.
――――, and Henry Miller. *A Private Correspondence*. Edited by George Wickes. New York: E. P. Dutton, 1963.
Eliot, T. S. *After Strange Gods*. New York: Harcourt, Brace, 1934.
――――. *American Literature and the American Language*. St. Louis: Washington University Studies, 1953.
――――. "Charles Williams." *The Listener*, 9 January 1947.
――――. "Commentary." *The Criterion* 12 (October 1932).
――――. *The Complete Poems and Plays, 1909–1950*. New York: Harcourt, Brace, 1952.
――――. *The Confidential Clerk*. New York: Harcourt, Brace, 1954.
――――. *The Cultivation of Christmas Trees*. London: Faber and Faber, 1954.
――――. "Defense of the Islands." In *Britain at War*, edited by Monroe Wheeler. New York: Museum of Modern Art, 1941.
――――. *The Elder Statesman*. New York: Farrar, Straus and Cudahy, 1959.
――――. *Essays Ancient and Modern*. New York: Harcourt, Brace, 1932.
――――. *For Lancelot Andrewes*. London: Faber and Gwyer, 1928.

Bibliography

———. *The Idea of a Christian Society* and *Notes towards the Definition of Culture*. New York: Harvest, 1940.

———. "Introduction." In *Leisure, the Basis of Culture,* by Josef Pieper. Translated by Alexander Dru. New York: Pantheon, 1952.

———. "Introduction." In *The Need for Roots,* by Simone Weil. Translated by Arthur Wills. New York: G. P. Putnam's Sons, 1952.

———. *Knowledge and Experience in the Philosophy of F. H. Bradley*. London: Faber and Faber, 1964.

———. "Leibniz' Monads and Bradley's Finite Centers." *The Monist,* October 1916.

———. "On Conversion." *The Listener,* 19 December 1946.

———. *On Poetry and Poets*. New York: Farrar, Straus and Cudahy, 1957.

———. *Quatre Quatuors*. Translated by P. Leyris. Notes by J. Hayward. Paris: Editions du seuil, 1950.

———. *The Sacred Wood*. London: Methuen, 1920.

———. *Selected Essays*. New York: Harcourt, Brace, 1932.

———. *A Sermon Preached in Magdalene College Chapel*. Cambridge: Cambridge University Press, 1948?.

———. "Talk on Dante." *Adelphi,* October 1951.

———. *Times Literary Supplement,* 21 February 1929.

———. "*Ulysses*: Order and Myth." *Dial* 75 (November 1923).

———. *The Use of Poetry*. Cambridge: Harvard University Press, 1933.

Eliot, Valerie. "Introduction." *The Waste Land: A Facsimile and Transcript of the Original Drafts*. New York: Harcourt Brace Jovanovich, 1971.

Lewis, C. S. *Miracles*. New York: Macmillan, 1974.

Mann, Thomas. *The Magic Mountain*. Translated by H. T. Lowe-Porter. New York: Vintage, 1969.

Saint John of the Cross. *The Dark Night of the Soul*. Translated by K. Reinhardt. New York: Ungar, 1957.

Tolkien, J. R. R. *Tree and Leaf*. Ballantine, 1966.

Williams, Charles. *Arthurian Torso, Containing the Posthumous Fragment of The Figure of Arthur by Charles Williams and a Commentary on the Arthurian Poems of Charles Williams by C. S. Lewis*. London: Oxford University Press, 1948.

Yeats, William Butler. *Collected Plays*. London: Macmillan, 1935.

———. *The Collected Poems of W. B. Yeats*. New York: Macmillan, 1962.

———. *The Cutting of an Agate*. New York: Macmillan, 1912.

———. *Early Poems and Stories*. New York: Macmillan, 1925.

———. *A Vision*. New York: Macmillan, 1961.

Bibliography

Secondary Sources

Ault, Norman, ed. *Elizabethan Lyrics.* New York: Capricorn, 1960.

Baillie, John. *The Idea of Revelation in Recent Thought.* New York: Columbia University Press, 1956.

Bergsten, Staffan. *Time and Eternity: A Study in the Structure and Symbolism of T. S. Eliot's Four Quartets.* Stockholm: Svenska bokfor laget, 1960.

Braybrooke, Neville, ed. *T. S. Eliot: A Symposium for His Seventieth Birthday.* New York: Farrar, Straus and Cudahy, 1958.

Brooks, Cleanth. *The Hidden God.* New Haven: Yale University Press, 1963.
———. *Modern Poetry and the Tradition.* Chapel Hill: University of North Carolina Press, 1939.

Drew, Elizabeth. *T. S. Eliot: The Design of His Poetry.* New York: Charles Scribner's, 1949.

Eliade, Mircea. *Cosmos and History.* Translated by Willard Trask. New York: Harper, 1959.
———. *Myths, Dreams and Mysteries.* Translated by Philip Mairet. London: Harvill, 1960.
———. *Patterns in Comparative Religion.* Translated by Rosemary Sheed. New York: Sheed and Ward, 1958.

Frazer, Sir James George. *The New Golden Bough.* Edited by T. H. Gaster. New York: Criterion, 1959.

Gardner, Helen. *The Art of T. S. Eliot.* New York: E. P. Dutton, 1959.

Heath-Stubbs, John. *Charles Williams.* London: Longmans, Green, 1955.

Howarth, Herbert. *Notes on Some Figures behind T. S. Eliot.* Boston: Houghton Mifflin, 1964.

Jones, Genesius. *Approach to the Purpose.* London: Hodder and Stoughton, 1964.

Kenner, Hugh. *The Invisible Poet: T. S. Eliot.* New York: Ivan Obolensky, 1959.
———, ed. *T. S. Eliot: A Collection of Critical Essays.* Englewood Cliffs, N.J.: Prentice-Hall, 1962.

March, Richard, and M. J. Tambimuttu, eds. *T. S. Eliot: A Symposium.* Chicago: Henry Regnery, 1949.

Martz, Louis L. "The Wheel and the Point: Aspects of Imagery and Theme in Eliot's Later Poetry." In *T. S. Eliot: A Selected Critique,* edited by Leonard Unger. New York: Holt, Rinehart and Winston, 1948.

Matthiessen, F. O. *The Achievement of T. S. Eliot.* With a chapter on Eliot's later work by C. L. Barber. New York: Oxford University Press, 1959.

Moorman, Charles. *Arthurian Triptych: Mythic Materials in Charles Williams, C. S. Lewis, and T. S. Eliot.* Berkeley: University of California Press, 1960.

Bibliography

Nicolson, Marjorie Hope. *The Breaking of the Circle*. New York and London: Columbia University Press, 1965.

Pellegrini, Allesandro. "A London Conversation with T. S. Eliot." Translated by Joseph Frank. *Sewanee Review* 57 (1949).

Pétrement, Simone. *Simone Weil: A Life*. Translated by Raymond Rosenthal. New York: Pantheon, 1976.

Pound, Ezra. *The Letters of Ezra Pound, 1907–1941*. Edited by D. D. Paige. New York: Harcourt, Brace, 1950.

Rajan, B., ed. *T. S. Eliot: A Study of His Writings by Several Hands*. London: D. Dobson, 1948.

Scott, N. A. *Rehearsals of Discomposure*. London: J. Lehman, 1952.

Smidt, Kristian. *Poetry and Belief in the Work of T. S. Eliot*. London: Routledge & Kegan Paul, 1961.

Smith, Grover. *T. S. Eliot's Poetry and Plays: A Study in Sources and Meaning*. Chicago: University of Chicago Press, 1956.

Spender, Stephen. *Eliot*. Glasgow: Collins, 1975.

Tillyard, E. M. W. *The Elizabethan World Picture*. New York: Vintage, n.d.

Time, 6 March 1950.

Unger, Leonard, ed. *T. S. Eliot: A Selected Critique*. New York: Holt, Rinehart and Winston, 1948.

Vickery, John B. *The Literary Impact of the Golden Bough*. Princeton: Princeton University Press, 1973.

Weston, Jessie L. *From Ritual to Romance*. New York: Anchor, 1957.

Williamson, George. *Reader's Guide to T. S. Eliot*. New York: Noonday, 1957.

Wilson, Edmund. *Axel's Castle*. New York: Charles Scribner's Sons, 1931.

ALDOUS HUXLEY

Primary Sources

Huxley, Aldous. *After Many a Summer Dies the Swan*. New York: Avon, 1939.

———. *Antic Hay*. New York: Modern Library, 1923.

———. *Ape and Essence*. New York: Harper, 1948.

———. *The Art of Seeing*. London: Chatto and Windus, 1943.

———. *Beyond the Mexique Bay*. London: Chatto and Windus, 1934.

———. *Brave New World*. New York: Modern Library, 1946.

———. *Brave New World Revisited*. New York: Bantam, 1960.

———. *Brief Candles*. London: Chatto and Windus, 1930.

———. *The Burning Wheel*. Oxford: B. H. Blackwell, 1916.

———. *The Cicadas and Other Poems*. London: Chatto and Windus, 1931.

———. *Collected Essays*. New York: Bantam, 1960.

———. *Collected Short Stories*. New York: Bantam, 1960.

Bibliography

———. *Crome Yellow*. London: Chatto and Windus, 1949.

———. *The Defeat of Youth and Other Poems*. Oxford: B. H. Blackwell, 1918.

———. *The Devils of Loudon*. New York: Harper, 1959.

———. *"The Doors of Perception" and "Heaven and Hell."* New York: Harper, 1963.

———. *Ends and Means*. New York: Harper, 1937.

———. *Eyeless in Gaza*. New York: Harper, 1936.

———. "The Farcical History of Richard Greenow." In *Quintet*. New York: Pyramid Books, 1961.

———. *The Genius and the Goddess*. New York: Bantam, 1956.

———. *Grey Eminence*. New York: Meridian, 1959.

———. *Island*. New York: Bantam, 1963.

———. *Jesting Pilate*. London: Chatto and Windus, 1948.

———. *The Letters of Aldous Huxley*. Edited by Grover Smith. New York: Harper and Row, 1971.

———. *Music at Night and Other Essays*. London: Penguin, 1950.

———. *On Art and Artists*. Edited by Morris Philipson. New York: Harper, 1960.

———. *On the Margin*. New York: George H. Doran, 1923.

———. *The Perennial Philosophy*. New York: Harper, 1944.

———. *Point Counter Point*. New York: Avon, 1928.

———. *Proper Studies*. London: Chatto and Windus, 1933.

———. *Those Barren Leaves*. New York: Avon, 1925.

———. *Time Must Have a Stop*. New York: Harper, 1944.

Secondary Sources

Altizer, Thomas, et al. *Truth, Myth, and Symbol*. Englewood Cliffs, N.J.: Prentice-Hall, 1962.

Bedford, Sybille. *Aldous Huxley: A Biography*. New York: Alfred Knopf, 1974.

Brooke, Jocelyn. *Aldous Huxley*. London: Longmans, Green, 1954.

Clark, Ronald W. *The Huxleys*. London: Heinemann, 1968.

Coomaraswamy, Ananda. *The Dance of Shiva*. New York: Noonday, 1957.

———. *The Transformation of Nature in Art*. New York: Dover, 1956.

Fromm, Eric. *The Forgotten Language*. New York: Grove Press, 1957.

Henderson, Alexander. *Aldous Huxley*. London: Chatto and Windus, 1935.

Hesse, Hermann. *The Journey to the East*. Translated by Hilda Rosner. New York: Noonday, 1957.

———. *Siddharta*. Translated by Hilda Rosner. New York: New Directions, 1957.

Bibliography

———. *Steppenwolf.* Translated by Basil Creighton. New York: Ungar, 1957.

Huxley, Julian, ed. *Aldous Huxley: A Memorial Volume.* New York: Harper and Row, 1965.

Huxley, Laura. *This Timeless Moment: A Personal View of Aldous Huxley.* London: Chatto and Windus, 1969.

Isherwood, Christopher, ed. *Vedanta for Modern Man.* New York: Harper, 1951.

———, ed. *Vedanta for the Western World.* Hollywood, Calif.: Marcel Rodd Co., 1945.

Manuel, Frank, ed. *Utopias and Utopian Thought.* Boston: Beacon Press, 1967.

Obituary. *New York Times,* 24 November 1963.

O'Faoláin, Seán. *The Vanishing Hero.* New York: Grosset and Dunlap, 1956.

Pandey, Nand Kumar. "The Influence of Hindu and Buddhist Thought on Aldous Huxley." Ph.D. dissertation: Stanford University, Department of English, 1963.

Radhakrishnan, S. *Eastern Religions and Western Thought.* New York: Oxford University Press, 1959.

Rolo, Charles, ed. *The World of Aldous Huxley.* New York and London: Harper, 1947.

Watts, Alan. *Psychotherapy: East and West.* New York: Mentor, 1963.

———. *The Way of Zen.* Harmondsworth: Penguin, 1962.

Williams, Charles. *The Greater Trumps.* New York: Noonday Press, 1950.

Woodcock, George. *Dawn and the Darkest Hour: A Study of Aldous Huxley.* New York: Viking, 1972.

Yeats, William Butler. *Early Poems and Stories.* New York: Macmillan, 1925.

Zimmer, Heinrich. *Philosophies of India.* Edited by Joseph Campbell. Princeton: Princeton University Press, 1971.

C. G. Jung

Primary Sources

Jung, C. G. *Aion: Researches into the Phenomenology of the Self.* Translated by R. F. C. Hull. New York: Pantheon, 1959.

———. *Analytical Psychology: Its Theory and Practice.* New York: Vintage, 1968.

———. *The Archetypes and the Collective Unconscious.* Translated by R. F. C. Hull. Princeton: Princeton University Press, 1971.

———. *Civilization in Transition.* Translated by R. F. C. Hull. New York: Pantheon, 1964.

———. *The Freud/Jung Letters.* Edited by William McGuire. Translated by Ralph Manheim and R. F. C. Hull. Princeton: Princeton University Press, 1974.

Bibliography

————. *Memories, Dreams, Reflections.* Translated by Richard and Clara Winston. Rev. ed. New York: Pantheon, 1963.

————. *Mysterium Coniunctionis.* Translated by R. F. C. Hull. New York: Pantheon, 1963.

————. *Psyche and Symbol.* Edited by Violet de Laszlo. New York: Anchor, 1958.

————. *Psychology and Alchemy.* Translated by R. F. C. Hull. New York: Pantheon, 1953.

————. *Psychology and Religion.* New Haven: Yale University Press, 1960.

————. *Psychology and Religion: West and East.* Translated by R. F. C. Hull. New York: Pantheon, 1958.

————. *The Structure and Dynamics of the Psyche.* Translated by R. F. C. Hull. New York: Pantheon, 1960.

————. *Symbols of Transformation.* Translated by R. F. C. Hull. New York: Pantheon, 1952.

————. *Two Essays on Analytical Psychology.* Translated by R. F. C. Hull. New York: Pantheon, 1953.

————, ed. *Man and His Symbols.* New York: Doubleday, 1964.

Secondary Sources

Bennet, E. A. *C. G. Jung.* New York: E. P. Dutton, 1962.

Campbell, Joseph, ed. *Man and Time.* New York: Pantheon, 1957.

Freud, Sigmund. *Studies in Parapsychology.* Introduction by Philip Rieff. New York: Collier, 1963.

Glover, Edward. *Freud or Jung?* New York: Meridian, 1963.

Goodenough, Erwin R. *Jewish Symbols in the Greco-Roman Period.* Vol. 4. New York: Pantheon, 1954.

Harding, M. Esther. *Psychic Energy.* 2d ed., rev. & enl. New York: Pantheon, 1963.

Jacobi, Jolande. *Complex/Archetype/Symbol in the Psychology of C. G. Jung.* Princeton: Princeton University Press, 1959.

————. *The Psychology of C. G. Jung.* New Haven: Yale University Press, 1962.

Köhler, Wolfgang. *Gestalt Psychology.* New York: Mentor, 1959.

Koestler, Arthur. *The Roots of Coincidence: An Excursion into Parapsychology.* New York: Vintage Books, 1973.

————. *The Yogi and the Commissar.* New York: Collier, 1961.

Langer, Susanne. *Philosophy in a New Key.* Cambridge, Mass.: Harvard University Press, 1942.

Neumann, Erich. *The Origins and History of Consciousness.* Translated by R. F. C. Hull. New York: Pantheon, 1954.

Nock, A. D. *Conversion.* London: Oxford University Press, 1961.

Bibliography

Progoff, Ira. *Jung's Psychology and Its Social Meaning*. New York: Grove Press, 1955.

———. *Jung, Synchronicity, and Human Destiny*. New York: Dell, 1973.

Radin, Paul. *Primitive Man as Philosopher*. New York: Dover, 1957.

Rhine, J. B. *The Reach of the Mind*. New York: William Sloane, 1962.

Schaer, Hans. *Religion and the Cure of Souls in Jung's Psychology*. Translated by R. F. C. Hull. New York: Pantheon, 1950.

Serrano, Miguel. *C. G. Jung and Hermann Hesse*. Translated by Frank MacShane. New York: Schocken, 1966.

Snell, Bruno. *The Discovery of Mind: The Greek Origins of European Thought*. Translated by T. G. Rosenmeyer. New York: Harper, 1960.

von Franz, M.-L. "Time and Synchronicity in Analytical Psychology." In *The Voices of Time,* edited by J. T. Fraser. New York: George Braziller, 1966.

Wach, Joachim. *Sociology of Religion*. Chicago: University of Chicago Press, 1962.

INDEX

Index

Index

Miller, Henry, 158
Modern Man in Search of a Soul (Jung), 170
Mounier, Emmanuel, 19, 36, 57, 135
Muir, Edwin, 2, 142
Murder in the Cathedral (Eliot), 70, 108
Mysticism, 11–14, 19, 41, 43–45, 96, 151–57, 182–83
Myth, 7, 42, 49–51, 80, 82–83, 165–66, 180; of the eternal return, 83–84, 87–88

Nicoll, Maurice, 19
Niebuhr, Reinhold, 65, 133, 134
Nietzsche, Friedrich, 46, 59, 60, 175
Nilsson, Martin P., 200

On the Margin (Huxley), 145
Ortega y Gasset, José, 158
Orwell, George, 58
Ouspensky, P. D., 19

Perennial Philosophy, The (Huxley), 132
Picard, Max, 125
Point Counter Point (Huxley), 121, 128, 129
Positivism, revolt against, 22, 205 n. 29
Poulet, Georges, 3
Pringle-Pattison, A. Seth, 75
Proust, Marcel, 16, 99
Psychical Research, Society for, 22, 204 n. 22
Psychology of the Unconscious, The (Jung), 164, 166, 167

Revolt against time, twentieth-century, 1–25
Rhine, J. B., 13, 23, 204 n. 18
Riesman, David, 158
Rolland, Romain, 200
Roszak, Theodore, 201

Saint-Simon, Comte de, 51, 187, 188, 197
Sayers, Dorothy, 19, 101, 200
Schweitzer, Albert, 58
Secularism, 15, 16
Secularization, 15, 119
Sheldon, William, 139–40
Silesius, Angelus, 43
Sinclair, May, 19, 200
Slavery and Freedom (Berdyaev), 46
Solitude and Society (Berdyaev), 46

Space, sacred, 94–95, 97, 99
Spengler, Oswald, 35, 58, 118, 200
Steiner, Rudolf, 22
Symbolism, 6, 153, 174–76; mandala, 161–62, 176–83
Synchronicity, 184–96

Teilhard de Chardin, Pierre, 9, 18, 19, 190
Thomas, Dylan, 1, 2, 142
Those Barren Leaves (Huxley), 125, 126
Tillich, Paul, 46, 56, 135
Time: cyclical, 4, 7–9, 58–59, 63, 83–85, 87–88, 106–109, 118, 148, 150, 185–89; historical, 3, 20, 21, 63, 75, 171, 200; human, 3, 4; linear, 4, 6, 7, 63, 71, 93, 108–109, 200; sacred, 87–88; scientific, 3, 4; spatialization of, 4, 5, 7, 9, 60, 63, 107, 148; spiral, 9, 109, 186. *See also* Images; Space
Time Must Have a Stop (Huxley), 115, 125
Tolkien, J. R. R., 101, 216 n. 108
Toynbee, Arnold, 56

Underhill, Evelyn, 19

von Hügel, Baron, 19

Waste Land, The (Eliot), 81, 82–88
Watkins, Vernon, 67
Waugh, Evelyn, 222 n. 109
Weber, Max, 22
Weil, Simone, 76
Wells, H. G., 16, 58
Weston, Jessie L., 84
Willey, Basil, 56
Williams, Charles, 100–101, 149, 151, 152, 182
Windelband, Wilhelm, 22
Wolfe, Thomas, 17
Woolf, Virginia, 17, 200

Yeats, W. B., 10, 95, 97–98, 148, 150, 153, 190, 198

Zaehner, R. C., 12, 13, 105, 138, 151, 182. *See also* Mysticism
Zimmer, Heinrich, 139

[245]